Research Methods in
Educational Leadership
and Management

Educational Management Research and Practice
Series Editor: Tony Bush

Managing People in Education
Edited by Tony Bush and David Middlewood

Strategic Management in Schools and Colleges
Edited by David Middlewood and Jacky Lumby

Managing External Relations in Schools and Colleges
Edited by Jacky Lumby and Nick Foskett

Practitioner Research in Education: Making a Difference
David Middlewood, Marianne Coleman and Jacky Lumby

Managing Finance and Resources in Education
Edited by Marianne Coleman and Lesley Anderson

Managing Further Education: Learning Enterprise
Jacky Lumby

Managing the Curriculum
Edited by David Middlewood and Neil Burton

The Principles and Practice of Educational Management
Edited by Tony Bush and Les Bell

This book, *Research Methods in Educational Leadership and Management* is the reader for the module Research Methods in Educational Management, one of the core modules of the MBA in Educational Management offered by the CELM (previously EMDU), University of Leicester.

The reader for the course is *The Principles and Practice of Educational Management*: edited by Tony Bush and Les Bell.

Other books accompanying the modules in this course are:
Leadership and Strategic Management in Education Tony Bush and Marianne Coleman
Managing Finance, Resources and Stakeholders in Education Lesley Anderson, Ann R. J. Briggs and Neil Burton
Human Resource Management in Schools and Colleges David Middlewood and Jacky Lumby
Managing Effective Learning and Teaching Ann R. J. Briggs and Daniela Sommefeldt

For further information about the MBA in Educational Management, please contact the CELM at celm@le.ac.uk. For further information about the books associated with the course, contact Paul Chapman Publishing at www.paulchapmanpublishing.co.uk.

University of Leicester

Research Methods in Educational Leadership and Management

Edited by
Marianne Coleman
and
Ann R. J. Briggs

SAGE Publications
London • Thousand Oaks • New Delhi

ISBN 0-7619-7184-X (hbk)
ISBN 0-7619-7185-8 (pbk)

Paul Chapman Publishing Ltd
A SAGE Publications Company
1 Oliver's Yard, 55 City Road
London EC1Y 1SP

SAGE Publications Inc
2455 Teller Road
Thousand Oaks, California 91320

SAGE Publications India Pvt Ltd
B–42 Panchsheel Enclave
PO Box 4109
New Delhi 110 017

British Library Cataloguing in Publication data
A catalogue record for this book is available from the British Library

Library of Congress Control Number: 2002103295

Typeset by Anneset Ltd., Weston-super-Mare, Somerset
Printed and bound in Great Britain by
Cromwell Press Limited, Trowbridge, Wiltshire

Contents

Foreword

Researchers in educational management have for some time had ready access to social science research methods texts which provide very detailed advice on specific aspects of research methodology. Whilst these dense tomes are useful reference sources, they do not often engage with what is potentially a wide international readership of researchers into educational management and leadership, nor with the specific needs of new researchers. This current volume, edited by Marianne Coleman and Ann Briggs, identifies a particular niche in the field of research methods, namely a book that is required by researchers — including practitioner researchers — who are working in this particular field throughout the world. The advantage this book has over some previous texts is that it contains specially commissioned pieces that are appropriate for the field of educational management and leadership, and addresses issues of concern to the experienced researcher, the new researcher and those engaged in practitioner research.

The contributions provided by various authors demonstrate the rich range of methodologies that social scientists use when studying educational settings. As with any volume on research methodology, the authors indicate the 'different voices' in which research methodology can be discussed. The range of chapters provided within this volume is indeed impressive and includes essays that take on tough philosophical issues, as well as technical discussions of validity and reliability and contributions that have the potential to develop our understanding of research approaches, such as case studies and action research. A particular feature of this book is the way in which it focuses on data analysis, writing and dissemination as well as some of the standard topics including research techniques and data collection. In this respect, this volume is an important contribution to the literature which I am sure will be of great value to students who wish to whet their appetites before doing more detailed work on particular aspects of research methods; but who also require a background against which further work can be done. It is this facility that this collection provides. Overall, it is a volume that will be of great use to those engaged in teaching and learning about the research process and research methods. I am sure it will become essential reading for students engaged in the study of educational leadership and management.

Professor Robert G. Burgess
Vice-Chancellor
University of Leicester
May 2002

Series editor's foreword

Research is increasingly regarded as an essential aspect of educational policy and practice. In England, the National College for School Leadership has appointed a director of research and school improvement, and has also appointed practitioners as research associates. The Learning and Skills Council, which now oversees post-16 education in England, has set up a Research Centre which was launched in 2001 by Education Minister Margaret Hodge. The Department for Education and Skills has given a higher profile to research, and both the General Teaching Council and the Teacher Training Agency have research budgets and initiatives.

These developments are underpinned by the recognition that taking account of research evidence is likely to improve the quality of educational policy-making and practice. The outcomes will include an increase in the volume of research and improved dissemination of existing knowledge, in ways which are more likely to engage practitioners than by publishing solely in academic journals. This should enable teachers, and leaders and managers, to take account of research findings in reflecting on their own practice.

Perhaps even more important is the notion of teachers and managers researching their own practice. Joyce (1991) identifies school-based research as one of the five 'doors' to school improvement. Investigating their own practice provides teachers and leaders with the evidence to justify change and increases the likelihood that they will embrace innovation, because they have been directly involved in identifying the need for it. The international trend towards site-based management, although it takes many forms, provides the potential to enhance the value of school-based research by leaders and managers. As more decisions are made within the institution, the research findings can be incorporated into policies without the need for external approval. An earlier book in this series (Middlewood *et al.*, 1999) demonstrates that research 'makes a difference' in a wide range of educational contexts in many countries.

It is now widely accepted that managers in education require specific preparation if they are to be successful in leading schools and colleges. The development of effective leaders and managers requires a range of strategies, including high quality courses and tuition, mentoring by experienced and successful principals, opportunities to practise management at appropriate stages in professional careers, and an appreciation of research methods. It also needs the support of literature which presents the major issues in clear, intelligible language while drawing on the best theory and research. The aim of this series, and of this volume, is to develop a body of literature with the following characteristics:

- directly relevant to school and college management;
- prepared by authors with national and international reputations;
- using an analytical approach based on empirical evidence but couched in intelligible language; and
- integrating the best theory, research and practice.

Research Methods in Educational Leadership and Management, the seventh volume in the series, aims to provide a thorough grounding in research methods for leaders and managers in education. Many readers will already be engaged in research activity as part of a higher degree but this text will also be valuable for those leaders who wish to conduct research that will inform the decision making of governing bodies and leadership teams, or will underpin subject reviews. It provides a comprehensive introduction to the main broad issues, research approaches and specific research methods in educational leadership and management leading to a consideration of analysis and dissemination. The editors have attracted contributions on these topics from well-established authors, and the chapters they have written will provide a most valuable starting point for postgraduate students as well as for practitioners engaging in educational research. This volume will make an important contribution to developing the research skills required to help leaders and managers to conduct worthwhile and meaningful research exercises within their own educational organisations.

Tony Bush
The University of Reading
May 2002

References

Joyce, B. (1991) 'The doors to school improvement' in *Educational Leadership*, May, pp. 59–62.
Middlewood, D., Coleman, M. and Lumby J. (1999) *Practitioner Research in Education: Making a Difference*, London: Paul Chapman.

Preface

This book has been written specifically for students, and practitioner researchers of educational management and leadership. It will be of particular use to those studying for a Master's or Doctoral qualification in the field of educational leadership and management, for example, students at the University of Leicester, registered either for a Master's degree such as the MBA in Educational Management, or for the programme leading to a Doctorate in Education. However, it is hoped that this book will be a useful reference source, and provide a good grounding in research methods, for all those who undertake research in education, whether they are undertaking an accredited programme of study or not.

One of the major themes that runs through the book is that research in educational management and leadership is likely to be embedded in practice. A companion book in the series, *Practitioner Research in Education: Making a Difference* (Middlewood *et al.*, 1999) is based on the premise that research in schools and colleges and in other educational settings will lead to change and improvement. At the very least, research will impact on the professional development of the individual, but it may also encourage small changes in practice, such as the development of a policy; it may even underpin a major change in the ethos that affects the whole institution, particularly where multiple research projects are involved.

Since this book is intended primarily for students engaged in postgraduate study, it is likely that the research that you the reader undertake will be the central feature of assignments, a dissertation or a thesis. Although it is not written directly as a guide to the preparation of such scholarly work, the steps that you will need to follow in constructing your research for an academic outcome have been taken into account in the book's construction. It starts with a consideration of broad overview issues, moves to research approaches and then to specific research instruments, before finishing with a discussion of analysis and academic writing.

You will notice that many of the chapters refer to research as being systematic; this is exemplified by the number of lists that appear either as a structure for a chapter, or as a reminder at the end of the chapter (examples are Chapters 7, 8, 10 and 15). Typically, these lists include: establishing the focus of the research; framing research questions; deciding on the appropriate research approach and instruments; collecting, classifying and storing the data; and analysing and writing up. However, even though research is systematic it demands more than following a list of instructions. If it is to meet the highest standards, carrying out research requires the examination of values and constant reflection on the part of the researcher.

The first part of the book establishes some of its over-arching themes. As you carry out the various stages of your research you may need to refer several times to each of these chapters. In Chapter 1, for example, Marlene Morrison challenges us to think about the nature of knowledge and being and how it relates to the methodological issues that will tax your mind as a researcher. This is a chapter that will be illuminating both to new researchers and to those with more experience.

Chapter 2 exemplifies one of the main themes of the book: the recognition that much that has been written about research is based on an unthinking assumption that what applies in the Western world, particularly in the USA and the UK, will also apply elsewhere. In this chapter Clive Dimmock shows clearly, not only that research is seen differently in different cultures, but that the focus of any research can only be fully understood within its cultural context. This point is endorsed and further exemplified in other chapters, including in Chapter 12 by Martin Cortazzi where he discusses the interpretation of narrative and documentary analysis.

One of the first things that you will need to do as a researcher is to establish the focus of your research. In order to do this, you will need to undertake library research to discover what has already been written in your chosen area. This will include an examination both of existing research and of the theoretical and conceptual areas that relate to your research focus. In Chapter 3, Roy Kirk shows the importance of systematically making use of all available tools, whether paper or electronic, to provide a clear foundation for your work.

The remaining chapters in the first part of the book are those of Tony Bush, who discusses reliability, validity and triangulation: what he calls the 'authenticity' of research, and of Hugh Busher who considers the ethics of research in education. These chapters deal with two of the book's most consistent themes. Virtually every chapter refers to some aspect of validity, very often incorporating Michael Bassey's notion of the 'trustworthiness' of the data. Similarly, the desire to ensure that research is carried out with due regard to ethics, and that no one is damaged by your research, is a theme that most of the authors in this book take into consideration. The particular ethical difficulties that an insider researcher encounters are ones that most of you who are reading this book will need to take into account.

The second part of the book presents you with three broad methods of research: surveys, case studies and action research. The three chapters dealing with these types of research amplify the themes of the basic choices about research you will have to make, and the need to consider your own values and understanding, that are introduced by Marlene Morrison in Chapter 1. In Chapter 6, Ken Fogelman presents an introduction to survey and sampling, even dealing with thorny questions such as: 'How many questionnaires do I need?'. He outlines the ways in which a researcher can ensure that research outcomes are as generalisable as possible, whilst Michael Bassey makes the case for 'fuzzy' generalisations in Chapter 7. Here, he presents an authoritative account of an approach that will be taken by many insider researchers, that of the case study. In Chapter 8, Pam Lomax shows how action research is truly embedded in practice and how it sets out to change a situation rather than to observe and record it, an approach which practitioner researchers in particular will need to consider.

The third part of the book is concerned with the research tools that may be used within any of the three wider approaches covered in Chapters 6, 7 and 8, or may be used in their own right. In some ways Chapters 9 and 10 are companion chapters, in that they provide clear, practical, and sometimes light-hearted, guides to undertaking two of the most commonly used types of research: interviews and questionnaires. Both make links with the survey method, particularly with the issues of sampling discussed in Chapter 6, and also refer to validity and reliability and the ethics of research. In Chapter 11, Janet Moyles draws on her own experience of using observation as a research tool to show how it can be used systematically in classrooms or in management settings such as meetings or, alternatively, in a more interpretive way through participant observation and the use of field notes. Her helpful thoughts on the analysis of data from observation provide a useful link to the work of Rob Watling in Chapter 15. Two further chapters complete the section on tools, and both refer to the written word. In Chapter 12, Martin Cortazzi shows how documents and texts can be analysed and introduces the analysis of narrative and life history. In this rich chapter, the techniques referred to include quantitative content analysis but he makes the point that each text: 'is surrounded by a context of expectations and patterns of knowledge and meaning held by those who use the text and who inevitably — and quite normally — bring these to their own interpretation and use of the text'. The importance of maintaining sensitivity to context and to culture in undertaking research is re-inforced. In Chapter 13, the final chapter in this section, Marlene Morrison draws on her extensive experience with the use of diaries as research instruments. In this chapter, diaries are seen as potentially useful to researchers in a variety of ways whether as diaries kept by researchers themselves, as respondent diaries, or as diaries accompanied by interviews.

The final section of the book considers analysis and writing and dissemination. In Chapter 14, Anthony Pell and Ken Fogelman outline some of the ways in which quantitative data can be analysed and presented, while in

Chapter 15 Rob Watling shows the steps that can be followed in the analysis of qualitative data, making the point that analysis is not necessarily something that you only consider at the end of a research project. Although research has to be carried out sequentially, it is vital that you consider at the outset how your work is to be analysed and in particular whether you have the resources to undertake the sort of analysis that is consequent on the collection of a large amount of a particular type of data. Transcribing even one interview is a painstaking process and the extraction of themes from a number of transcriptions should develop as the work progresses rather than being left to the end. Similarly inputting and analysing a large amount of quantitative data requires skills that may have to be learnt and practised.

Chapter 16, the final chapter, has been written by Ann Briggs with you, the practitioner/student/researcher/writer, very much in mind. You may find yourself short of the necessary time, and sometimes confidence, to carry out the research and undertake the writing up that is required of you if you are aiming for a master's or a doctoral qualification. But we hope this book will give you the insight and the practical tools you need to develop your skills as a researcher and as a writer. We hope too that your research will lead not only to the achievement of your desired qualification, but also to the publication of research that will disseminate your findings, and add to the understanding and improvement of educational processes and their leadership and management.

The editors were delighted to receive contributions to this volume from colleagues in the world of education who have each been able to bring their own strengths and experience as researchers to bear. We would also wish to thank Tony Bush as series editor, Marianne Lagrange of Paul Chapman Publishing and our colleagues at the University of Leicester's School of Education, for their advice and support. Finally we would like to thank Christopher Bowring-Carr for indexing and Joyce Palmer and Julie Hardisty for their help in production.

Marianne Coleman and Ann Briggs
May 2002

Notes on contributors

Judith Bell has worked as a college lecturer, head of department and vice principal, as a university lecturer in several universities, as a course team writer in the Open University and as one of Her Majesty's Inspectors specialising in further and higher education. She works now as a writer and lecturer and holds the honorary position of Special Professor in the School of Continuing Education at the University of Nottingham.

Michael Bassey is an Emeritus Professor of Education of Nottingham Trent University and an Academician of the Academy of Learned Societies for the Social Sciences. He is Academic Secretary of the British Educational Research Association and editor of its house journal *Research Intelligence*. His major claim to knowledge is offering a solution to the problem of generalisation in the form of fuzzy generalisation and best-estimate-of-trustworthiness.

Ann Briggs is a lecturer in Educational Management at the Centre for Educational Leadership and Management previously the Educational Management Development Unit of the University of Leicester. Prior to taking up her post in Higher Education, her main teaching areas were in English and Communications. Her principal research interests are the management of learning and learning resources, and management in Further Education Colleges.

Professor Robert Burgess is Vice-Chancellor of the University of Leicester. His research interests include social research methodology and the sociology of education. He has researched and written extensively on research methodologies and the ways in which they can be used in the study of educational settings.

Tony Bush is Professor of International and Comparative Education at The University of Reading. He was previously Professor of Educational Management and Director of the Educational Management Development Unit now the Centre for Educational Leadership and Management at the University of Leicester. He has directed research projects in the UK on grant-maintained schools (Leverhulme Trust) and on mentoring (Esmee Fairbairn Foundation) as well as projects in China and South Africa funded by the British Council.

Dr Hugh Busher is a senior lecturer in the School of Education, University of Leicester. He has long-standing research interests in leadership and change processes in educational organisations in their policy contexts, and in issues of equity, social justice and inclusivity in education. He is co-ordinator of the British Educational Research Association (BERA) Special Interest Group (SIG) on Leading and Managing Schools and Colleges and a series editor for BELMAS books with Paul Chapman.

Dr Marianne Coleman is a senior lecturer in educational management at the Institute of Education, University of London and was previously in the Educational Management Development Unit of the School of Education at the University of Leicester. She has written and researched extensively in the field of educational management and has a particular research interest in women in educational management and leadership.

Martin Cortazzi is Professor of Education at Brunel University and was previously a senior lecturer at the University of Leicester's School of Education. He has written extensively on narrative and is an experienced researcher in China and elsewhere.

Clive Dimmock is Professor of Educational Management and Director of the Centre for Educational Leadership and Management previously the Educational Management Development Unit at the University of Leicester, UK. He is particularly interested in the application of grounded theory and inductive analysis research methods to educational leadership and management and has published extensively in the areas of culture and leadership.

Ken Fogelman is Professor of Education, Director of the School of Education and Dean of the Faculty of Education and Continuing Studies at the University of Leicester. His previous career was as a full-time researcher, at the National Foundation for Educational Research, at the National Children's Bureau and at City University.

Roy Kirk is Education Librarian at the University of Leicester Education Library. He has held the offices of Chair and Secretary for both the Library Association Education Librarians Group (ELG) and the Librarians of Institutes and Schools of Education (LISE) group over the last decade. He is currently editor of *Technical Education and Training Abstracts,* a quarterly abstracting journal.

Pamela Lomax was Professor of Educational Research at Kingston University until July 1999. Since then she has been working as an independent consultant for a number of universities, mainly supporting doctoral students who are using action research. She has published many books and papers in the field of action research.

Dr Marlene Morrison is Deputy Director of Research at the School of Education, University of Leicester. An experienced educational researcher and Deputy Director of the Centre for Citizenship Studies in Education, her research interests include citizenship, health education, and race equality; libraries for teaching and learning; and the professional development of teachers, including temporary teachers. Her publications reflect those interests. She is the postgraduate tutor for research students in education, and she teaches widely on the research methods training programme with specific interests in qualitative and ethnographic research.

Janet Moyles is Professor of Education and Research at Anglia Polytechnic University, Chelmsford, and an early childhood education specialist, particularly in the area of effective teaching and learning and children's play. She has directed a number of funded research projects for government departments, unions and charitable bodies related to early years and primary teaching and has also written a number of books and a variety of journal articles on different aspects of early years and primary education.

Dr Anthony Pell is a research associate at the University of Leicester. His research interests include the construction and use of attitude and psychological scales and their use in quantitative research.

Dr Rob Watling is a lecturer and Deputy Director of Research at the School of Education, University of Leicester. He has extensive experience of designing and conducting educational research, and his recent work has concentrated on issues of social inclusion, citizenship, school inspection, and partnerships.

Ted Wragg is Professor of Education at Exeter University. He is the author of over fifty books on education, former President of the British Educational Research Association, editor of the international journal *Research Papers in Education* and has directed numerous research projects studying teaching and learning processes.

Part A
The Concept of Research

1

What do we mean by educational research?

Marlene Morrison

Thinking about educational research

The aim of this chapter is ambitious though, on the surface, straightforward. It is to convey a sense of educational research as twin-focused — a systematic inquiry that is both a distinctive way of thinking about educational phenomena, that is, an *attitude*, and of investigating them, that is, an *action* or *activity*. Others have dubbed this as 'a mode of interrogation for education' (Brown and Dowling, 1998). To trumpet its distinctiveness is a necessary though insufficient starting point; educationists are living through times when research outputs have often received a hostile reaction, interestingly, if disturbingly, from both within the educational research community (Hargreaves, 1996; Tooley with Darby, 1998) and without (Woodhead, 1998; Barber, 1996). At first sight, such 'spats' may seem far removed from the world of the first-time or small-scale researcher in educational management. Yet they remain critical because the published outcomes of educational research form the bedrock from which postgraduate researchers start their own research journeys. As importantly, at the macro-level, they raise awareness about the extent of political manipulation in which research intentions and frameworks are bounded, and sound warnings about possible replications at the micro-level, especially the balance between what is 'researchable' and what is permitted or celebrated as research. More broadly, I want to argue that making visible the various debates that determine what constitutes educational research is complex and fruitful for *all* researchers, whether incoming or continuing.

My experience of conducting research over the past fifteen years, and of encouraging others, would suggest that for managers of educational institutions, departments, and classrooms, some but not all criticisms of educational research are well founded. Tendencies towards academic elitism, the inaccessibility of research outcomes, and the perceived irrelevance of educational research may have left some managers, and teachers, in 'a vacuum, with the so what? or what next? factors failing to be addressed' (Clipson-Boyles, 2000, 2–3). The growth of professional doctorates and research-focused postgraduate degrees is seen as a counterpoint to such tendencies. Educational managers might now feel that they have an ownership of research knowledge and practice. Yet, becoming researchers rather than research recipients brings other challenges, described graphically by Brown and Dowling (1998) in terms of the emergence of 'all singing/all dancing practitioner researcher[s]' (1998: 165) with attendant tendencies to deny the existence of 'research as a distinctive activity' and a 'plundering' of techniques which may lead to 'a fetishizing of methods' (1998: 165).

Such tendencies may fail to distinguish 'professional educational practice' from 'educational research practice' (*ibid.*). One manifestation is training in educational research that is almost totally associated with the acquisition of research skills that enable individual small-scale researchers to collect, process, and analyse research data. Asking important 'Why?' questions may be sacrificed upon the altar of immediacy and urgency in the rush to answer 'how to' questions, as if research were 'only' a matter of skills acquisition for a technical craft. If educational research *is* both an attitude and an activity, then the task of this chapter is to invite readers to consider and re-consider educational research not just as a 'rule-driven' means of 'finding out' what educational managers did not know before (even if they suspected!), but as an approach to skilful and intellectual inquiry that is rooted in, and shaped by a number of research traditions, and, as importantly, multiple ways of viewing the educational worlds we inhabit.

Some, but not all of this discussion will focus upon the appropriateness of quantitative and qualitative approaches to educational research, and the extent to which earlier debates about usefulness have been superseded by more recent methodological debates. This will not be a focus upon 'isms' or, indeed, research jargon for its own sake. It is well understood that small-scale researchers need to balance the practicalities of doing research with the philosophies that underpin, sometimes implicitly, their engagement with it. Yet research in educational management, whatever its primary concerns, makes claims about what counts as legitimate 'knowledge' and for whom. Traditionally, educational researchers have justified those claims by pointing to the robustness of the methods that inform their research. Some educational researchers may spend months, even years, convincing themselves and others that the techniques associated with their research endeavours are necessarily 'objective' whilst failing to recognise that the term 'objectivity' — being neutral, unbiased, and making sure one's personal values do not enter the research — is *itself* a value-implicit position in which it is assumed that there is a world of educational management 'out there' to be studied that is 'independent of knowers' (see also Usher, 1997: Introduction).

So, in order to explore the meanings of educational research, we need to consider the range of intentions, claims, and purposes that underpin it, paying specific attention to educational management. Let us begin with definitions.

Exploring definitions

What do we mean by 'research'?

Bassey (1999) provides readers with a useful starting point:

> Research is systematic, critical and self-critical enquiry which aims to contribute towards the advancement of knowledge and wisdom. (1999: 38)

Some key terms are used here. 'Systematic' implies a sense of order and structure: whilst some research relies more on innovative design than others, the implication is that there is a connectedness about research which involves the planning and integration of design, process, and outcomes. The terms 'critical' and 'self-critical' are clearly important: the assumption is that the research design, and in particular, its methodological integrity, should be open to the scrutiny and judgement of others, and that all aspects of research are subject to reflection and re-assessment by the researcher.

In her text on research methods in educational management, Johnson (1994: 3) substitutes the adjective 'focused' for 'critical' as part of her definition, considering that research needs always to concern itself with a specific issue/topic/question. In these terms, 'educational management' is an insufficiently specific topic for enquiry although 'structures for the introduction and development of a staff appraisal system in a college of further education', for example, might well be. Furthermore, for Johnson, the processes and outcomes of such an enquiry will be that the researcher obtains data that moves 'beyond generally available knowledge to acquire specialised and detailed information, providing a basis for analysis and elucidatory comment on the topic of enquiry' (1994: 3). What does this mean? For Johnson, research conclusions 'should not' derive from 'received wisdom about a subject' but rather from what the researcher discovers during the course of the study; this will 'help other interested parties think freshly about the subject' (1994: 4). One discerns hesitancy, even reluctance, on Johnson's part to consider the values implicit in the choice of research subject, design, process, or data analysis. There is little such hesitancy in Bassey's definition. The terms 'critical', 'self-critical', and 'advancement of knowledge and wisdom' are each value-laden. Research will bring 'more' knowledge and 'more' wisdom, though at this point of definition we might be less sure about who benefits.

So far, our definitions seem to imply that research will make known, or at least make known in terms of a new or different situation, location, or context, that which was not known before; for small-scale researchers, this might be to themselves *or* those colleagues with whom they work *or* to a much wider audience if the successful thesis is published. To explore this further, researchers need to look at the empirical and theoretical fields in which they operate. For Brown and Dowling (1998), research should always justify the claims it makes to knowledge 'in terms of reference to experience of the field to which these knowledge claims relate' (1998: 7). Specifically, 'it must justify those claims further in relation to the empirical settings, which is the local space in which the researcher is operating' (1998: 9). What is meant by the word 'justify'?

Let us consider the role of 'manager'. Readers will not embark upon research that has a management focus without having some idea about what management means to them, or indeed what they think it means to and for others. For example, we all carry preconceptions about what we think 'effective' management is or ought to be. Though researchers may not always be fully conscious of the preconceptions they bring to their research, they need to make as overt as possible the conceptual structures that they bring to their projects. This is what Brown and Dowling (1998) have called 'the theoretical problem' and this is, in turn, embedded in a range of published literature that the researcher will unpack as part of 'the theoretical field' (1998: 10). But researchers do not, and probably could not, study all there is to know in their area of interest; theoretical development occurs as researchers progressively focus their areas of research; at different stages in the research process more attention is given to theoretical than to empirical development, and to the theoretical and empirical fields or sites for investigation, and vice versa. Focused upon our understanding of the subject of research and the fitness for purpose of the research design, the movement between theoretical and empirical development is ongoing. Depending upon the research questions asked, some aspects of the theoretical field will become more relevant than others.

As an example, readers might wish to consider differences in the theoretical fields that writers like education management consultant Daphne Johnson and academic Professor Stephen Ball might bring to their investigation of management principles and practices, and of the relationship between those fields and the research questions addressed. For Johnson (1994):

> The ethos of research into educational management is to assist the development of effective school and college management. Your [she refers to researchers in educational management] research-based enquiry is meant to lead to professional reflection and, where appropriate, a commitment to change. The hope is that all concerned with your enquiry will be helped by it (1994: Preface)

Links between effective management and professional reflection are assumed, and these are, in turn, linked to different aspects of management such as:

- the principles of educational management and their translation into practice;
- leadership and strategic management;
- curriculum management;
- the management of staff; and
- managing finance and external relations. (1994: 93–4)

For Ball (1999) a core educational 'myth' is the assumption that 'good management makes good schools'. He paints a 'grim picture' (1999: 88) that questions 'the social and moral costs' of an increasingly pervasive managerialism in which, the head teacher, for example:

> is the main carrier and embodiment of managerialism and is crucial to the transformation of the organisational regimes of schools. That is, the dismantling of professional organizational regimes and their replacement with market-entrepreneurial regimes .... Some heads have been aggrandized and others damaged by the requirements of managerial leadership and its attendant responsibilities. (Ball,1999: 89)

Furthermore:

> one aspect of the effectivity of managerialism is its 'dislocation', that is, management is no longer identified simply with the activities of one group, or role or office. ... We need to evaluate the desirability of these changes carefully. We need to ask the question — what are we doing to ourselves? (1999: 90–11)

Even if agreement can be reached about the overall purposes and intentions of research enquiry, the preceding extracts would suggest that as an attitude and an activity, research in educational management does not exist in an objective or neutral vacuum in which understandings about the term 'management', for example, remain uniform or uncontested.

What do we mean by 'education'?

The concerns of this book are to do with empirical research in the field of educational management. All researchers, including first time researchers, need to revisit the term 'education' because, as Bassey (1999) has pointed out, 'every researcher needs to be clear what he or she means by [the term]' (p.37). For Bassey, education is:

> First, the experience and nurture of personal and social developments towards worthwhile living.

7

Second, the acquisition, development, transmission, conservation, discovery, and renewal of worthwhile culture. (1999: 37)

A noteworthy feature of this definition is its open-endedness; 'worthwhile' and 'culture' are or might be what others recommend or prescribe or denounce. Meanings that underpin research frameworks are therefore always imbued with values. The term 'lifelong education' provides another example; it is a slippery concept which seems attractive to a wide variety of distinctive and differing 'totalitarian' and 'liberal' interests (Tight, 1996: 36). As Bagnall (1990) points out:

> The term 'lifelong education' has been used in recent educational literature to advocate or denote the function of education as being: the preparation of individuals *for* the management of their adult lives, the distribution of education *throughout* individual lifespans, the educative function *of* the whole of one's life experience, and the identification of education *with* the whole of life. (Bagnall, 1990: 1, original emphasis)

Lacking a standard model of what lifelong education might look like, researchers need to makes their meaning frameworks explicit and comprehensible if research problems linked to lifelong education are to be addressed coherently.

So, what is 'educational research'?

The study of education is both multi-disciplinary and inter-disciplinary. In part this is what makes educational studies exhilarating as well as challenging! A range of aims and purposes guides all educational research; decisions to 'settle upon' one research project rather than another are guided implicitly and explicitly by researchers' practical, personal, professional and/or disciplinary interests, even if, at the start of the research journey, such interests may lack the coherence of later stages. Bassey (1999) is in no doubt about what constitutes educational research, and expresses this as:

> Critical enquiry aimed at informing educational judgements and decisions in order to improve educational action. This is the kind of value-laden research that should have immediate relevance to teachers and policy makers, and is itself educational because of its stated intention to 'inform'. It is the kind of research in education that is carried out by educationists. (1999: 39)

For others, research may be about *using* research for 'working towards justice, fairness, and openness in education' (Griffiths, 1998: 1). Although, for Griffiths, 'research into organizations — or into educational management —

8

is not, routinely, described as "for social justice"' (1998: 19), educational management, she argues, does not need to be excluded:

> On the face of it, research related to organizational theory (and educational management) could be thought of as one of the less promising areas, since it has a history of being theorized to reflect the interests and needs of educational managers (Ball,1987: 5)... A closer look [at some examples of educational research output in the area] reveals the underlying concern with social justice. (1998: 19)

Stances advocated by Michael Bassey and Morwenna Griffiths show some similarity. Here are views that educational research 'can lay no claim to abstract neutrality or being a curiosity-driven quest for knowledge . . . rather, in the short run and in the long run, it is action-orientated' (Griffiths,1998: 67). Whilst such an orientation implies no one particular methodological approach, educational action is foregrounded, and the making of knowledge claims, for the claim's sake, is relegated. Bassey (1999) distinguishes between action-oriented research, with its intentions to effect action, and what is described as 'discipline research' which is primarily concerned with *understanding* the phenomena of educational activities and actions. Thus:

> Discipline research in education aims critically to inform understandings of phenomena pertinent to the discipline in educational settings. (1999: 39)

Such perspectives on educational research do not go uncontested. Writers like Burgess (in Bryman and Burgess, 1994), Bryman (1988), Jonathon (1995) and Hammersley (1995) in varying degrees come closest to a view of educational research as 'disinterested inquiry' which follows the methods and methodologies of sociology, psychology, anthropology and so on. Other researchers deploy a *hybrid* approach in which problems may be conceived primarily as 'sociological' or 'psychological'; the whole panoply of theoretical discourse derived from specific disciplines is then applied to the research problem.

With regard to policy-orientated research, for example, Ozga (2000) draws upon a social scientific framework in order to explore the ways in which theoretical positions inform all aspects of research design including the selection and analysis of evidence. She refers to Cox (1980) in order to elaborate the difference between problem-solving and critical theory as they are applied respectively to policy research in education:

> Theory can serve two distinct purposes. One is a simple, direct response, to be a guide to help solve the problems posed within a particular perspective which was the point of departure. The other is more reflective upon the processes of theorising itself, to become clearly

aware of the perspective which gives rise to theorising, and its relation to other perspectives (to achieve a perspective on perspectives), and to open up the possibility of choosing a different valid perspective from which the problematic becomes one of creating an alternative world. Each of these purposes gives rise to a different kind of theory. . . .

The first purpose gives rise to *problem-solving theory*. It takes the world as it finds it, with the prevailing social and power relationships and the institutions into which they are organised, as the given framework for action. The general aim of problem-solving is to make these relationships and institutions work smoothly by dealing effectively with particular sources of trouble [such troubles may constitute the research problem]. . . .

The second purpose leads to *critical theory*. It is critical in the sense that it stands apart from the prevailing order of the world and asks how that order came about. Critical theory, unlike problem-solving, does not take institutions and social and power relations for granted but calls them into question by concerning itself with their origins and how and whether they might be in the process of changing. . . .

As a matter of practice, critical theory, like problem-solving theory, takes as its starting point some aspect of a particular sphere of human activity [for our purposes, the management of education at whatever level]. But whereas the problem-solving approach leads to further analytical sub-divisions and limitation of the issues to be dealt with, the critical approach leads towards the construction of a larger picture of the whole . . . and seeks to understand the processes of change in which both the parts and the whole are involved. (Cox, 1980: 128–30, quoted in Ozga, 1999: 45–6)

Whilst readers of this chapter are likely to be researchers who will conduct research single-handedly and on a small scale, they will be joining an educational research community in which there is 'a lively and sometimes agitated debate within the traditions of educational studies about its status and forms of inquiry' (Ranson, 1996: 528). In trying to make sense of the world in which educational research operates, researchers work within a range of beliefs about the ways in which education and research are/can be understood as practice. Sometimes disputes about forms of enquiry appear to be conducted at the level of method or technique, with relatively little attention paid to issues of epistemology, ontology, or methodology. Yet, researchers need to consider how and why such issues matter, and to whom, and it is to those issues that the chapter now turns.

Epistemology, ontology and methodology

Why do we need to make connections?

Research enquiry is full of challenges and uncertainties. As researchers we want to know if the conclusions we reach are the 'right' ones; at the same time, our literature searches and reviews tell us that the history of published research into educational management, as for other educational areas, is one in which a range of published authors appear to reach different as well as similar conclusions about the same or very similar phenomena. As McKenzie (1997) points out, 'research is embedded in a churning vortex of constructive and destructive tensions in which old educational 'certainties' are replaced by new 'certainties' (1997: 9). That tension is historical. For researchers, two questions are key:

> What is the relation between what we see and understand [our claims to 'know' and our theories of knowledge or *epistemology*] and that which is reality [our sense of being or *ontology*]?

> In other words, how do we go about creating knowledge about the world in which we live? (McKenzie, 1997: 9)

Epistemology, then, is central to research endeavour. All researchers ask questions about knowledge — how we find it, how we recognise it when we find it, how we use it, and how it distinguishes truth from falsehood. Educational researchers bring a wide range of theoretical perspectives to their work. Perhaps the widest of these is an *ontology*. This consists of a range of perceptions about the nature of reality. *Methodology* is also critical in this regard since ontology and epistemology affects the methodology that underpins researchers' work; crucially, methodology provides a rationale for the ways in which researchers conduct research activities.

From this perspective, methodology is much more than *methods* or *techniques* or *tools* for research like 'conducting an interview' or 'keeping a research diary'. The methodological rationale provides researchers with underlying reasons for 'conducting an interview'; as importantly, in choosing to conduct serial life history interviews with a secondary school head of science, for example, rather than a questionnaire survey with a number of heads of science, the researcher is arguing that interviews provide a 'more informed' way of claiming knowledge than a questionnaire could provide in order to address one or more of his/her specific research questions. (This is not to argue that a questionnaire might not be appropriate to address *another* research question.)

Epistemological and methodological concerns are implicated at every stage of the research process. There might be a tendency to think that the information collected by researchers is transformed into 'data' and then into 'knowledge' as if this were both automatic and linear. Not so. Information is transformed into data by the process of analysis; information is collected in a range of forms, as qualitative or quantitative information, or as combinations of both.

Paradigms

In making sense of research information and transforming it into data, researchers draw implicitly or explicitly upon a set of beliefs or a *paradigm* about how that analysis might be patterned, reasoned, and compiled. Researchers who adhere to a specific paradigm will hold a kind of consensus about what does or should count as 'normal' research. (The term 'normal' is set in inverted commas deliberately; a range of practitioners, researchers, and policy makers may hold rather different perceptions about what constitutes 'normal' research. This may leave some readers feeling rather uncomfortable, especially those who seek assurance that all research proceeds according to rules 'set in stone'; it is to be hoped that such discomfort will reduce as readers progress.)

Bassey (1999) describes a paradigm as:

> a network of coherent ideas about the nature of the world and the function of researchers which, adhered to by a group of researchers, conditions the patterns of their thinking and underpins their research actions. (1999: 42)

One way of illustrating the important connections between *epistemology*, *ontology*, *methodology* and *paradigm* is to recognise that a range of 'isms' (Silverman, 2001: 38) and/or 'idioms' (Gubrium and Holstein, 1997) implicitly or explicitly underpin the activities and language of educational research. *Feminism* and *post-modernism* are examples of two such 'isms' and readers are warmly encouraged to engage with the literature on either or both. The brief excursion into feminist research that follows should at least alert readers to the potential and actual influence of 'isms' upon the subject, design, processes, and outcomes of educational research. An exploration of the terms *positivism* and *interpretivism* — also introduced in the next section — will be expanded in the second half of the chapter.

Feminist research

All discussions about the methodology of educational research require researchers to familiarise themselves with philosophical debates about the meaning of education, the nature of educational enquiry, and whether that enquiry will be influenced by individual ontologies. From a feminist ontology, the focus will be specifically and primarily upon gender inequalities in education, and upon epistemologies that provide greater understanding of such inequalities. Crucially, feminists will be drawn towards a set of ideas which provides an explanatory framework for the existence and persistence of male domination in all aspects of society, including education. The critical framework is extended to the educational research community which, it is argued, has provided and continues to provide knowledge that supports the continuation of male domination. Such criticism extends to the selection of research problems and topics for enquiry.

For example, the recent and persistent outcry about the under-achievement of predominantly white, male, and working-class boys, has been seen by some feminists as a 'moral panic' in which policy makers attempt to regain or reinforce patriarchal forms of education and power that have been central to education (Weiner *et al.*, 1997). As more research funding is given to the 'problem' of male under-achievement, these writers question why and how female success is being viewed 'as a corollary to male failure' (1997: 620). Instead, they call for research that first, pays particular attention to the way in which the curriculum continues 'to implicitly produce the gender differences it seeks to eradicate' (1997: 629); second, focuses upon *all* 'low-fliers', whether male or female; and third, mounts a strong challenge to 'new, hegemonic educational orthodoxies such as those of so-called male under-achievement. . . . What we are seeing may be, in fact, merely a new rendition of the old patriarchal refrain'(1997: 629).

Feminists are especially critical of research that treats people studied as objects rather than subjects, and they challenge and reject claims to value-neutrality and objectivity in educational research. Instead, research is seen as an inter-subjective experience which should empower rather than exploit. Not surprisingly, the methodology that has underpinned feminist approaches has tended to be interpretive, and often (but not always) micro in nature. Thus the micro-details of gender-as-lived and gender-as-experienced by girls and women, who constitute the subjects of research *and* the researchers, have been central concerns. Research provides not only a source of politicisation and consciousness raising, but also raise questions about the wider functioning of society.

It has also been argued that there is an interpretive and constructivist methodology that is distinctively feminist. This is mainly conducted *by* women *for* and *with* women rather than *upon* women as objects. Feminist criticisms of educational research extend beyond positivist approaches to conventional ethnography where, they would argue, the emphasis has been upon 'mere' description rather than a focus upon emancipation and positive change for women. The extent to which feminist methodology *is* distinctive from other methodologies has been the focus for vigorous debate (Hammersley, 1992a; Ramazanoglu,1992). Currently, feminists are turning their attention to the epistemological and methodological relationships between feminist research and recent strands of post-modernism, some readings of which might be variously described as supportive or anathema to feminist goals.

So far, we have briefly considered the effect on research of one 'ism'. Feminism makes reference to the over-arching and distinctive contributions of positivism and interpretivism (if only to reject or amend aspects of them). In the following sections, discussion turns to the respective influences of positivism and interpretivism upon a range of educational research activities and environments. Whilst academic debates between these traditions have often been heated, the core aim here is to introduce readers to epistemological and methodological issues that are frequently reduced to matters of 'quantity' and 'quality'. Finally, arguing against a 'naïve' use of any one paradigm, prospects for combination will be considered and implications for research practice summarised.

Readers should again be alert to over-simplifications that an introductory chapter may engender. Alan Bryman's text on *Quantity and Quality in Social Research* (1988) still provides one of the most cogent accounts of the debate about the nature and values of quantitative and qualitative approaches to research.

Introducing positivism

Four issues confront readers who wish to explore the term *positivism* for the first time.

1. As Bryman (1998) articulates, there is a range of definitions attributed to positivism.
2. The term is not always recognised by educational researchers who may work implicitly within the paradigm. Especially with regard to first-time researchers, it is not always easy to discern whether the approach being used is seen 'simply' as the most appropriate or 'scientific' way of conducting research, and/or whether this reflects a cultural preference for one paradigm or methodology over another (see also Dimmock, Chapter 2 of this volume).
3. The term is sometimes used pejoratively, particularly by those who would reject this paradigm in favour of (an) alternative(s).
4. The educational community includes researchers who, for reasons that might be ideological, technical, or pragmatic, engage in 'mix-and-match' approaches to research methodology and method. They may not perceive, or indeed value, the need for a specific distinctiveness in paradigmatic approaches to research activities. Readers will be invited to consider 'combination' frameworks in the final section of this chapter. (Meanwhile, 'mix-and-match' approaches may also be viewed as a research response to criticisms from research sponsors who berate the boldness or 'exaggera-

tion' of research claims emanating from one paradigm, frequently interpretive.)

The key point about positivist approaches to educational research is its adherence to the scientific method. The positivist tradition has a number of key
features:

- People — pupils, students, heads of departments, principals, and parents
  — are the *objects* of educational research, notwithstanding their uniqueness as one from another and from the other objects of the natural world.
- Only educational phenomena that are amenable to the researcher's senses,
  in other words, are *observable* through experience, can validly be considered as knowledge. 'Feelings' as the objects of educational research activity, therefore, need to be ruled out, unless they can be rendered observable
  and measurable.
- Scientific knowledge is obtained through the collection of verified 'facts'.
  Such facts can be observed 'out there' in an educational world that is distinct from the observer. These facts feed into theories about educational
  management, for example; theories, in turn, represent the accumulated
  findings of educational research. Theories are likely to have law-like characteristics because they are based upon empirically established *regularities*.
  The notion that a theory of educational management . . . or learning . . .
  or leadership can be built upon an edifice of empirically established facts
  is called *inductivism*.
- Theories also provide a backdrop to empirical research because *hypotheses* can be generated from them, usually in the form of postulated *causal
  connections*. This implies that educational research is also *deductive*.
- Positivists take a particular stance with regard to values. As Bryman (1988:
  15) articulates, they do so in two senses. The first involves the need for
  educational researchers to 'purge' themselves of values which may impair
  their objectivity and undermine the validity of the research. The second
  is to draw a distinction between scientific statements and normative ones.
  Thus 'whilst positivists recognise that they can investigate the implications
  of a particular normative position, they cannot verify or falsify the position itself' (1988: 15).
- Human characteristics and attributes can be considered as *variables*. When
  combined, they can capture the essence of either human beings or the educational activities in which they are engaged. Discoveries about the relationship between variables should enable positivists to explain the world
  they have uncovered. Because positivists do not consider themselves as
  'inside' the research milieux they investigate, then it should not matter
  who does the research, provided that others are as 'expert' as they are in
  applying the scientific method. One would expect that other researchers
  handling similar data would come to similar conclusions.

- Positivists may predict, in the sense that observations in the past may enable them to predict what will happen in the future, given similar circumstances and significant associations between variables.

What is the relation between positivism and quantitative research?

Quantitative research as a rational, linear process has been heavily influenced by the application of the scientific method which has, in turn, been seen mainly in positivist terms. Bryman (1998) provides an 'idealised' model in which he reminds us that 'the truth' is often messier than the ideal, with theory playing a smaller role in quantitative research than is frequently assumed:

> Quantitative research is often conceptualised by its practitioners as having a structure in which theories determine the problems to which researchers address themselves in the form of hypotheses derived from general theories. These hypotheses are invariably assumed to take the form of expectations about likely causal connections between the concepts which are the constituent elements of the hypotheses. Because concepts in the social sciences are frequently believed to be abstract, there is seen a need to provide operational definitions whereby their degrees of variation and co-variation can be measured. Data are collected by social survey, experiment ... Once the survey or experimental data have been collected, they are then analysed so that the causal connection specified by the hypothesis can be verified or rejected. The resultant findings then feed back into, and are absorbed by, the theory that set the whole process going in the first place. (1998: 18)

Quantitative research has a number of core features:

1. The relation between *concept formation*, observation and *measurement* is central. How we objectify, observe and measure 'leadership styles', 'intelligence', 'educational attainment', 'reading ages', and 'home-school partnerships', for example, are key concerns; with this comes the important notion of 'breaking down' the research problem into manageable 'bits' that can be observed and measured. The use of structured observation and questionnaires are common in educational research for measurement purposes.
2. Quantitative research is also interested in *causality*, or what Babbie (1979: 423) described as 'some things are caused by other things'. So, quantitative researchers will make frequent use of independent and dependent variables, frequently associated with experimental and cross-sectional survey design, and more recently, mathematical modelling. What makes a school 'effective'? How can we tell a 'good school' from a 'bad school'? How do we know that a school has 'improved'? By 'how much' and 'why'?

3. In cross-sectional studies, three conditions have to be met in order to establish causal relations (Bryman, 1988: 30-34). First, researchers need statistical techniques to show that there is a relationship between variables; second, they need to show that the relationship is non-spurious; third, the analyst needs to show that there is a temporal order to the data being studied.

4. Following the model of the natural sciences, quantitative researchers have a central interest in showing that their findings can be *generalised* beyond the location of their project. Hence the concern among such researchers about the representativeness of survey samples, or the extent to which the results of experiments can be generalised beyond the circumstances of the original experiment.

5. As suggested in the introduction, few educational researchers, whether disposed towards qualitative or quantitative research, subscribe to the view that research can be *entirely* value-free. Therefore, the interest of the quantitative researcher turns more generally on whether the research can be (rather than is) replicated.

6. In quantitative research, the emphasis is very much upon the individual as the object of research; the aggregation of individualised data provides overall measures. Thus in a survey sample of 300 women managers and 300 male managers designed to ascertain a 'measure' of gendered leadership styles, individual responses may be aggregated in order to give a summative measurement. Following Bryman (1988), there may be a kind of perversity in reifying aggregated data on 'gendered management styles' on the one hand, and placing an emphasis upon individual, unconnected, and discrete responses on the other.

Introducing interpretivism

As with positivism, a range of issues confronts readers who may be exploring the term 'interpretivism' for the first time:

1. The term 'interpretivism' encompasses a number of philosophical traditions. The substitute term *anti-positivism* sets the paradigm in binary opposition to positivism. In the following section, the terms 'phenomenology', 'ethnomethodology', 'symbolic interactionism', 'naturalism', and 'ethogenics' are introduced; boundaries overlap and some traditions are excluded (see Silverman, 2001: 38–40 for additional terms and approaches, for example.) For some, ethnography is also a branch of this paradigm, although it is not always clear that there is agreement about whether ethnography is a philosophy or a method. (Pole and Morrison, forthcoming)

2. The term is not always recognised by educational researchers who work within the paradigm. Recognising the inter-subjectivity of educational

research may be viewed as 'obviously' the most appropriate way of conducting resesearch on/with or for human beings.
3. The term is not always recognised by educational researchers who work within the paradigm. Recognising the inter-subjectivity of educational research may be viewed as 'obviously' the most appropriate way of conducting research on/with or for human beings.
4. The educational community includes researchers who, for reasons that might be ideological, technical, or pragmatic, engage in 'mix-and-match' approaches to research methodology and method. Some researchers may not perceive, or indeed value a specific distinctiveness in paradigmatic approaches to research activities.

The starting point for interpretive researchers is to operate within a set of distinctive principles regarding what it means to conduct educational research *with* people. Thus the world of the educational researcher is different from the world of the natural science researcher — all educational research needs to be grounded in people's experience. For interpretivists, reality is not 'out there' as an amalgam of external phenomena waiting to be uncovered as 'facts', but a construct in which people understand reality in different ways. (It may be that some human groups perceive reality similarly, but this does not diminish the potential for reality to be construed differently.)

Interpretive researchers recognise that they are part of, rather than separate from, the research topics they investigate. Not only does their work impact upon research participants but participants impact upon researchers. For interpretivists, the core task is to view research participants as research subjects and to explore the 'meanings' of events and phenomena from the subjects' perspectives.

- *Phenomenologists.* From the writings of the 'father' of *phenomenology*, Albert Schutz (1967), through to more recent proponents, comes the view that 'the phenomenologist attempts to see things from the person's point of view'. (Bogdan and Taylor, 1975: 14)
- *Ethnomethodologists* have also been influenced by the work of Schutz; early work drew largely upon participant observation, unstructured interviews, and ethnographic studies in specific settings. More recently, the emphasis has been upon conversation analysis, and upon recordings of conversations with subjects, presented in as unadulterated forms as possible.
- *Symbolic interactionists* view life as an unfolding process in which individuals interpret their environment and act upon it on the basis of that interpretation. Best known proponents of this approach are G.H. Mead (1934) and Herbert Blumer (1969). Blumer (1969) argued that symbolic interactionism rests upon three premises:

> The first premise is that human beings act towards things on the basis of the meanings that the things have for them . . .
>
> The second is that the meaning of such things is derived from, or arises out of, the social interaction one has with one's fellows [*sic*] . . .
>
> The third premise is that these meanings are handled in, and modified through an interpretative process used by the person in dealing with the things he [*sic*] encounters. (1969: 2)

A key implication of this approach has been an emphasis upon participant observation, a common feature of school ethnographies of the 1980s (Burgess, 1983; Ball, 1981) in which the researcher becomes a participant in the activity s/he is observing.

- *Naturalism* implies a reluctance among researchers to interfere 'artificially' in the world around them and in particular emphasises the need to record the educational world in a way that would be consistent with the images of the world that participants carry with them.
- A key aspect of *ethogenics* is the understanding of 'episodes' in social life. The early study by Marsh, Rosser, and Harre (1978) of disorder in classrooms, and on football terraces, is cited by Bryman (1988) as an example of the ways in which ethogenics provides a framework for the analysis of social action:

> The material collected on schools and football terraces reveals that the apparently disordered events that often occur in these milieux, can be seen as 'conforming to a very distinct and orderly system of roles, rules, and meanings' (1978: 97); in other words, peoples' accounts of particular episodes and the observation of their acts . . . reveal a structure in the midst of apparent disorder. (1988: 61)

What is the relation between interpretivism and qualitative research?

What is apparent from the previous section is that there is an over-arching view that all human life is experienced and constructed from a subjective perspective. For an interpretivist there *cannot be* an objective reality which exists irrespective of the meanings human beings bring to it (though they may disagree about the extent to which reality is re-constructed by researchers).

Qualitative research has a number of key features:

1. Strategies that take the subject's perspective are central and draw heavily from the philosophical traditions introduced above. Understanding those perspectives is critical, regardless of whether the subjects are children or adults. Indeed, recent research, which emphasises the importance of

children's perspectives, as research 'with' and 'for' rather than 'on' children (for example, Mayall, 2000), reflects a powerful (re)emergence not only of the need to empathise with research subjects but also to penetrate the meaning frames in which they (in this case, children) operate. For researchers observing school management meetings or school playground activities, there is, therefore, an imperative to acquire and understand a specialised, even new language. The need to penetrate the subject's world suggests a preference for lengthy immersion 'in the field' as a participant observer, or for detailed unstructured or serial life history interviews. The approach is replete with challenges, not least of which may be seeing 'through *whose* eyes' and the pressure to produce research outcomes over reduced time spans. Nonetheless, the aim is to investigate 'from the inside' through a process of *verstehen* or empathetic understanding.

2. Qualitative researchers play much attention to detailed observation. Indeed, the essence of their work is 'rich' and 'deep' description. This provides contexts for description and interpretation when researchers ask 'What is going on here?' Few details are excluded. Thus the layout of the chairs and tables in a principal's office in preparation for a senior management meeting, for example, can offer important descriptive insights about the ways a principal might construe the purposes and operation of such a meeting.

3. In qualitative research, detailed consideration is given to the holistic picture in which the research topic is embedded. This is more than attention to setting; the approach taken is that researchers can *only* make sense of the data collected if they are able to understand the data in a broader educational, social, and historic context. For example, school improvement studies look at individual institutions 'as a whole' in order to understand the processes of change that have led to improvement in that school, but not necessarily in other schools. (Such studies do not, of course, always endear themselves to policy makers who may prefer 'the attractiveness of school effectiveness research . . . resulting from the prospect it offers of identifying the characteristics of effective schools, and then using them to improve less effective schools' (Ozga 2000: 80).)

4. Because qualitative research is frequently concerned with process(es) — of learning, adaptation, innovation, change, professional development, etc, there is often a longitudinal element to the research, and no shrinking from the commonplace, or what Miles and Huberman (1994) describe as the 'banal':

> Qualitative research is conducted through an intense and/or prolonged contact with a 'field' or life situation. These situations are typical 'banal' or normal ones, reflective of the everyday life of individuals, groups, societies, and organizations. (1994: 6)

5. There may be a reluctance on the part of qualitative researchers to impose prior structures on their investigation so as not to foreclose issues which may be invisible at the start of the research. Moreover, 'the researcher is the main "measurement device" of the study' (Miles and Huberman, 1994: 7). An absence of foreclosure should not be misconstrued as a reluctance to be systematic, and a case can be made for 'tight prestructured qualitative designs' (especially for those new to qualitative studies) as well as for 'loose, emergent ones' (1994: 17).

6. Linked to the previous point, there may be a reluctance to impose prior theoretical frameworks. Instead, notable writers in the field discuss the importance of 'sensitising concepts' (Blumer, 1954) and 'conceptual frameworks' (Miles and Huberman, 1994). 'Frameworks can be rudimentary or elaborate, theory-driven or commonsensical, descriptive or causal' (Miles and Huberman, 1994: 18).

7. In contrast to quantitative research, the emphasis in interpretivism is upon words rather than numbers. This should not, of course, be exaggerated, from either perspective, but the key issue for qualitative researchers is that textual analysis predominates: 'Words can be broken into semiotic segments. They can be organised to permit the researcher to contrast, compare, analyse and bestow patterns upon them' (Miles and Huberman,1994: 7). More recently, photographs and video images have complemented rather than replaced words (for example, Harrison, 1996).

Prospects for combining approaches

The educational research landscape has become increasingly diverse. Regardless of whether this is seen as fundamentally problematic, or, more positively, an opportunity to examine educational management and leadership from a rich diversity of perspectives, some notes of caution are necessary.

- There may be a tendency for tutors of research methods courses to encourage their students to discuss the advantages and disadvantages of qualitative and quantitative 'methods' as if in isolation from either the epistemological roots in which they are located, or their appropriateness to particular research problems/topics. In the absence of either, the question is pointless and lacks meaning.
- In previous sections, the distinction between methods and methodology has been made. Yet, there may still be a tendency to confuse methods and methodology, a confusion that may be magnified when mixing-and-matching methods in a non-reflective 'cook book' style.
- At the risk of repetition, not all researchers exhibit strong epistemological 'leanings' towards any one philosophical tradition. (This, of course, begs the question about which levels of knowledge and understanding

about diverse traditions researchers bring to their research when they embark upon their studies.)

• What may flow from the previous point is the tendency of some researchers to engage in rationalisations about their epistemological positions 'after the event'. Brown and Dowling (1998) comment:

> We have chosen not to present the choice of a particular way of collecting data as indicating a strong affiliation to a specific epistemological position. In our view these associations are commonly *post-hoc* and are of limited help in either the design or interrogation of research. It is of greater importance in deciding how to collect your data, that the methods are consistent with the theoretical framework in which you are working. (1998: 57)

Again, this begs the question of the extent to which the 'theoretical frameworks' in which researchers work are, in turn, nested in deeper epistemological frameworks that are concerned with what counts as worthwhile educational knowledge and how to get it. This brings us almost full-circle to the starting points for this chapter: namely the relationship between the nature of our research enquiry and the attitudes and activities of educational researchers. Almost, but not quite. One bridging point remains and that is known as reflexivity.

Reflexivity

At one level, reflexivity denies the possibility of researchers ever achieving an entirely objective position in relation to research, because they are part of the social, political and educational worlds they are studying. Such 'worlds' vary from person to person, from one country to another, and between cultures. Readers will recall that earlier in the chapter, the term 'isms' was introduced to illustrate that some researchers work with self-conscious political or ideological intent. Positivism and interpretivism are also shown to be underpinned by philosophical traditions, though it has been suggested that research has not always been conducted with overt commitment to, or understanding about underlying epistemological ideas. From the perspective of reflexivity, such awareness, or lack of it, is not just implicated in an understanding of epistemology but also requires researchers to consider that 'the sense' they make of the world is reflected in, and affected by, the norms and values that have been absorbed as part of life experience.

In brief, reflexivity means two things: first, that all research orientations are shaped by and reflected in the social, political and educational worlds in which individual researchers operate; and second, that researchers need to be aware of the way such orientations affect all research aspects, including decisions about the selection of research topics. Such awareness is challenging since it may bring to the fore features of research that might otherwise have remained hidden, assumed, or denied.

Take, for example, the 'extreme' forms of positivism or interpretivism, especially naturalism. Naturalists share with positivists a commitment to accounts of 'other' educational phenomena, including people; research reports from both are supposedly untainted by the researcher. Perhaps surprisingly, positivism and naturalism show important similarities. Positivists want to eliminate the researcher (or distance him/her, sometimes physically, through postal questionnaires, for example) as much as possible from the research, and attempt to do this via statistical procedures. For naturalists, the key to their 'absence' from the research is to 'write' the other's actions and words, as if the other were unaffected by the researcher's presence, leaving research participants to 'tell it as it is'. Is this possible? Reflexive researchers appreciate that *it isn't*.

> Once we abandon the idea that the social character of research can be 'standardised out' or avoided by becoming a 'fly on the wall' or 'full participant', the role of the researcher as active participant in the research process becomes clear. He or she is the research instrument *par excellence*. (Hammersley and Atkinson, 1995: 19)

So, reflexivity is not exclusive to either positivist or interpretive research. Whilst challenging in its implications, I would want to argue that such awareness is both empowering for researchers and those with whom they work. Researchers of educational management and leadership are empowered to produce insightful, critical, systematic and skilful accounts without placing overwhelming 'emphasis upon futile appeals to naïve empiricism of either the positivist or naturalistic variety' (Hammersley and Atkinson, 1995: 20–1). This allows researchers to reflect upon, and even celebrate, their key roles as contributors to, and participants in, the principles and practices of their educational research projects, and also 'denies the supremacy' (*ibid.*) of qualitative or quantitative approaches.

Finally

In presenting the philosophical traditions that underpin *positivism* and *quantity, interpretivism* and *quality* in educational research, a tendency to underestimate the degree of overlap, and indeed, similarity between them has been noted. In part, this is a consequence of establishing, for analytical purposes, a distinction between 'qualitative' and 'quantitative'; hopefully, evaluative distinctions between 'good' and 'bad' have been avoided. Two further examples are illustrative. Bryman (1988), for example, asserts that 'there does not seem to be any obvious reason why qualitative research cannot be used to test theories in the manner typically associated with the model of the quantitative research process' . . . or to deny that 'much quantitative research shares a concern for subjects' interpretations which is supposed to be the province of the qualitative researcher' (1988: 172–73). Secondly, both qualitative and quantitative researchers can and do use numerical data. Recent developments in qualitative software packages, for example, make it possible for researchers to collect and analyse responses from many unstructured interviews as from pre-coded questionnaire sample returns.

The educational research community often appears to veer between cautious optimism and a less than reflective 'cook book' approach towards combining qualitative and quantitative approaches. In the past, adherence to paradigmatic positions has tended to focus mainly upon idealised versions of a debate that, for epistemological fundamentalists, remains ongoing. Systematic and focused enquiry into educational management requires, in combination, an awareness of:

- the philosophical tradition(s) that underpin(s) the approach taken; and
- its appropriateness to the research topic selected.

and an awareness that:

- some, *but not all* topics lend themselves to methodological integration; and that
- decisions to integrate or not need to be justified on theoretical and empirical grounds.

Perhaps the key issue for all educational researchers is to engage with either or both approaches knowingly and self-consciously as a counterpoint to naïvety. According to Brown and Dowling:

> The naïve use of quantitative methods imagines that statistical techniques themselves will guarantee the quality of the work. Correspondingly, naïve qualitative research tends to substitute narrative for analysis. On the other hand, the adoption of a dual approach involving both qualitative and quantitative techniques can help in overcoming such tendencies to what we might refer as naïve empiricism. The qualitative imagination will tend to demand that quantitative analysis explains itself in terms of non-statistical concepts that it is claiming to measure. The quantitative imagination will demand a degree of precision in definition that qualitative work may want to slide away from. (1998: 83).

Again, caution needs to be exercised in relation to the view that using a combined approach to educational research *necessarily* provides a balance between the shortcomings of one approach and the strengths of another. The critical issue for researchers is to choose the approach that best addresses the questions asked; and, as importantly, that researchers are aware of the implications of choosing one approach over another (or combining them), and its impact upon the things that researchers will find. Hammersley (1992b) evokes the image of the research journey:

> What is involved here is not a cross-roads where we go left or right. A better analogy is a complex maze where we are repeatedly faced with decisions, and where paths wind back on one another. (1992b: 172)

Such methodological awareness, I would argue, has seldom been more necessary. I would agree with Bassey (1999) that the 'public' world of educational policy, practice and research has become more 'positivist' (1999: 44). When writers of research guides advocate adherence to the conventional styles of research writing in 'the third person' (Denscombe, 1998: 229–31) and caution against 'breaking the rules', it is not difficult to recognise the extent to which the conventions of positivist approaches to research remain the norm. (Interpretive researchers recognise that they are part of the reality they study and may use personal pronouns when writing up research to emphasise and illustrate their approach.) Interpretive research may no longer be the 'Cinderella' of the educational research world, but when 'in the field of education the dominant ideology of positivism/empiricism becomes perhaps even more dominant' (Scott, 2000: 1), researchers need to be very clear not only about *how* they are doing research on educational management and leadership but also '*why* this approach rather than another?'

References

Babbie, E. R. (1979) *The Practice of Social Research*, 2nd edn., Belmont, California: Wadsworth.

Bagnall, R. (1990) 'Lifelong education: the institutionalisation of an illiberal and regressive concept', *Educational Philosophy and Theory*, 22(1): 1–7.

Ball, S. (1981) *Beachside Comprehensive: A Case Study of Secondary Schooling.* Cambridge: Cambridge University Press.

Ball, S. (1987) *The Micro-Politics of the School: Towards a Theory of Social Organisation.* London: Routledge.

Ball, S. (1999) 'School management. Myth: good management makes good schools', in O'Hagan, B. (ed.), *Modern Educational Myths. The Future of Democratic Comprehensive Education*, London: Kogan Page.

Barber, M. (1996) *The Learning Game: Arguments for an Educational Revolution*, London: Victor Gollancz.

Bassey, M. (1999) *Case Study in Educational Settings*, Buckingham: Open University Press.

Blumer, H. (1954) 'What is wrong with social theory?', *American Sociological Review*, 19(1): 3–10.

Blumer, H. (1969) *Symbolic Interactionism*, Englewood Cliffs, NJ: Prentice Hall.

Bogdan, R. and Taylor, S. J. (1975) *Qualitative Research for Education. An*

Introduction to Theory and Methods, Boston: Alleyn and Bacon.

Brown, A. and Dowling, P. (1998) *Doing Research. Reading Research. A Mode of Interrogation for Education*, London: Falmer Press.

Bryman, A. (1988) *Quantity and Quality in Social Research*, London: Routledge.

Burgess, R. G. (1983) *Experiencing Comprehensive Education: A Study of Bishop McGregor School*, London: Methuen.

Bryman, A. and Burgess, R. G. (eds.) (1994) *Analysing Qualitative Data*, London: Routledge.

Clipson-Boyles, S. (2000) 'Introduction', in Clipson-Boyles, S. (ed.) *Putting Research into Practice in Primary Teaching and Learning*, London: David Fulton publishers.

Cox, R.W. (1980) 'Social forces, states, and world orders', *Millenium: Journal of International Studies*, 10(2): 126–155.

Denscombe, M. (1998) *The Good Research Guide for Small-Scale Research Projects.* Buckingham: Open University Press.

Griffiths, M. (1998) *Educational Research for Social Justice. Getting off the Fence*, Buckingham: Open University Press.

Gubrium, J. and Holstein, J. (1997) *The New Language of Qualitative Method.* New York: Oxford University Press.

Hammersley, M. (1992a) 'On feminist methodology', *Sociology*, 26: 187–206.

Hammersley, M. (1992b) '*Deconstructing the Qualitative Divide: What's Wrong with Ethnography?* London: Routledge.

Hammersley, M. (1995) *The Politics of Social Research*, London: Sage.

Hammersley, M. and Atkinson, P. (1995) *Ethnography. Principles in Practice*, 2nd edn., London: Routledge.

Hargreaves, D. (1996) 'Educational research and evidence-based educational research. A response to critics', *Research Intelligence*, 58: 12–16.

Harrison, B. (1996) 'Every picture 'tells a story': uses of the visual in sociological research', in Lyons, E. S. and Busfield, J. (eds.) *Methodological Imaginations*, Macmillan Press for the British Sociological Association, pp. 75–94.

Jonathon, R. (1995) 'Liberal philosophy of education: a paradigm under strain', Journal of the Philosophy of Education, 29(1): 93–107.

Johnson, D. (1994) *Research Methods in Educational Management*, London: Pitman Publishing.

McKenzie, G. (1997) 'The Age of Reason or the Age of Innocence?', in McKenzie, G., Powell, J. and Usher, R. (eds.) *Understanding Social Research. Methodology and Practice*, London: Falmer Press.

Marsh, P., Rosser, E. and Harre, R. (1978) *The Rules of Disorder*, London: Routledge and Kegan Paul.

Mayall, B. (2000) 'Conversations with children: working with generational issues', in Christensen, P. and James, A. (eds.) *Research with Children. Perspectives and Practices*, London: Falmer Press.

Mead, G. H. (1934) *Mind, Self, and Society*, Chicago: University of Chicago Press.

Miles, M. B. and Huberman, A.M. (1994), *Qualitative Data Analysis* (2nd edn.), London: Sage.

Ozga, J. (2000) *Policy Research in Educational Settings*, Buckingham: Open University Press.

Pole, C. and Morrison, M. (forthcoming) *Ethnography for Education*, Buckingham:

Open University Press.

Ramazanoglu, C. (1992) 'On feminist methodology: male reason versus female empowerment', *Sociology*, 26: 207–212.

Ranson, S. (1996) 'The future of educational research', *British Educational Research Association Journal*, 22(5): 532–536.

Schutz, A. (1967) *The Phenomenology of the Social World*, Evanston, IL: Northwestern University Press.

Scott, D. (2000) *Realism and Educational Research. New Perspectives and Possibilities.* London: Routledge/Falmer Press.

Silverman, D. (2001) *Interpreting Qualitiative Data. Methods for Analysing Talk, Text, and Interaction*, 2nd edn., London: Sage.

Tight, M. (1996) *Key Concepts in Adult Education and Training*, London: Routledge.

Tooley, J. with Darby, D. J. (1998) *Educational Research: A Critique.* London: Ofsted.

Usher, R. (1997) 'Introduction' in McKenzie, G., Powell, J. and Usher, R. (eds.) *Understanding Social Research. Methodology and Practice*, London: Falmer Press.

Weiner, G., Arnot, M. and David, M. (1997) 'Is the future female? Female success, male disadvantage, and changing gender patterns in education', in Halsey, A. H., Lauder, H., Brown, P. and Wells A. S. (eds.) *Education, Culture, Economy, and Society*, Oxford: Oxford University Press.

Woodhead, C. (1998) 'Foreword', in Tooley, J. with Darby, D. J. *Educational Research: a Critique*, London: Ofsted.

2

Cross-cultural differences in interpreting and doing research

Clive Dimmock

Introduction

There is little doubt that research in different cultures, and the comparative study that often results, is rapidly assuming greater significance than at any time during the past century. Interest in cross-cultural research is a consequence of powerful trends acting at the macro-social level, in particular, the emergence of a global economy, and a cadre of policy makers who increasingly 'sing from the same hymn sheet' (Lauder, 2000: 465).

For too long, assumptions, policies and practices emanating from Western Europe and North America have been imposed on societies with very different cultures. As Broadfoot (1997: xii) puts it, 'There has been no shortage of individual researchers, government agencies and international aid organisations ready to define problems and prescribe solutions according to their own priorities and their own cultural assumptions'.

More recently, however, a growing awareness of the need for cultural and contextual sensitivity when conducting empirical research and when drawing conclusions from comparative and cross-cultural studies, seems to be emerging (Dimmock, 2000). The need for raised sensitivity applies particularly to postgraduates and academics researching in at least one of the following three situations. First, it is pertinent to researchers wishing to conduct empirical and non-empirical research in cultures other than their own; secondly, it is applicable to those aiming to conduct studies in their own cultures while using methods, assumptions, models, theories and even conclusions drawn from elsewhere; and thirdly, it is relevant to researchers wishing to draw comparisons between the education systems of different societies.

While this chapter raises issues of relevance to academic researchers in general, it is primarily written with the interests and concerns of postgraduate students in mind. The chapter explores two main avenues of educational management research in different cultures. The first concerns the cultural effect of attributing different meanings or understandings to such research, and the second raises issues concerning the conduct of research in different cultures. Accordingly, the chapter is structured to reflect these two themes.

Societal culture and the implications for understanding the meaning of research

It is fitting to begin with words of caution to the novice researcher. A large part of the accumulated body of literature in educational management and leadership has been generated by a culturally homogeneous cadre of scholars from English-speaking backgrounds. These scholars represent societies that constitute no more than eight percent of the world's population yet they claim to speak for the vast majority. In many instances they fail to de-limit the geo-cultural boundaries within which their models, theories, ideas, findings and conclusions apply. On other occasions, they advocate the transfer and adoption of policies and practices from one society to another with relative impunity and naïvety. Policy makers, too, are not slow to adopt policies that are culturally borrowed from elsewhere. We have come to expect this as part of the globalised world. Bajunid (1996) summarises the issues well in posing the following questions to non-Western societies:

- Is the wholesale acceptance of Western educational practices appropriate to their national goals?
- Are the educational practices they have adopted from the West consistent with and sustaining of their cultural heritage?
- What are their own intellectual traditions and indigenous approaches to education and cultural transmission?
- How does the indigenous knowledge embedded in their culture fit with the theories, assumptions, and practices embedded in Western-derived educational programmes?

Paradoxically, the same questions apply equally well, but in reverse, to the USA and the UK as they look to Japan, Taiwan and other Asian 'Tigers' for direction on how to improve teaching and student learning outcomes. For probably the first time, there is now reciprocal interest between East and West in each other's education systems.

The point to make, however, is not that such international cross-cultural awareness is negative and should cease. Indeed, quite the reverse. There is a strong case for encouraging more postgraduates and academics to research the influence of societal culture on schooling and educational management since relatively little is known about it. Through learning about other societies and cultures, each society can learn more about itself. A key issue is that successful policies and practices cannot simply be replicated and transplanted from one society to another, even with some adaptation. Before a particular policy or practice is adopted in a given system, there is a need to know why it is working in other societies and with what effects. This demands an understanding of the indigenous culture, its values, beliefs, customs and ways of life, all of which interact.

The problem is that our knowledge base for understanding culture and its intricate connections with policy and practice is extremely sketchy. Cultural variables mediate between society on the one hand and school policies and practices on the other. Orthodox school effectiveness and school improvement studies have generally failed to build cultural variables into their equations. This has repercussions for postgraduates and academics when designing future research proposals.

It is thus timely that research in educational leadership and management take more cognisance of societal culture. It is fair to claim that the cultural and cross-cultural dimension in the field has been ignored or neglected for too long. Among the reasons why societal culture and cross-cultural comparison are beginning to attract attention are the following:

- narrow ethnocentrism of Anglo-American research;
- international comparison of test results;
- the work of international agencies;
- globalisation of policy and practice;
- increased mobility of ideas and people;
- internationalisation of schools, especially the private sector;
- internationalisation of higher education; and
- multi-culturalism within societies.

This list may itself provide a framework of ideas for potential research proposals. A growing interest in cross-cultural research and in culture more generally in educational management has a number of consequences. First, the foundation concept of 'culture' itself needs clarification. Second, to the extent that cultures differ, the meanings that societies impart to particular ideas, actions, behaviours, processes and structures may differ. Third, there is a need to develop more rigorous and systematic methods of authentic comparison and measurement of cultural differences and their impact on educational management. The first two points are matters concerning the meanings attributed to research and will be discussed in this section, while the last relates to the following section on the conduct of research.

Clarifying the concept of culture

For the intending researcher in the field, a key early stage is to appreciate the different interpretations and nuances of the term 'culture'. The present argument suggests that the concept of culture and societal culture in particular, is a promising base on which to build a comparative and international branch of educational leadership and management. Elsewhere, a justification for this approach has been provided (see, for example, Dimmock and Walker,

1998a, 1998b). However, the researcher should be mindful of potential difficulties.

Culture is an amorphous, ambivalent and contested concept (Brislin, 1993). Anthropologists and sociologists, 'culturalists' and 'modernists' tend to attribute different emphases, if not meanings, to the term. Anthropological and 'culturalist' approaches dwell on the values, beliefs and customs of distinct groups of people, whether they be at national/regional level (societal culture), local level, or school level (organisational culture). From these perspectives, culture is based on the traditional values that have built up over a long period of time. Sociologists, on the other hand, adopt a more institutionalist position, viewing culture as an amalgam of values, institutional and structural arrangements, political and historical forces that together configure a society. 'Modernists' stress the world as a changing environment where traditional values are constantly eroded. They tend to see 'culture' as a mix of older and newer values, all in a state of flux.

While it is clear that culture does not account for all of the influences on schooling and educational management, it is difficult to know where exactly to draw its boundaries in delimiting it from say, history, politics, economics and religion. From a culturalist perspective, the latter may be considered part of, and certainly influential in shaping, culture. A further issue concerns the increasing phenomenon of multi-cultural societies with distinctive sub-groups of people within a society, rendering the emergence of a homogeneous, typical and representative societal culture even more difficult.

The purpose of the present discussion is to encourage the postgraduate researcher to undertake studies in educational leadership and management from a cultural perspective, but to do so with insight and awareness of the complexities. There are many challenges confronting, as well as attractions enticing, the researcher when applying the concept of culture (for a full discussion, see Dimmock, 2000, Dimmock and Walker, 1998a, 1998b, Walker and Dimmock, in press). It is not an easy concept to work with, but it is too important an influence to be ignored.

Examples of cultural context and differences of meaning

Since culture permeates all levels of society, it provides rich opportunities for researchers to explore the interrelationships between schools and their micro- and macro-environments. Studying the influence of societal culture is particularly rewarding at the level of the school, since it is here that the macro and micro-levels of culture interact at the point of policy implementation.

'Culture' is a particularly useful analytical concept in situations where the characteristics of different organisations appear on the surface to possess similarity, but are, in fact, quite different in their actual *modus operandi*. For example, schools in different societies often appear to have similar, formal leadership hierarchies and organisational structures, while subtle differences in values, relationships and processes are hidden or disguised (Walker and Dimmock, 2000a). Likewise, while different societies may appear to adopt the same policy agenda and framework, the meanings and interpretations each attaches to the core ideas and concepts may vary dramatically. These are important considerations for researchers, as the following illustrations demonstrate.

A policy shift towards school-based management and devolution has been gathering momentum in very different cultures and societies for the past two decades. Associated with these reforms in the management and organisation of school systems are new configurations for curriculum, teaching and learning, as well as changes to assessment and evaluation. These are broad sweeping reform packages that are complex in affecting just about every part of an education system — its rules, roles and relationships. They are thus attractive themes for postgraduate research.

In the global push to introduce such measures, a new educational lexicon has been invented based on core concepts such as, 'school-based management', 'accountability', 'collaborative decision making', 'appraisal', 'national curriculum', 'curriculum frameworks', 'outcomes curriculum', 'student-centred learning', 'constructivism', 'league tables', 'performance indicators', 'creativity' and 'quality schools'. Educators across the world — policy makers, practitioners and researchers alike — increasingly communicate by using this lexicon. The problem is that often, without realisation, educators in different cultures attribute different meanings and significance to the same core concepts and ideas. Researchers need to be alert not only to how globalisation spreads the same policy agenda across many societies, but how different cultures mediate the meanings and significance of these policies.

This latter point is well illustrated by the current press in many societies for a national curriculum based on student-learning outcomes. In the UK, a national curriculum was introduced in 1988 to replace a situation where each school and local authority exercised considerable discretion as to what was taught and how much time was allocated to each subject. Teaching, especially in primary schools, had come to rely on so-called progressive, student-centred methods. The aim of the British Government, therefore, was to establish a clear and detailed prescribed curriculum specifying learning outcomes, where none existed before, and to pare back the progressive methods by advocating direct whole-class teaching and testing. Contrast this with Hong Kong, which already had a prescribed curriculum for many decades, though not one framed in learning outcome terms. In Hong Kong, the problem — as perceived by the Special Administrative Region Government — has been too great a reliance on direct whole-class teaching, too much standardisation, insufficient attention to individual student differences and too little variation of teaching methods. While the push in both societies is towards a national curriculum based on learning outcomes, the means of achieving the aims is very different. Each starts from a different position. Each culture attributes different importance and meanings to the same ideas.

Hong Kong, along with others of its Asian neighbours, aims to introduce more student-centred methods into their otherwise teacher-centred classrooms. United Kingdom governments, fearing that student-centredness had gone too far, have sought to introduce more basic education and direct teaching. At the policy level, the tendency is for each to move towards the other. In practice, however, culture along with other factors, makes this global tendency difficult to achieve.

If the analysis is continued, the practicality of student-centred methods is influenced by class size. Class sizes in Hong Kong are typically 40 or 45, while in mainland China, they can be 65 to 70. It is worth asking the question 'Is it possible for Hong Kong or mainland Chinese teachers to practise student-centred learning?' In addressing this question, Stevenson and Stigler (1992) show how Chinese teachers manage to combine both direct teaching and student-centredness in a uniquely Chinese style of teaching. They show convincingly that Chinese culture enables teachers to conduct lessons with such large classes and yet still attend to individual needs. Chinese culture is manifested in early childhood socialisation in the family, preparing children to conform more readily to school authority and traditional teaching, than do Western cultures, thus presenting few disruptive problems and enabling teachers to focus on learning. Home and school values seem to align more closely in Asian than Western societies, with ramifications for teaching.

Elsewhere, Watkins (2000) has argued that there are major cultural differences between Anglo-American and East Asian connotations of rote memorisation and learning. The Western view of rote learning and memorisation is derogatory, contrasting it with deep learning for understanding. In contrast, Watkins (2000) shows that for the Chinese student, memorisation is highly valued as a necessary prior step towards learning for understanding. The Chinese student typically learns in a different way from their Western counterparts.

Many other examples are to be found of how culture imparts different meanings and connotations to the same concept. For example, in Singapore, 'creativity' is seen as a set of skills to be acquired, while in the UK and the USA it is viewed as the product of 'free' expression and original thought. Likewise, the notion of appraisal assumes a different connotation in Chinese societies such as Hong Kong, where the direct face-to-face exchange of views associated with Anglo-American cultures, is considered threatening (Walker and Dimmock, 2000b).

The foregoing discussion is not exhaustive. Rather, its purpose is to illustrate how researchers in educational leadership and management need to take cognisance of how apparently identical concepts, policies, ideas and behaviours may hide important differences in meaning and connotation, depending on their cultural context. Other important considerations for post-graduate and academic researchers, however, centre on the conduct of research in different cultural settings.

Differences in societal culture and the implications for conducting research

If, as this chapter suggests, postgraduate research in educational management is to take greater cognisance of societal culture, then there is a need to establish robust frameworks and rigorous methodologies. The field of cross-cultural comparative and international educational management is still in its infancy (Dimmock and Walker, 1998a, 1998b). Besides new frameworks and models, careful thought about the techniques and instruments to facilitate data collection and analysis is needed. Without this rigour, there is a danger that superficial cross-cultural analysis and comparison will result. The same pitfall awaits researchers investigating an educational management problem or issue within a culture rather than between cultures. Failure to distinguish the part that culture plays may seriously weaken their thesis.

Postgraduate students, as well as academics, require a foundation for studying the influence of societal culture at school level and for making cross-cultural comparisons. In earlier work, a framework was presented for the systematic study of cross-cultural comparative educational leadership and management (see for example, Dimmock, 2000; Dimmock and Walker 1998a, 1998b; Dimmock and Walker, 2000). This framework identifies four elements that make up a school:

- organisational structures;
- leadership and management processes;
- curriculum; and
- teaching and learning.

In addition, the concept of culture is operationalised for research application. This entails identifying generic dimensions that are present in all cultures, but to different degrees. Since they are generic, they provide common reference points, thereby enabling more rigorous and systematic comparison. As an integral part of the framework, the dimensions of societal culture are as follows:

- power-concentrated/power-dispersed;
- self-oriented/group-oriented;
- aggression/consideration;
- proactivism/fatalism;

34

- limited relationship/holistic relationship;
- long-term oriented/short-term oriented; and
- male influence/female influence.

Having identified the elements of schools and key dimensions of culture, the next stage in the development of our research programme has been to use both as a source of generating instruments for data collection and analysis. The instruments developed to date reflect a mixed methodology, that is, both quantitative and qualitative. Through the process of administering the instruments and collecting cross-cultural data on school management and schooling in different cultures, the validity, reliability and 'trustworthiness' of the instruments can be tested and refined.

Ultimately, the research development process outlined above aims to build and test new theory. A fundamental assumption, however, is that the researcher will be able to gain access in different societal cultures to those cases and samples considered important for investigation. Regrettably, this may not always be the case.

Difficulties of access

Conducting research in some cultures can present difficult if not insurmountable problems regarding access for even the most experienced academic researcher, let alone the postgraduate student. In some schools considered 'highly researchable' access might be difficult because so many researchers wish to study them. They become 'over-researched' and access may be denied simply because of disruption to normal school life. There is always the need for researchers to cultivate good relationships with potential participants, and where possible, to offer them some benefit in return for their willingness to participate.

These problems fade into insignificance, however, when compared with the challenges of researching in countries such as mainland China. There, research in school leadership and management is often seen as 'intrusive', the more so if the researcher is from outside the country. School principals, in particular, are extremely sensitive to requests to collect data in their schools for fear of upsetting their superiors; teachers are equally sensitive for much the same reason. Normally, successful access to mainland schools requires the penetration of an elaborate bureaucratic network, highly trusted co-operative relationships with eminent local academics and bureaucrats, and even the payment of fees.

Undertaking research projects in some cultures — even if they are for personal master's or doctoral theses — may require the permission of government authorities as is the case in Singapore. Large bureaucracies are not the easiest of organisations to penetrate unless key people in prominent positions are known to the researcher. Even when government bureaucracies do respond positively by granting permission for a research study to proceed, they may insist on changes to the research design that fundamentally weaken it. For example, the authorities may insist that a large sample be reduced in size before it can proceed, with the effect that generalisation is rendered impossible.

Gaining the willing participation of subjects and respondents may also present a problem in cultures where power, influence and status are of great importance. In societies such as those of Arabia, Israel and China, participation is more likely if the researcher is perceived by the respondents to have power, standing and status. In such circumstances it is useful if postgraduate students can enlist allies in the system with some influence.

In general, it appears that the more democratic, open and liberal the society, the easier is access to the subjects to be researched. It also appears that a wider array of research paradigms and methodologies are tolerated and practised in such societies.

Preference for different paradigms and methodologies

A host of factors related to culture warrant consideration at the early stage of planning and designing a research study. For example, in certain societies there might be a tradition of using one research paradigm rather than another. Even within the same paradigm, some research methods might be more difficult to apply in certain cultures than others. For example, within the qualitative paradigm, the present author has in the past encouraged some of his postgraduate students in Hong Kong to adopt the life history approach. These attempts have usually met with only partial success because of a reticence on the part of potential participants to talk openly about themselves, their life histories and the lives of others. Similarly, many subjects and respondents may be reluctant to participate in studies that involve their criticism of authority or government. In addition, cultural differences can account for why certain research paradigms or methodological approaches are particularly inappropriate in some settings. The adoption of a critical perspective or a feminist perspective in Singapore, for example, might be a case in point.

A further issue concerns the preference for a particular research methodology or paradigm that researchers in some cultures display. In many developing countries and some developed societies, such as Hong Kong, the preference for quantitative methods over qualitative is quite apparent. This phenomenon in the case of Hong Kong might simply be a reflection of the natural aptitude that Chinese students seem to have for mathematics and statistics, a characteristic borne out in their superior performance in international achievement tests at school. Some have even attributed this gift for mathematics to the Chinese language and its construction of characters based on symbols. Others account for it by recognising that the Chinese prefer to think synthetically and to gain the big picture (and hence, to undertake large sampling from which generalisations can be made), while Westerners tend to think analytically and creatively. With the recent expansion of higher education in Hong Kong, however, there is now a growing awareness of, and desire to learn more about, qualitative research methods in educational management.

Besides the marked preference for quantitative studies in such cultures, there is also a tendency to focus on policy and descriptive, system-wide studies, a phenomenon recognised by Vulliamy, Lewin and Stephens (1990). Comparative studies of a macro-system level in educational management typify this phenomenon. School-level and classroom-level research, especially of an empirical kind, is less prevalent and case studies of individual principals and teachers are a rarity. There are many promising avenues for future research projects in these latter areas.

Overcoming cultural difference in conducting research — cross-cultural research teams

In conducting research into educational leadership and management that takes societal culture into account, a key issue concerns the researcher's understanding of the particular culture(s) being studied. This is less of a problem where the culture of the researcher and the education system under investigation are the same. One would expect a native to possess a full appreciation of his or her own culture. Against this, however, is the view that people can be 'blind' to some aspects of their own culture and can take for granted many otherwise interesting characteristics, thus failing to give them due recognition.

'Outsider' researchers also present problems in possibly lacking detailed knowledge and appreciation of the indigenous culture. As Lauder asserts when describing comparative, cultural research in education:

> there is an experiential component necessary to good comparative research. It involves . . . a range of cognitive and emotional understandings that enable individuals to get 'beneath the skin' of another culture. In turn, this raises all the problems about the difficulties of translation (2000: 466).

On the other hand, 'outsiders' may bring a 'fresh' perspective, one which may not only highlight key aspects of a particular culture, but recognise salient differences between it and other cultures.

A way of capitalising on the strengths of both 'insider' and 'outsider' researcher is to bring both together in cross-cultural teams. There may be difficulties of language and communication in such teams, especially initially, but these may ease over the course of time (see Chapter 11). For individual masters or doctoral students, however, the possibility of forming teams is rare, unless the supervisor has a number of students investigating the same research themes cross-culturally.

Examples of contrasting cultures and the promotion of research in educational leadership and management

It was noted above that the conduct of research in some cultures may be inhibited for political and social reasons. In contrast, three countries with very different societal cultures — Papua New Guinea (PNG), Sierra Leone and the UK — provide examples of governmental encouragement of educational research. In the first two cases, independent research has been encouraged in order to reduce the dependence on expertise and funding from foreign agencies. Guthrie (1989) reports that Papua New Guinea 'is a comparatively uncommon example of a developing country with an extensive, critical and readily available research literature which does inform educational policy and practice' (1989: 46). The country's Ministry of Education has supported educational research with a strong applied focus since the mid-1960s, when the *Papua New Guinea Journal of Education* was established. In the 1970s, the Educational Research Unit at the University of Papua New Guinea was established and since then research by foreigners has been encouraged.

The main reason underpinning the PNG Government's enlightened policy with regard to research has been its avowed desire to improve educational practice. There is close co-operation between educational researchers, policy makers and administrators at both national and provincial levels towards that end.

A rather different model of government sponsorship of educational research is provided by Sierra Leone. According to Vulliamy (1990: 23), research there has been 'more self-consciously national' and has been angled at influencing practitioners directly rather than through policy makers and planners. Many projects begin with teachers who are encouraged to apply case study and action research methods in tackling their school-level problems. Although the Government was initially sceptical, its policy has been to allow these projects to proceed.

Vulliamy (1990) goes on to draw three interesting conclusions from the successful examples of educational research in PNG and Sierra Leone. The first is the need for clear mechanisms whereby educational research can influence policy and practice; the second is the need for appropriate places to publish research findings; and the third is the benefit that can flow from co-operation between developed and developing countries. In PNG, this co-operation has been through the engagement of overseas researchers on locally defined projects and in Sierra Leone through the use of financial aid and external consultants to facilitate national research.

The recent UK experience provides a third example of government endorsement of research in education, more particularly in educational management and school leadership. Clearly, the British culture is very different from that of the developing societies of PNG and Sierra Leone. The Blair Labour Government has made expenditure on education its top priority since taking office in the mid-1990s. A key aim of the Government has been school improvement; that is, improvement in student-learning outcomes. Among the motivating forces for such a policy are the development of a globalised competitive world economy and its accompanying knowledge-based society, and the superior performance of East Asian and South-East Asian students on international achievement tests in maths and science. British students are seen as lagging behind their Asian counterparts in these subjects.

Consequently, a raft of policies has been introduced to secure improvement in the quality of teaching, learning and leadership. These include the establishment of national standards for all grades of teachers and head-teachers; an elaborate system of school evaluation and inspection to affirm the standards; protected time each day for literacy and numeracy; and the establishment of a national college to promote school leadership. However, the most interesting initiative, and one that is particularly relevant to this chapter, has been the focus on what is called 'evidence-informed policy and practice' (EIPP).

In the late 1990s, Hargreaves (1999) and others expressed concern that educational policy and practice was insufficiently grounded in research findings of what works. He challenged educators, somewhat contentiously, to identify a body of confirmatory research which would underpin a more robust set of practices for the profession to adopt. Only then could the teaching profession enjoy the level of rigour and credibility traditionally enjoyed by the legal and medical professions.

For some years, scholars, practitioners and policy makers had made reference to 'best practice' as a set of standards and processes for schools to target. The meaning of the term 'best practice' was never clear either in the minds of those who used it, or those who tried to implement it. The term itself, as the present author has argued (Dimmock, 2000), was misleading in presuming that there was a clear-cut best way to practise education. For that reason, he coined the phrase 'informed practice' for teachers and school leaders (Dimmock, 2000: 21–3). The argument was much the same as that which Hargreaves (1999) had advanced, namely that teaching and leadership should, wherever possible, be founded on research evidence of effective practice.

Coincidentally, others in the UK had begun to use the phrase 'evidence-informed policy and practice', signalling an emphasis on the relationships between the three communities of researchers, policy makers and practitioners. As Levǎcić and Glatter (2001) report, the Government believes the lessons learnt from high quality research can improve decision making at all levels of education. Moreover, well-founded evidence on key issues is needed and the newly formed Centre for Management and Policy Studies in the Cabinet Office is promoting strategies for knowledge-based policy making. More recently, there has been a shift from 'evidence-based' to 'evidence-informed' policy and practice.

While these trends generate debate about the meaning of 'well-founded evidence', 'research', and the strategies by which evidence-based research informs policy and practice, the main point that emerges from the present discussion is the recent acknowledgement by the British Government of the nexus between research, evidence and policy and practice as part of its effort to secure school improvement. It remains to be seen how this policy will in the future manifest itself in re-configuring institutional arrangements and relationships between the three communities of researchers, policy makers and practitioners. A further complication for British educators centres on the issues discussed in this chapter. From which parts of the world is research evidence drawn considered legitimate? Or, perhaps more aptly, for research evidence from different cultures to be valid for the British context, what processes of cultural sensitisation need be undertaken? The same question applies equally to other contexts than Britain. There are many aspects to this development in the UK that will provide rich research opportunities for post-graduate students, and for academics.

Conclusions

This chapter has highlighted the relative neglect of societal culture as an influence in research on educational leadership and management. Many compelling forces account for the recent upsurge of interest in an international perspective in the field, particularly one that takes cognisance of societal culture. Among these are globalisation and the urge to borrow or import 'successful' ideas from other cultures. While a willingness to learn from other countries is desirable, drawing simplistic or superficial lessons from research or practice conducted in different cultures can be misleading as well as dangerous. The same lessons are as relevant for researchers conducting investigations in their own cultures — failure to bound their studies and to consider societal culture as an influence may seriously detract from their work and lead others to draw misleading conclusions.

At the same time, as this chapter has argued, there are rich research opportunities for postgraduate students wishing to examine educational leadership and management from a societal cultural perspective. The chapter has argued the case firstly, for a more 'culture sensitive' approach to study and research in educational management; and secondly, for a more systematic and robust approach to research involving culture and cultural difference in the field. Along the way, it has also highlighted methodological issues that will be of concern to postgraduate and academic researchers in what is bound to be an exciting and challenging avenue for future investigation. In this way, let us hope that a more sophisticated culture-sensitive field of educational leadership and management emerges in the future.

References

Bajunid, I. A. (1996) 'Preliminary explorations of indigenous perspectives of educational management: The evolving Malaysian experience', *Journal of Educational Administration*, 34(5): 50–73.

Brislin, R. (1993) *Understanding Culture's Influence on Behavior*, Orlando, FL: Harcourt-Brace.

Broadfoot, P. (1997) Foreword in Crossley, M. and Vulliamy, G. (eds.) *Qualitative Research in Developing Countries*, London: Garland Publishing.

Dimmock, C. (2000) *Designing the Learning-centred School: A Cross-cultural Perspective*, London: Falmer Press.

Dimmock, C. and Walker, A. (1998a) 'Towards comparative educational administration: building the case for a cross-cultural, school-based approach', *Journal of Educational Administration*, 36(4): 379–401.

Dimmock, C. and Walker, A. (1998b) 'Comparative educational administration: developing a cross-cultural comparative framework', *Educational Administration Quarterly*, 34(4): 558–595.

Dimmock, C. and Walker, A. (2000) 'Developing comparative and international educational leadership and management: a cross-cultural model', *School Leadership and Management*, 20(2): 143–160.

Guthrie, G. (1989) 'Higher degree theses and educational decision making in developing countries', *International Journal of Educational Development*, 9: 43–52.

Hargreaves, D. (1999) 'The knowledge-creating school', *British Journal of Educational Studies*, 47(2): 122–144.

Levačić, R. and Glatter, R. (2001) 'Really good idea'?: Evidence-informed policy and practice in educational leadership and management, Educational Management and Administration, 29(1), 5–25.

Lauder, H. (2000) 'The dilemmas of comparative research and policy importation: an extended book review', *British Journal of Sociology of Education*, 21(3): 465–475.

Stevenson, H. W. and Stigler, J. W. (1992) *The Learning Gap: Why our Schools are Failing and What we can Learn from Japanese and Chinese education*, New York: Summit Books.

Vulliamy, G. (1990) 'The potential of qualitative educational research strategies in developing countries', in Vulliamy, G., Lewin, K. and Stephens, D. (eds.) *Doing Educational Research in Developing Countries*, London: Falmer Press.

Vulliamy, G., Lewin, K. and Stephens, D. (1990) *Doing Educational Research in Developing Countries*. London: Falmer Press.

Walker, A. and Dimmock, C. (2000a) 'Leadership dilemmas of Hong Kong principals: sources, perceptions and outcomes', *Australian Journal of Education*, 44(1): 5–25.

Walker, A. and Dimmock, C. (2000b) 'One size fits all? Teacher appraisal in a Chinese culture', *Journal of Personnel Evaluation in Education*, 14(2): 155–178.

Walker, A. and Dimmock, C. (in press) 'Moving school leadership beyond its narrow boundaries: developing a cross-cultural approach', in Leithwood, K. and Hallinger, P. (eds.) *The Second International Handbook of School Leadership*, Netherlands: Kluwer Academic Publishers.

Watkins, D. (2000) 'Learning and teaching: a cross-cultural perspective', *School Leadership and Management*, 20(2): 161–174.

3
Exploring the existing body of research
Roy Kirk

Recognising a need for information

When starting out on your research, one of the most important tasks that you face is to review the literature relevant to the area you intend to research. It is vital that this is carried out, but if done haphazardly, it can take up a disproportionate amount of time. To give some idea of the size of the exercise, there are, on average some 33,000 academic books published each year in the UK alone. There are over 400 education journals published in the UK, and more than 1,000 in the USA. As a researcher in educational management and leadership you will be principally looking for publications in that area, which can only make your research even more difficult. A 'needle in a haystack' task, no less. In addition, you should be aware that the information you seek may lie in publications which may have no apparent relevance to your specific area of interest, making your task even more difficult. This chapter aims to help you develop the information skills you need to carry out this task, and to carry it out efficiently, both in terms of time spent and results achieved.

You need to review the literature relating to your research field in order to find out what has been published to date in it. This will help you set the parameters for your research by showing you what has yet to be researched. It will also give some indication of the research methods that have been used and it may produce further ideas for development suggested by those who have carried out earlier research and identified areas that merit further investigation (Lofthouse and Whiteside, 1994: 185–9; Birley and Moreland, 1998: 80–101).

However, the researcher will need to conduct more than just a literature review — examining secondary sources. You will also need to acquire data from primary sources to support ideas springing from the research. In the area of educational management statistical data may be essential. Up-to-date government information, financial information, and also information relating to management as a discipline in general, are other areas which may provide important support for the research being carried out. Three major research questions spring from this (Wiersma, 1986: 47–8):

- Where is the information to be found?
- What should be done with the information?
- What use is to be made of the information?

The second and third of these questions are dealt with in Chapter 16. They are concerned with issues which involve weaving your findings into your research arguments and producing considered conclusions. The first question is the concern of this chapter. There are many sources to be checked. Some will be traditional print sources, some are in the form of databases. More and more is available from web sites and other electronic information tools. There are useful annotated lists of such sources (Smeaton, 1999; Clarke, 1993). The rest of this chapter tries to show you how to use them and to emphasise some of the most useful.

Using appropriate kinds of resource

Understanding the structure of literature and being able to identify what information can be found in specific formats is an extremely important skill for the researcher. Information, as we have seen in the previous section, is available in a variety of formats and from a wide range of sources. These can range from general sources not aimed at a specific audience, to very specific sources designed for the subject specialist. To complicate the picture further, you will need to distinguish between *published* (formal) sources and *unpublished* (informal) sources (Hinton, 2000).

Formal sources are typically published research in the form of conference papers or journal articles. Once accepted for publication in this form, this information may be republished in reviews and textbooks and, in summarised form, in encyclopaedias. Literature reviews, therefore, may involve reviewing information contained in a number of different formats:

- *dictionaries* give specific subject definitions and are, therefore, very specialised;
- *directories* contain useful information about organisations;
- *encyclopaedias* provide overviews of topics in specific areas and often give basic bibliographies of seminal titles in the field;
- *statistical tables* contain data representing local, national and international concerns;
- *books* contain accepted information, but they do become out of date;
- *journals* are primary sources of information based on current research. The most important journals are refereed, which means that articles published are looked at critically by peer experts in the particular field involved. More and more journals are available in an electronic format.

Informal communication is a source of information not published in the usual sources as listed above. Disseminating this information need not necessarily involve publication at all, as these examples show.

- *Grey literature*. In order to disseminate information quickly, the early results of research are published as reports, pamphlets or just information sheets.
- *Academic colleagues*. Research conclusions and themes need to be disseminated. Clearly the oldest way of publicising research conclusions, when researchers or academics communicate informally with each other by talking to each other at conferences, by telephone or by email.
- *Theses and dissertations*. These are the end results of work carried out for doctorates and masters' degrees. They are not published in the conventional sense, but are made available within the libraries of the institutions awarding the qualifications. They are important sources of front-line research.

It goes without saying that accessing these sources of information may present difficulties to researchers not 'in the know' and this is where a word with your librarian or your tutor could be very profitable!

The Internet is proving to be a fruitful source of information. It is a source that is growing both in terms of the quantity of data available and the usefulness of that data (though care must be exercised, as will be seen later in this chapter); as with traditional publishing sources, Internet information is available in a variety of formats.

Here is a review of some of the types of Internet resources that are available at the time of writing.

- *Electronic journals*. Many journals are now available electronically, but they are not easy to access unless as a student, you belong to the library of your parent institutution.
- *Databases*. We will be looking at bibliographic databases in the next sections. Library catalogues, usually available through university web site home pages, are also useful sources of information.
- *Discussion lists*. Electronic communication networks within specific subject areas. Subscribing members exchange ideas, ask questions and compile results of surveys for the common use of other members eg. ADMIN, EDPOLICY.
- *Internet search tools*. Search engines, subject gateways and Internet guides are all useful Internet search tools.
- *Organisations*. Thousands of organisations have web sites on the Internet which offer information in a variety of formats from annual reports to full text research papers.

Faced with such a wide range of sources, how do researchers decide which will best suit their needs? Perhaps some of the answers to this question are obvious. For example, if statistical sources are required, then the printed sources in the area under review will without doubt be the obvious source. Statistical sources from many organisations are available on the Internet. Good examples of UK sources are the web sites of the Department for Education and Skills (DfES) and the British Educational Leadership, Management and Administration Society (BELMAS). Governments in other countries will produce their own statistics. The web sites of the European Union (EU), the Centre for Educational Research and Innovation (CERI) and similar organisations are also good places to begin your search. Check what information organisations in your own country produce.

Choosing the right database is not easy for the beginner. There are some simple guidelines to follow. They are not completely foolproof (database searching is seldom that anyway), but you may avoid some very basic errors if you follow them.

- Check the subject coverage of the database to be used. Take care that you do not miss important sources because you have narrowed your search too much. Check the obvious databases, but look at the not-so-obvious databases as well. Perhaps your tutor or librarian can advise you here.
- What does the database cover in terms of publications? Does it cover just journals, for example, or does it cover other documents as well?
- What time periods does the database cover? For example, the on-line version of *British Education Index* (BEI) only covers 1986 to the present day. The CD-Rom version covers 1976 to the present day and the paper version covers 1954 to the present. The Educational Resources Information Center (ERIC) database, sponsored by the US Department of Education, goes back to 1966, both electronically and in paper format.
- How frequently is the database updated (daily, monthly, quarterly, or yearly)? This is a very important piece of information to have in your possession.

Constructing strategies for locating information

Now you can begin to plan your search. This process is called constructing a search strategy. *This is one of the most important steps in your literature search and can be the key to your success or failure.*

Most students wishing to carry out an electronic database, or Internet search will start by sitting at their terminal, logging on to the database and typing in at the appropriate place as many subject headings as they can think of that are appropriate to their specific research topic. But there is a better way of approaching the task. The first step is to prepare carefully for the search. The 'instant' approach will produce a very inefficient search result. It will lead you to discover too much information, much of which will be peripheral, or may lead you to find nothing relevant at all, wasting your precious time. The strategic approach may seem to take longer (we all like to hasten on with any task) but the results it yields will be infinitely better and will enable you to conduct your search much more efficiently. It is a little like decorating in that your success will depend on the level of meticulous preparation you are prepared to undertake.

So how should this preparation be made? The strategic process is described as follows.

1. Put your research topic into one sentence as concisely as possible. Not only is this the key to your whole search strategy, but it will also make you think carefully about your topic. Your research topic could be:

School improvement and the role of middle managers in secondary schools

2. Next, underline the key concepts in your sentence. Again, this will help clarify your thinking. In our example, key concepts would be underlined as follows

School <u>improvement</u> and the <u>role</u> of <u>middle managers</u> in <u>secondary schools</u>

3.   We now come to the third and most interesting stage of the process. In order to ensure that you make as full a search as possible, it is important to identify synonyms for each of the concepts you have underlined. This is where the dictionaries, encyclopaedias and thesauruses (such as Marder (1991) the *British Education Theasaurus*) mentioned earlier in this chapter can come into their own. The results of this exercise may produce the following

   A <u>Improvement</u>: achievement gains, development, innovation, success
   B <u>Role</u>: role perception, perspective taking
   C <u>Middle managers</u>: department heads, administrators, leadership
   D <u>Secondary schools</u>: comprehensive schools, city technical colleges, community schools, high schools

4. You are now ready to log into the appropriate bibliographical database or web site. Most bibliographical databases incorporate the Boolean Logic operator search facility using the commands 'OR', 'AND' and 'NOT'. 'OR' links two terms and expands a search. Thus, each of the terms in each of the individual concepts A, B, C and D need to be joined together with OR. The command 'AND' links terms and narrows a search. Thus, each of the combined concepts A, B, C and D now need to be joined together with AND to narrow the search to just those concepts together. It is here that your hard work begins to bear fruit as the results of your search should be very relevant to your needs. As an aside, the command 'NOT' is used to eliminate a concept completely. If our example was intended to search for information relating to all countries but France, we would add

'NOT' France to the search command, thus cutting from the search any references to French educational management.

We have now completed our search strategy. Although it may have taken some time, it will produce an efficient result with relevant and manageable information. Most databases allow you to search a subject by controlled vocabulary. An on-line thesaurus is available. Some databases will automatically map the term(s) you type to the closest match in the database thesaurus. Almost all electronic databases allow free-text or keyword searching where the term, or terms, are searched in every field of the database.

The search strategy you devise can be used to conduct searches in other formats too. For example, many sources are still only available in paper format. You can use the same keywords for your search, even if the searching is not as quick. Internet web sites use similar techniques and the concepts carefully worked out will prove just as useful here, also. The keys to finding information on the web are search engines, which operate at different levels. Web browsers (such as Netscape Navigator and Internet Explorer, for example) allow documents to be searched by a particular string of words, or part words. At the other end of the scale are the many global search engines, which create indexes to every web page; so you will see that correctly identifying key concepts is essential to the success of your search. In between there are local search engines for particular sites, subject gateways and a host of other tools (Peters, 1998; Forrester and Rowlands, 2000).

Locating and accessing research information

Now you are ready to carry out your search. *This, the next most important step in your literature search, needs careful thought.* This section lists some important sources, giving some indication of their importance to the educational management researcher. It is not possible to give detailed instructions on how to use each source in this brief chapter. However, most are 'user friendly', and there is a help facility in most cases while a librarian will be pleased to offer advice.

Examples will be selected from the following categories:

- electronic bibliographical databases;
- 'paper' abstracting and indexing journals;
- theses;
- library catalogues;
- web sites; and
- mail lists.

Electronic bibliographical databases (general)

A number of major general databases will produce reference information in educational management publications. Most will have a bias towards the particular country in which they are produced. In some cases this is very obvious (the name of the country appears in the title); in others it is not. Some databases only include periodical articles while others offer a wider range of material, including chapters from edited books, research papers, Internet resources and theses. Some include abstracts of the items indexed, others do not. If in doubt, read carefully the information details of the database you are using. All of these databases are only accessible to students registered with their parent university or HE institution and all, except Educational Research Abstracts (ERA), require ATHENS authentication (a nationwide access management system that controls access to numerous datasets and information services). You will need to ask your 'home' library or Computer Centre for details of how to register for a user name and password.

BIDS education databases

The Bath Information and Data Services (BIDS) offers three education databases, all using the same interface.

- British Education Index (BEI): 1986 onwards;
- ERIC (Educational Resources Information Center): 1966–1983; and
- ERIC (Educational Resources Information Center): 1984 onwards.

The British Education Index is produced by the University of Leeds and provides references to journal articles and, increasingly, to chapters from books. There are many references of use to educational management students. ERIC is sponsored by the US Department of Education and a search will provide many sources on management, not just from periodicals but also from report literature. Searching is easy and ERIC is also available through the FirstSearch gateway. The search technique is different, but equally easy.

Manchester Information and Associated Services (MIMAS) database

Two major databases are associated with this gateway:

- *ISI Web of Science*. This is a citation index: for each article found it lists the articles cited in the found article, together with where that found article has been cited.
- *ZETOC*. Based on the top requested 20,000 journals at the British Library Document Supply Centre, the 'hit rate' for very specific subject areas is quite high.

EUDISED database

EUDISED (European Documentation and Information System for Education) is an educational research database. Together with the *European Education*

Thesaurus, its aim is 'to extract from the large amount of educational research in progress, data of interest to educational policy and practice. About 2,000 project descriptions a year are added to the database which is available in 17 language versions. (http://culture.coe.fr/her/eng/esused.html)

Australian Education Index database
The Australian Education Index is Australia's largest source of educational information. It contains abstracts of over 100,000 documents and journal articles and covers the period 1979 to the present.

CBCA Fulltext Education database
Formerly the Canadian Education Index, this database provides indexing and full text access to the principal education literature published in Canada.

Electronic bibliographical databases (specific)

Two databases are of particular importance in the subject area of educational management and leadership.

ERIC Clearinghouse on Educational Management
This database is part of the US national Educational Resources Information Center network. Its scope includes 'all aspects of the governance, leadership, administration and structure of public and private educational organizations at the primary and secondary levels'. (http://eric.uoregon.edu/)

ERA (Educational Research Abstracts)
This database gives access to seven leading international abstracting journals, including *Educational Management Abstracts*. (http://www.tandf.co.uk/era)

'Paper' abstracting indexes and journals

Only one *specific* example is given here — beware that you do not miss the wealth of information that will be available in more general databases.

Educational Management Abstracts
A paper version of this Carfax/Taylor & Francis publication available to anyone who does not have access to the ERA service.

Theses

Theses completed for higher degrees are very important sources of research. Finding out about them is now relatively simple. These are the main databases to use.

Index to Theses
This is an electronic version of the *Index to Theses accepted for Higher Degrees by the Universities of Great Britain and Ireland*. It includes theses accepted from 1970 to the present and includes abstracts. (http://theses.com/)

ProQuest Digital Dissertations
The Dissertation Abstracts International (DAI) database can be searched, but not by subject. Theses can be purchased on-line with credit card details. (http://www.umi.com/hp/Support/DServices)

Networked Digital Library of Theses and Dissertations (NDLTD)
This database provides access to theses and dissertations in electronic format from around the world. (http://www.theses.org/)

Library catalogues

Nearly every university and HE institution library catalogue across the world is available now over the Internet. All have their own Uniform Resource Locators (url, an internet address that is used to connect servers, sites, or pages around the world) but access is easiest via most university home pages. Why not try your own institution's home page and click onto the catalogue page pointing to UK HE library catalogues?

Web sites

The message has already been sounded throughout this chapter that more and more valuable information is becoming available on web sites. The web sites themselves are authored in a variety of ways as the following examples will illustrate. All of them, to a greater or lesser degree, will offer invaluable help to the educational management student.

- *British Educational Leadership Management and Administration Society.* 'The Society seeks to advance the practice, teaching and study of educational management, administration and leadership in the United Kingdom and to contribute to international developments.' (http://www.shu.ac.uk/belmas)
- *Educational Administration and Supervision.* A resource containing a wide range of links to subjects within educational administration and supervision. (http://mhhe.com/socscience/education/edadmin/resource)
- *The Directory of Organizations in Educational Management.* The purpose of this on-line database is to 'guide users to sources of information on a wide range of topics related to educational policy, management, leadership and organization in K12 (3–18-year-old) schools.' (http://eric.uoregon.edu/directory/index.html)
- *Education-line.* Gives access to educational documents on-line. (http://brs.leeds.ac.uk/~beiwww/beid.html)
- *SOSIG (Social Science Information Gateway).* A gateway giving access to data that has been given peer approval. Research reports are a significant feature of this database. (http://www.sosig.ac.uk/)
- *Virtual Teachers Centre.* Part of the UK's National Grid for Learning, this

is a discussion group 'chat line'. Of the four current groups, one is for senior managers. (http://www.vtc.ngfl.gov.uk/vtc/meeting.current.html)

- *Education 2000*. A web site for managers and administrators in schools, colleges and universities. (http://education2000.co.uk/)
- *NISS Education*. A nationwide organisation providing access to organisations concerned with education. (http://niss.ac.uk)
- *BUBL News WWW Subject Tree for Education*. Provides over five hundred resources from around the world. (http://link.bubl.ac.uk/education/)

Discussion lists

The Internet contains literally thousands of special interest discussion lists, each managed by an individual list server. Anyone may join a list and each has its specific (but similar) protocols. Lists are available (Carvin, 2000), but their contents are open to rapid change. Here are some examples in the field of educational management and leadership.

- *ADMIN*. Educational administration discussion list. (listproc@bgu.edu)
- *EDPOLICY*. Educational policy analysis. (listserv@asuvm.inre.asu.edu)
- *EFFSCHPRAC*. Effective school practices list. (mailserv@oregon. uoregon.edu)

Help with all these bibliographic databases and information web sites will be available from your subject librarian, or distance-learning support librarian. Developments take place constantly and changes occur in unlikely places.

Finding a copy of your source

One area in which everyone needs help is how to find a copy of all the interesting sources that have been uncovered in a search. Finding the web site information is easy. It is there on your screen. But take care about copyright. More information is available later in this chapter.

Finding copies of books and journals can present more of a problem. The first move is to check to see whether your usual library — be it the one belonging to your parent institution or your local library — has copies of the relevant monograph or journal. It is surprising how few researchers do. Once it has been ascertained that the items are not in stock there, then is the time to approach your library again to make use of any national inter-library loan facility that may be available. In the UK there is a sophisticated national inter-loan service. Set up in 1957 as the National Lending Library for Science and Technology, and now re-titled British Library Document Supply Centre, the service operates through most UK public and academic libraries across the country. More than 4 million requests are dealt with annually from the UK and throughout the world. The phrase 'throughout the world' is important because if you have difficulty finding a copy of your source in your own country, help is at hand — though at a cost. Other countries may lend you books and send you photocopies of articles through a national inter-loan service. There is certain to be a charge, of course, but each library has its own way of dealing with that.

Comparing and evaluating information

Once your search is completed, no matter what the source, you need to evaluate what you have found. This is one further fundamental step in the search process.

Evaluation has to be made on a number of levels.

- Have you found the right sources, appropriate to your needs?
- Have you found enough resources appropriate to your needs?
- What is the value of the data found?

It is comparatively easy to carry out a search (once you have identified your key concepts), but you have to be careful that what you have found is really appropriate to your needs. Most bibliographical databases offer, initially, a brief list of the references that fit your search terms. This list normally contains information on title, author, publication details and type (e.g. journal article, report or thesis). This information can be very misleading, however, as titles often promise more than they can deliver. It is therefore vital to review the full database entry for the item(s). This will give you full bibliographic records, including keywords used and, in most cases, an abstract of the article. It is from this that you can really judge if the item is what you want. If it is not, you should reject it which may mean carrying out your search again, using a slightly different strategy. Only you can judge.

Some searches, even with the best forethought and planning, produce a substantial list of references. It might seem slightly odd, therefore, to suggest that you may not have found enough resources appropriate to your needs. Nevertheless, this can be a problem if you do not check the extent of the database(s), whether electronic or paper, or the web sites you are searching. You need to ensure that the source you have used really covers the subject you are researching. What literature formats does the database cover — just periodicals, or does it include book chapters, government documents, dissertations and theses, for example, as well? You will also need to know the time period that the database covers and the frequency with which it is updated.

Finally, and most important of all, you will need to consider the academic value of the items you have found. Just because they are in a database does not guarantee their quality. Is the author a well-known authority in his or her field? In the case of books, is the publisher reputable in the field? Many journal articles are refereed by peers in the relevant subject area. The status of the editorial board membership is also important. Check the journal itself

53

to find out this information. Is the journal linked to a major professional association? Is the item, whether it is a book, a journal article, or any other type of document up-to-date? Early web sites were criticised for the poor quality of the information they contained. There are still some dubious sites on the Internet, but there is much valuable information, too. Judge web site information by the same criteria you would use for traditional publications. Is it from a leading organisation? Is its author well-known academically? When did the information appear and how often is it updated? Does the web site provide the kind of information you seek? Above all, try to conduct your Internet searches by using subject gateways which filter the information that can be found. Two good examples are Social Science Information Gateway (SOSIG) and Resource Discovery Network (RDN).

Communicating what has been found to others in meaningful ways

Once you have carried out your searches, found the documents you need and read them, you will begin to write up your findings for that assignment, dissertation or thesis. That skill is covered by another chapter, but you need to bear in mind two important aspects of communicating your findings:

- your bibliography; and
- copyright and plagiarism.

It is essential that you construct your bibliography accurately, honestly and in a standard way. Your bibliography is vital: not only does it illustrate what you have read, but it also supports what you have written and gives your reader access to further information in an informed way. You have come a long way in your research by now, but ensuring that you have an accurately cited bibliography is one of the milestones in the research process. Bibliographies can take two forms, neither of which excludes the other. A simple list of references contains all the references you have actually cited (quoted directly, or indirectly) in the text of your research paper. A bibliography also contains references to additional works to which you have not directly made reference, but which have helped you construct your essay, dissertation or thesis.

Either way, it is essential is that you choose a particular reference style and maintain that style throughout your bibliography. You can choose from a number of styles including:

- the Harvard system;
- the British Standard system;
- the Vancouver System; and
- the American Psychological Association guidelines system.

All are equally acceptable. But whichever you choose, make sure you follow that style faithfully. Most academic departments tend to adopt the Harvard system. The key feature of this system is that the date of publication immediately follows the author(s) in the citation (Loft, B. and Jones, R. H., 2000). The best advice is to check with your tutor, although the chosen style is usually set out in the course rubrics. Here are some examples of bibliographic references constructed using the Harvard system (the first two citing books, the third citing a journal).

> Curry, B. K. (2000) *Women in Power: Pathways to Leadership in Education,* New York and London: Teachers College Press.
> Oliver, P. (ed.) (1996) *The Management of Educational Change: a Case-study Approach,* Aldershot: Arena (Monitoring change in education series).
> Evans, M. (1997) 'Shifting the leadership focus from control to empowerment — a case study', *School Leadership and Management* 17 (2): 273–283.

Of course, electronic publishing and web sites now form a growing proportion of sources for literature and there are guidelines laid down for the way such sources should be cited, too. They all follow the generic format of the systems already outlined. Help is available through relevant publications and web sites (Winship and McNab, 2000: 155–8), but if in doubt consult your tutor, or librarian. Remember, the main reason for using standard ways of citing sources is to ensure that the document cited can be recognised, and found again if necessary.

One vital secret of success in citing documents is to make sure that you have made a note of all the publication details whilst you have the document *in your possession.* You may have borrowed the book from another library in person, or through the inter-library loan system. To look at it again may be difficult, costly, or impossible. You may have made a copy of an article — and then mislaid it. Always note the relevant publication details on index cards, or make use of the bibliographic software now available. Examples of these are *EndNote* and *ProCite* which do all the work for you once you have been trained in their use. Even more important, it is possible to import bibliographic records from a database into your software package as you do your search. You may decide not to read some of the references. You may decide not to put all the publications you have referred to into your bibliography. It may be easier to exclude titles than to find their full details again, particularly when the end of your research seems to be in sight.

Copyright and plagiarism are important legal issues to bear in mind. The copying of another author's work is forbidden in most countries by national copyright legislation. Make sure you know exactly what you are allowed to copy and you are *not* allowed to copy. In the UK the 1988 Copyright, Designs and Patents Act is the operative legislation in this area. When collecting articles, chapters from books and other documents, the availability of photocopiers and on-line printing facilities makes it very tempting to make copies of any item you need, no matter how much, or from where. But you may be breaking the law, so check first. The same legal restrictions apply to electronic publishing. Be careful what you print off or download — if in doubt, *don't*.

Plagiarism occurs when you deliberately copy someone else's work and pass it off as your own. This is becoming a major concern in the academic world where dissertations and theses are increasingly stolen and presented as someone else's work. Extracts from other people's writings should therefore always be put inside quotation marks and properly referenced in the reference list. Electronic communications and the computer's ability to 'cut and paste' have, like the photocopier before for paper works, made it much easier to yield to the temptation to steal other people's thoughts and pass them off as your own.

Learning how to keep up-to-date

At the beginning of this chapter we saw that carrying out a review of relevant literature is an essential prerequisite for your research. But you need to do more than review the literature — *you need to continue to review it throughout your research programme and up to the moment you complete the writing up of your research*. You will have already the concept keywords from your original search (modified by now, perhaps). Make use of them throughout your research so that you can take account of developments in the field. You will know the authors you are looking for — have they published something new lately? Look out for new developments, particularly in central and local government policies. Professional newspapers and quality daily newspapers are always a good source of information here.

Above all, keep looking for new journals. All academic libraries have a current journal shelf, or make their current journals obvious in some way. If possible, a once-a-week, or alternatively a once-a-month check will reap dividends by keeping you up-to-date and ensuring that you do not fail to take a vital new development into account just as you are about to submit your work.

If you really wish to be kept informed of new information, the ZETOC database (see above) offers a current awareness service. You inform them of your subject keywords (back to your strategy again) and once a month you are advised of the latest publications relating to those concepts. A similar service is provided by the Taylor & Francis Group. They offer an email service designed to deliver tables of contents for any journals published by them. The SARA (Scholarly Articles Research Alerting) service is provided free of charge and registration on the SARA web site is simple. (http://www.tandf.co.uk/SARA/SARA.html)

Conclusions

Exploring the existing body of research is a vital first step in any research project, be it for a university degree, a mid-term assignment or a major funded research project. All research benefits from an early search of the literature. A core transferable skill for all researchers is the ability to search the literature effectively and efficiently (Hart, 2001: 21). This chapter has tried to demonstrate that there are fundamental steps which need to be followed if the research task is to be carried out effectively. Clearly, there will always be advances in how information is disseminated and stored — just think of the developments that have taken place over the last five years — but, equally, there will always be over-arching guideline steps that should be followed, no matter how easily bibliographical sources can be accessed. The following steps have been identified as being the most important to follow.

- Prepare your search thoroughly before you do anything else. Then consult an electronic bibliographic database or search the Internet. The keyword list you construct will, more than anything else, determine the success and efficiency of your search.
- Think through the various sources that you will need to consult, be they in paper or electronic form. Try to be wide-ranging in your searches and use a variety of bibliographic tools and databases, certainly at the initial stages of your search.
- Begin to narrow your search at a later, rather than at an early stage.
- As you retrieve information, check the quality of your results. Are they appropriate? Are the dates relevant and to your timescale? What is the academic standing of the writers? Has the information been 'quality checked' in some way, e.g. by some form of peer review?
- Always make sure that you keep an accurate bibliographic record of the sources you have consulted. Do this when you have the document *in your hand, or on the screen.* Trying to remember it later invariably fails. Use one of the standard citation schemes, or the one chosen by your institution.
- Keep up-to-date by regularly checking what is published and announced during your research so that you do not miss vital information. Keep up-to-date too with search tools. They are developing all the time and may make your search easier and more accurate.
- Above all, consult with your institution's librarian or information manager at all times. He or she will be delighted to advise you and their experience could save hours of your time.

References

Birley, G. and Moreland, N. (1998) *A Practical Guide to Academic Research*, London: Kogan Page.

Carvin, A. (2000) *Email Discussion Lists and Electronic Journals*, http://www.ibiblio.org/edweb/lists.html

Clarke, P. (1993) *Finding Out in Education: a Guide to Sources of Information* (2nd edn.), Harlow: Longman.

Copyright, Designs and Patents Act 1988: Chapter 48. HMSO.

Forrester, W. H. and Rowlands, J. L. (2000) *The Online Searcher's Companion*, London: Library Association.

Hart, C. (2001) *Doing a Literature Search: a Comprehensive Guide for the Social Sciences*, London: Sage Publications.

Hinton, D. (2000) *Various help pages on the University of Leicester Library Distance Learning Web site*, http://www.leicester.ac.uk/li/distance/training/search/reference.html

Levačić, R. and Glatter, R. (2001) *Really good ideas?*: Evidence-informed policy and practice in educational leadership and management. Educational Management and Administration, 29(1), 5–25.

Loft, B. and Jones, R. M. (2000) *Reference styles: Harvard and Vancouver systems*, http://library.bma.org.uk/html/refsystem.html

Lofthouse, M. T. and Whiteside, M. T. (1994) 'The literature review II', in Johnson, D. (ed.) *Research Methods in Educational Management*, Harlow: Longman.

Marder, J.V. (ed.) (1991) British Education Thesaurus (2nd edn.), Leeds: Leeds University Press.

Ohio State University Libraries (2000) Evaluation of Web Sites, http://gateway.lib.ohio.state.edu/tutor/test

Peters, S. (1998) *Finding Information on the World Wide Web*, Guildford: University of Surrey (Social Research Update) http://www.soc.surrey.ac.uk/sru/SRU20.html

Smeaton, R. F. (1999) *Researching Education: Reference Tools and Networks*, Swansea: Librarians of Institutes and Schools of Education.

Wiersma, W. (1986) *Research Methods in Education: an Introduction* (4th edn.), Boston: Alleyn and Bacon.

Winship, I. and McNab, A. (2000) *The Student's Guide to the Internet 2000–2001* (3rd edn.), London: Library Association.

4

Authenticity — reliability, validity and triangulation

Tony Bush

Introduction

The purpose of this chapter is to examine different ways in which the authenticity and quality of educational research may be assessed. This is important for educational management researchers for two reasons:

- it helps in assessing the quality of studies undertaken by other researchers; and
- it helps in determining their research approach and methodology.

Although research methods should be determined largely by the aims and context of the research, they should also have regard to quality criteria. This will enable the researcher to respond with confidence when explaining methodology at a conference, seminar or viva voce examination. This notion of scrutiny is important: can the researcher defend and explain decisions about methodology to peers, professionals and examiners?

> The question asked [by researchers] is: will the research stand up to outside scrutiny and will anyone believe what I am saying about it? The technical language for examining this problem includes terms such as validity [and] reliability. (Easterby-Smith *et al.*, 1994: 89)

Validity, reliability and triangulation are all important and complex terms whose meaning and salience varies according to the stance of the researcher. These concepts were originally developed for use in positivist, or quantitative, research (see Chapter 1). Easterby-Smith *et al.* (1994) assess the argument that they are inappropriate constructs for interpretive, or qualitative, approaches:

> The language of validity and reliability was originally developed for use in quantitative social science. . . . There has been some reluctance to apply these ideas to phenomenological . . . research because they might imply acceptance of one absolute (positivist) reality. (Easterby-Smith *et al.*, 1994: 89)

Hammersley (1987: 73) responds to this proposition by pointing to the increasing use of these notions by researchers from both positive and interpretive traditions. '[Use of] the concepts of validity and reliability . . . is more frequent in "quantitative" than in "qualitative" research, but the basic issues apply to both'. Brock-Utne (1996) takes a similar view and asserts that they are equally important in both traditions:

> The questions of validity and reliability within research are just as important within qualitative as within quantitative methods though they may have to be treated somewhat differently. The commonly held assumption that qualitative methods pay attention to validity and not to reliability is false. (Brock-Utne, 1996: 612)

Reliability

Definition

Hammersley (1987: 73) claims that there is no widely accepted definition of reliability or validity. 'One finds not a clear set of definitions but a confusing diversity of ideas. There are substantial divergencies among different authors' definitions'.

Despite this claim, there is wide support for the view that reliability relates to the probability that repeating a research procedure or method would produce identical or similar results. It provides a degree of confidence that replicating the process would ensure consistency. These notions underpin definitions of this concept:

> Reliability is the extent to which a test or procedure produces similar results under constant conditions on all occasions . . . A factual question which may produce one type of answer on one occasion but a different answer on another is . . . unreliable (Bell, 1987: 50–51).

> [Reliability demonstrates] that the operations of a study — such as the data collection procedures — can be repeated, with the same results. (Yin, 1994: 144)

Sapsford and Evans (1984) emphasise that reliability applies to people involved in research as well as to the instruments which they may employ:

> Reliability is the consistency of the results obtained when using a measure in research. It is a word used of measuring instruments, including the human observer . . . , and refers to the basic scientific requirement that it should be possible for another worker to duplicate one's results or produce comparable evidence, at least in principle. (Sapsford and Evans, 1984: 259)

The concept of reliability can be applied to several different research methods.

Reliability in surveys

A survey aims to collect a substantial amount of data in order to draw conclusions about the phenomenon under investigation. Johnson (1994: 13) describes it as 'eliciting equivalent information from an identified population'. Fogelman provides an extended discussion of surveys in Chapter 6 of this volume.

Sapsford and Evans (1984) say that survey research places great emphasis on reliability of measurement, on the standardisation of measuring instruments and on the reliability of data collection techniques. Because the researcher may not be present as the data are collected, instrument design and testing, for example through piloting, are vital components of the reliability process.

One of the main ways of assessing reliability is through the 'test-retest' procedure. A reliable instrument should give more or less the same results each time it is used with the same person or group. 'When tests are developed, they are typically tested for reliability by giving them to a group of people then calling back those same people a week later to take the test again (Bernard, 2000: 49).

Youngman (1994: 263) refers to the notion of reliability in questionnaire research and suggests ways in which it might be checked:

* comparing findings with other sources, e.g. school records;
* direct questioning of respondents to see if personal responses match previous answers; and
* cross-checking findings with the pilot study.

These suggestions have certain similarities with validity as we shall see in the next section.

Wragg (1984: 191) asks two important questions in applying the concept of reliability to interviews:

* Would two interviewers using the schedule or procedure get similar results?
* Would an interviewer obtain a similar picture using the procedures on different occasions?

Fowler (1993) emphasises the need to ensure that all interviewees are asked the same questions in the same way if the procedure is to be reliable. This can work only if the interview schedule is tightly structured, with the properties of a questionnaire.

A survey data collection is an interaction between a researcher and a respondent. In a self-administered survey, the researcher speaks directly to the respondent through a written questionnaire. In other surveys, an interviewer *reads* the researcher's words to the respondent. In either case, the questionnaire is the protocol for one side of the interaction. (Fowler, 1993: 71, my emphasis)

Of course, in single-handed research such as postgraduate dissertations and theses, the interviewer and the researcher are the same person but the key point is that reliability depends on a highly structured instrument. When the researcher wants to modify the instrument to probe or prompt respondents, using a semi-structured approach, reliability may be compromised. However, Kitwood (1977), and Cohen and Manion (1994), express reservations about an overemphasis on reliability for interviews because this may have implications for validity:

In proportion to the extent to which 'reliability' is enhanced . . . , 'validity' would decrease. For the main purpose of using an interview in research is that it is believed that in an interpersonal encounter people are more likely to disclose aspects of themselves, their thoughts, their feelings and values, than they would be in a less human situation. At least for some purposes, it is necessary to generate a kind of conversation in which the 'respondent' feels at ease. In other words, the distinctively human element in the interview is necessary to its 'validity'. The more the interviewer becomes rational, calculating, and detached, the less likely the interview is to be perceived as a friendly transaction, and the more calculated the response is likely to be. (Kitwood, 1977, cited in Cohen and Manion, 1994: 282)

This argument goes to the heart of the earlier discussion about research paradigms. Structured interviews are similar to questionnaires in their design and both may be regarded as methods within the positivist tradition. They both provide potential for 'reliability'. However, unstructured or semi-structured interviews are often used by interpretive researchers and assume greater diversity in both the design and use of the research instrument and in the nature of responses from participants (see Wragg, Chapter 9). This may limit the scope for reliability while enhancing validity. We shall return to this debate later.

Reliability in case study research

Johnson (1994: 20) defines a case study as 'an enquiry which uses multiple sources of evidence. It investigates a contemporary phenomenon within its real-life context when the boundaries between phenomenon and context are not clearly evident.'

Yin applies the concept of reliability to case study research:

> The objective is to be sure that, if a later investigator followed exactly the same procedures as described by an earlier investigator and conducted the same case study all over again, the later investigator should arrive at the same findings and conclusions. . . . The goal of reliability is to minimise the errors and biases in a study. One prerequisite . . . is the need to document the procedures followed in the earlier case. . . . The general way of approaching the reliability problem is to conduct research as if someone were always looking over your shoulder. (1994: 146)

As Johnson (1994) implies, case study research involves several different methods. The main approaches are usually interviews, observation and documentary analysis. Bassey (1999: 81) refers to these methods as follows:

- asking questions;
- observing events; and
- reading documents.

We shall examine reliability issues in relation to each of these methods.

Interviews. Nisbet and Watt (1984: 82) regard the interview as 'the basic research instrument' in case study research. The nature and applicability of reliability procedures depend on the type of interview utilised by the researcher. In structured interviews, where the questions are predetermined, the approach to reliability is similar to that of a questionnaire survey. When interviews are undertaken as part of case study research, they may be semi-structured or unstructured, 'allowing each person to respond in his [sic] unique way' (Nisbet and Watt, 1984: 82). As we noted earlier, it is more difficult to ensure reliability using unstructured or semi-structured interviews because of the deliberate strategy of treating each participant as a potentially unique respondent.

Observation. Observation may be the basic tool in classroom research and can also be significant for studies of management issues, notably in observing meetings. Deem's (1993: 209) research on school governing bodies, for example, 'involved detailed observation of ten . . . governing bodies at their formal and working group meetings.'

Kleven (1995), and Brock-Utne (1996), apply the concept of reliability to participant observation and ask three questions 'of great relevance':

- Would we have seen the same and interpreted what we saw in the same way if we had happened to have made the observation at a different time? This question deals with the stability of the observations.
- Would we have seen the same and interpreted what we saw in the same

way if we had happened to pay attention to other phenomena during observation? We may here speak of parallel form reliability.

- Would a second observer with the same theoretical framework have seen and interpreted the observations in the same way? We may speak here of objectivity or intra-judge subjectivity. (Brock-Utne, 1996: 614–615)

Although these questions address the issue of reliability, Brock-Utne (1996: 615) concedes that assessing it is much more difficult. 'If the data exist in the form of verbal descriptions, we cannot estimate the numerical magnitude of the errors of measurement ... any observation, of whatever type, contains errors of measurement'.

Documentary analysis. Documentary analysis is an indispensable element in most case studies. Levačić's (1995: 86) research on the local management of schools, for example, involved both school and LEA documents, including 'budgets, minutes of meetings and supporting papers.'

The concept of reliability can be applied to documentary analysis, particularly when the approach is based on content analysis, a method which often involves counting words or terms found in the text (Cohen and Manion, 1994: 55). Robson (1994: 243) regards reliability as one of the advantages of content analysis using documents. 'The data are in permanent form and hence can be subject to re-analysis, allowing reliability checks and replication studies'. Robson (1994: 242) recommends that two people are involved in coding text to improve reliability, although this is difficult for single-handed researchers such as postgraduate students.

It is evident from this brief account that applying the concept of reliability to case study research is problematic, notably in semi-structured or unstructured interviews and in observation. This is unsurprising as reliability is a notion associated with positivist rather than interpretive research. This leads Bassey (1999) to dismiss it for case studies and to substitute the concept of 'trustworthiness' put forward by Lincoln and Guba (1985). 'This successfully illuminates the ethic of respect for truth in case study research' (Bassey, 1999: 75). In relation to data collection, Bassey asks three questions:

- Has there been prolonged engagement with data sources?
- Has there been persistent observation of emerging issues?
- Have raw data been adequately checked with their sources? (1999: 75)

Bassey addresses the 'probity' of case study research in Chapter 7 of this volume.

Reliability and validity

Aspinwall *et al.* (1994) regard reliability, along with validity and relevance, as one of the key tests in judging the adequacy of research:

Is it reliable? Would similar conclusions be drawn if the information was obtained by somebody else or by some other method? This is a tricky area. Again, quantitative indicators are often more reliable than more qualitative ones [but] their reliability may be bought at the expense of their validity. Where reliability is a problem, there is advantage in using more than one kind or source of data in relation to a particular criterion: [i.e.] triangulation. (Aspinwall *et al.*, 1994: 218)

The tension between reliability and validity in qualitative research is also noted by Kleven (1995) and Brock-Utne (1996) who question:

whether we need the concept of reliability at all as an independent concept since the question of reliability has little relevance except in connection with the question of validity. Reliability ... only has relevance because it is a necessary precondition for attaining validity. (Brock-Utne, 1996: 614)

Validity

Definition

The concept of validity is used to judge whether the research accurately describes the phenomenon which it is intended to describe. The research design, the methodology and the conclusions of the research all need to have regard to the validity of the process. The following definitions capture the main features of validity:

Validity ... tells us whether an item measures or describes what it is supposed to measure or describe. If an item is unreliable, then it must also lack validity, but a reliable item is not necessarily also valid. It could produce the same or similar responses on all occasions, but not be measuring what it is supposed to measure. (Bell, 1987: 51)

Validity is the extent to which an indicator is a measure of what the researcher wishes to measure. (Sapsford and Evans, 1984: 259)

Validity, like reliability, is a notion primarily associated with positivist research and has been questioned by those who favour qualitative, or interpretive, approaches. Denzin and Lincoln (1998) emphasise the central importance of validity within positivist paradigms and claim that it is inappropriate for other perspectives. Kincheloe and McLaren (1998) reject 'traditional' validity as unhelpful for 'critical' qualitative research and join Bassey (1999) in advocating the alternative concept of 'trustworthiness':

Where traditional verifiability rests on a rational proof built upon literal intended meaning, a critical qualitative perspective always involves a less certain approach characterised by participant reaction and emotional involvement. Some analysts argue that validity may be an inappropriate term in a critical research context, as it simply reflects a concern for acceptance within a positivist concept of research rigour. . . . Trustworthiness . . . is a more appropriate word to use in the context of critical research. (Kincheloe and McLaren, 1998: 287)

Types of validity

Several different types of validity have been identified by writers on research methods in education. The main distinction is between internal and external validity. *Internal* validity relates to the extent that research findings accurately represent the phenomenon under investigation, as the following definitions suggest:

> Establishing a causal relationship, whereby certain conditions are shown to lead to other conditions. (Yin, 1994: 143)

> How correctly the researcher portrays the phenomenon it is supposed to portray. (Brock-Utne, 1996: 615)

> The degree to which findings correctly map the phenomenon in question. (Denzin and Lincoln, 1998: 186)

Cohen and Manion (1994: 99–101) apply the notion of internal validity to several different research methods. In relation to survey research, they point to two potential causes of invalidity:

- Respondents may not complete questionnaires accurately. They suggest that validity may be checked by interviewing respondents. This is an example of triangulation, as we shall see in the next section.
- Those who fail to return questionnaires may have responded differently to those who did so. They suggest follow-up contact with non-respondents by trained interviewers to establish their views. This is an expensive strategy which is likely to be prohibitive for many single-handed researchers, including postgraduate students.

The main potential source of invalidity in interviews is bias. 'The sources of bias are the characteristics of the interviewer, the characteristics of the respondent, and the substantive content of the questions' (Cohen and Manion, 1994: 282). They suggest careful formulation of questions and interviewer training as possible solutions but bias is likely to be endemic, particularly in semi-structured and unstructured interviews, and is difficult to eliminate.

Similar problems arise in participant observation where the researcher's 'judgement [may] be affected by their close involvement in the group' (Cohen and Manion, 1994: 111). As we noted earlier, the concept of validity may be rejected as a positivist construct which cannot easily be applied to qualitative methods, including observation and most types of interview.

External validity relates to the extent that findings may be generalised to the wider population which the sample represents, or to other similar settings. The following definitions reflect this emphasis:

> The degree to which findings can be generalised to other settings similar to the one in which the study occurred. (Denzin and Lincoln, 1998: 186)

> External validity refers to the extent to which findings from research can be usefully generalised. In positivist research traditions, and especially in social survey analysis, this problem has been seen largely in terms of sampling strategies in order to ensure that the people studied are representative of the wider population to which generalisations are desired. (Brock-Utne, 1996: 617)

As Brock-Utne (1996) notes, external validity is usually applied in positivist research and both she, and Denzin and Lincoln (1998), are sceptical about applying this notion to qualitative methods. Case study research, for example, may be criticised because it does not match the survey approach in terms of generalisation. During the conduct of the study the description of the case will increasingly emphasise its uniqueness (Adelman *et al.*, 1984: 95).

Bassey (1999) addresses this issue by distinguishing between statistical and 'fuzzy' generalisations and linking these notions to quantitative and qualitative approaches:

> The statistical generalisation arises from samples of populations and typically claims that there is an x per cent or y per cent chance that what was found in the sample will also be found throughout the population: it is a quantitative measure. The fuzzy generalisation arises from studies of singularities and typically claims that it is possible, or likely, or unlikely, that what was found in the singularity will be found in similar situations elsewhere: it is a qualitative measure. (Bassey, 1999: 12)

Bassey (1999) refers to 'singularities' but generalisation may become less 'fuzzy' if several similar case studies are undertaken. Yin (1994) says that the problem of generalisation can be minimised by replicating the study in another similar setting. This process should lead to wider acceptance of the external validity of the findings:

The investigator is striving to generalise a particular set of results to some broader theory . . . the theory that led to a case study in the first place is the same theory that will help to identify the other cases to which the results are generalisable. . . . A theory must be tested through replication of the findings in a second or even third [case], where the theory has specified that the same results should occur. Once such replication has been made, the results might be accepted for a larger number of similar [cases], even though further replications have not been performed. (Yin, 1994: 145)

Triangulation

Triangulation means comparing many sources of evidence in order to determine the accuracy of information or phenomena. It is essentially a means of cross-checking data to establish its validity. Cohen and Manion (1994) explain this concept:

Triangulation may be defined as the use of two or more methods of data collection in the study of some aspect of human behaviour. . . . The use of multiple methods, or the multi-method approach, as it is sometimes called, contrasts with the ubiquitous but generally more vulnerable single-method approach that characterises so much of research in the social sciences . . . triangular techniques in the social sciences attempt to map out, or explain more fully, the richness and complexity of human behaviour by studying it from more than one standpoint. (Cohen and Manion, 1994: 233)

Cohen and Manion's (1994) definition links the notion of triangulation to a multi-methods approach but there is another way of understanding this concept. The two main types of triangulation are:

- using several methods to explore the same issue (methodological triangulation);
- asking the same questions of many different participants (respondent triangulation).

McFee (1992) clarifies the two different approaches to triangulation:

Triangulation *between* methods employs two or more approaches to a single problem . . . triangulation between methods compares (at least) two research 'solutions' to a single problem in an effort to 'validate' the outcomes of one approach in terms of the outcomes of another. (McFee, 1992: 215)

Triangulation *within* a method takes as its starting point the claim that the 'reality' of a situation is not to be apprehended from a single viewpoint. Thus it brings to bear two or more viewpoints on a particular occasion (say those of teacher, pupil and observer), with a view to characterising the occasion so as to accommodate, or account for, all these viewpoints. (McFee, 1992: 216)

Lee (2000) utilised both types of triangulation in her doctoral research on quality in vocational education in Hong Kong. She used a questionnaire survey, interviews and documentary analysis (triangulation between methods) to compare findings from these different methods. She also achieved triangulation within the interview method by interviewing both academic staff and managers at her case study college. This enabled her 'to respond to the multiplicity of perspectives present in a social situation. All accounts are considered in part to be expressive of the social position of each informant' (Adelman *et al.*, 1984: 98).

Cohen and Manion (1994: 235) say that triangulation may be used in either positivist or interpretive research but it is particularly valuable in case study research which depends on what Adelman *et al.* (1984: 94) call 'a family of research methods'. Nisbet and Watt (1984) apply the concept of triangulation to case study research:

In order to guard against being misled, either in interview or by documents, you must check one informant against another, and test what they say against any documents which exist. Similarly, observations in one context must be checked against others in comparable situations. This process is called triangulation. The basic principle in data collection for case study is to check your data across a variety of methods and a variety of sources. (Nisbet and Watt, 1984: 85)

Robson (1994) points to the value of using interviews and observations for triangulation in a study primarily based on content analysis of documents:

The documents have been written for some purpose other than for the research, and it is difficult or impossible to allow for the biases or distortions that this introduces . . . [There is a] need for triangulation with other accounts [and] data sources to address this problem. (Robson, 1994: 243)

Levăcić's (1995) research on local management of schools, cited earlier, provided for methodological triangulation through documents, observation and interviews as did the author's work on grant-maintained schools (Bush *et al.*, 1993) and foundation schools (Anderson *et al.*, 2001). Deem's (1993) project on school governing bodies included these three methods and also used questionnaires.

Triangulation is fundamentally a device for improving validity by checking data, either by using mixed methods or by involving a range of participants. While contributing to validity, its use is not a panacea. As McFee (1992: 215) suggests, 'its value is easy to overestimate'.

Conclusion

Educational research has the potential to influence policy and practice despite its many critics, notably in England and Wales during the 1990s (Hargreaves, 1996; Tooley and Darby, 1998). For these and other reasons, it is important to ensure that research findings are authentic. Reliability and validity are the two main issues to address when seeking to ensure authenticity while triangulation is one important way in which validity may be sought.

We noted earlier that reliability and validity may be regarded as constructs within the positivist research tradition. However, authenticity remains an important issue for qualitative researchers. It may be achieved through alternative concepts such as trustworthiness (Lincoln and Guba, 1985) or through a modification of the positivist concepts to enhance their applicability to interpretive, or phenomenological, research. Easterby-Smith *et al.* (1994), for example, apply reliability and validity to both research traditions (see table 4.1).

Easterby-Smith *et al.* (1994) acknowledge the many reservations about applying these concepts to interpretive research but assert that these notions are valuable for all researchers:

> Provided the researcher is committed to providing a faithful description of others' understandings and perceptions, then ideas such as validity and reliability can provide a very useful discipline. (Easterby-Smith *et al.*, 1994: 89)

Table 4.1 Reliability and validity in different research traditions

Concept	Positivist viewpoint	Phenomological viewpoint
Validity	Does an instrument measure what it is supposed to measure?	Has the researcher gained full access to the knowledge and meanings of informants?
Reliability	Will the same measure yield the same results on different occasions (assuming no real change in what is to be measured)?	Will similar observations be made by different researchers on different occasions?

(Adapted from Easterby-Smith *et al.*, 1994:90)

Lincoln and Denzin (1998) go beyond the debate about positivist and interpretive research to point out that validity is not an absolute concept:

> Validity represents the always just out of reach, but answerable, claim a text makes for its own authority ... the research could always have been better grounded, the subjects more representative, the researcher more knowledgeable, the research instruments better formulated, and so on ... validity is the researcher's mask of authority, which allows a particular regime of truth ... to work its way on the world. (Lincoln and Denzin, 1998: 415)

Authenticity may be an elusive target but it is an important objective for educational management researchers. While there is no perfect truth, a focus on reliability, validity and triangulation should contribute to an acceptable level of authenticity sufficient to satisfy both researcher and reader that the study is meaningful and worthwhile.

References

Adelman, C., Jenkins, D. and Kemmis, S. (1984) 'Rethinking case study', in Bell, J., Bush, T., Fox, A., Goodey, J. and Goulding, S. (eds.), *Conducting Small-Scale Investigations in Educational Management*, London: Harper and Row.

Anderson, L., Wise, C. and Bush, T. (2001) 'LEAs and foundation schools: headteachers' perceptions', *Management in Education*, 15(1): 21-25.

Aspinwall, K., Simkins, T., Wilkinson, J. and McAuley, J. (1994) 'Using success criteria', in Bennett, N., Glatter, R. and Levačić, R. (eds.), *Improving Educational Management Through Research and Consultancy*, London: Paul Chapman.

Bassey, M. (1999) *Case Study Research in Educational Settings*, Buckingham: Open University Press.

Bell, J. (1987) *Doing Your Research Project*, Milton Keynes: Open University Press.

Bernard, H. (2000) *Social Research Methods: Qualitative and Quantitative Approaches*, Thousand Oaks, California: Sage.

Brock-Utne, B. (1996) 'Reliability and validity in qualitative research within education in Africa', *International Review of Education*, 42(6): 605–621.

Bush, T., Coleman, M. and Glover, D. (1993) *Managing Autonomous Schools: The Grant-Maintained Experience*, London: Paul Chapman.

Cohen, L. and Manion, L. (1994) *Research Methods in Education*, London: Routledge.

Deem, R. (1993) 'Educational reform and school governing bodies in England 1986-1992: old dogs, new tricks or new dogs, new tricks', in Preedy, M. (ed.), *Managing the Effective School*, London: Paul Chapman.

Denzin, N. and Lincoln, Y. (1998) *The Landscape of Qualitative Research*, Thousand Oaks, California: Sage.

Easterby-Smith, M., Thorpe, R. and Lowe, A. (1994) 'The philosophy of research Design', in Bennett, N., Glatter, R. and Levačić, R. (eds.), *Improving Educational Management Through Research and Consultancy*, London: Paul Chapman.

Fowler, F. (1993) *Survey Research Methods*, Newbury Park, California: Sage.

Hammersley, M. (1987) 'Some notes on the terms 'validity' and 'reliability'', *British Educational Research Journal*, 13(1): 73–81.

Hargreaves, D. (1996) *Teaching as a Research-based Profession: Possibilities and Prospects*, London: Teacher Training Agency.

Johnson, D. (1994) *Research Methods in Educational Management*, Harlow: Longman.

Kincheloe, J. and McLaren, P. (1998) 'Rethinking critical theory and qualitative research', in Denzin, N. and Lincoln, Y. (eds.), *The Landscape of Qualitative Research*, Thousand Oaks, California: Sage.

Kitwood, T. (1977) 'Values in adolescent life: towards a critical description', unpublished Ph.D. thesis, University of Bradford.

Kleven, T. (1995) 'Reliability as an educational problem', doctoral lecture, Oslo: Institute for Educational Research.

Lee, M. C. (2000) 'Quality culture, academic practices and mechanisms: A case study of vocational education in Hong Kong', unpublished Ed.D. thesis, University of Leicester.

Levăcić, R. (1995) *Local Management of Schools: Analysis and Practice*, Buckingham, Open University Press.

Lincoln, Y. and Guba, E. (1985) *Naturalistic Inquiry*, Newbury Park, California: Sage.

Lincoln, Y. and Denzin, N. (1998) 'The fifth moment', in Denzin, N. and Lincoln, Y. (eds.), *The Landscape of Qualitative Research*, Thousand Oaks, California: Sage.

McFee, G. (1992) 'Triangulation in research: two confusions', *Educational Research*, 34(3): 215–219.

Nisbet, J. and Watt, J. (1984) 'Case study', in Bell, J., Bush, T., Fox, A., Goodey, J. and Goulding, S. (eds.), *Conducting Small-Scale Investigations in Educational Management*, London: Harper and Row.

Robson, C. (1994) 'Analysing documents and records', in Bennett, N., Glatter, R. and Levăcić, R. (eds.), *Improving Educational Management Through Research and Consultancy*, London: Paul Chapman.

Sapsford, R. and Evans, J. (1984) 'Evaluating a research report', in Bell, J., Bush, T., Fox, A., Goodey, J. and Goulding, S. (eds.), *Conducting Small-Scale Investigations in Educational Management*, London: Harper and Row.

Tooley, J. and Darby, D. (1998) *Education Research: An OFSTED Critique*, London: Ofsted.

Wragg, E. (1984) 'Conducting and analysing interviews', in Bell, J., Bush, T., Fox, A., Goodey, J. and Goulding, S. (eds.), *Conducting Small-Scale Investigations in Educational Management*, London: Harper and Row.

Yin, R. (1994) 'Designing single and multiple case studies', in Bennett, N., Glatter, R. and Levăcić, R. (eds.), *Improving Educational Management Through Research and Consultancy*, London: Paul Chapman.

Youngman, M. (1994) 'Designing and using questionnaires', in Bennett, N., Glatter, R. and Levăcić, R. (eds.), *Improving Educational Management Through Research and Consultancy*, London: Paul Chapman.

5

Ethics of research in education

Hugh Busher

Introduction

This chapter considers the development of an ethical framework for educational researchers that is a guide to inform their moral judgements in carrying out their work. However, as Sammons (1989) points out, it is individual people who, in the end, have to make ethical judgements. Zimbard) argues that:

> Ethics embody individual and communal codes of conduct based upon adherence to a set of principles which may be explicit and codified or implicit, and which may be abstract and impersonal or concrete and personal. (Zimbardo, 1984, cited in Cohen *et al.*, 2000: 58)

Pring (2000) takes a slightly different view, drawing a distinction between ethics and morals. 'Ethics [are] the philosophical enquiry into the basis of morals or moral judgements' (p. 141) whereas 'morals [are] concerned with what is the right or wrong thing to do' (p. 141).

This chapter begins by focusing on the principles that might underlie the moral dimensions of educational research rather than trying to exemplify what practical moral decisions researchers might take in particular situations. In doing this, it tries to go beyond the 'search for rules of conduct' that Simons (1995: 436) pursued in order to allow researchers to defend their work in various social and political contexts. Such technicist solutions imply an autocratic style of managing research that privileges the views of some people, researchers. This view of managing has 'at its core a set of values: a disrespectful and distrusting view of people as cogs or components in the machinery of organisations' (Shipley and Moir, 2001: iv) or other enterprises.

The underlying principles of educational research have been variously described as a commitment to honesty (Sammons, 1989) and an avoidance of plagiarism (Berger and Patchner, 1988). Pring (2000: 143) identifies them as respect for the dignity and privacy of those people who are the subjects of research; and the pursuit of truth — the right to try to find out as carefully and accurately as possible, but also the right of society to know (Cohen *et al.*, 2000).

Respect for the dignity and privacy of participants is often translated into the common practice, urged by various codes of conduct for researchers in Education and the Social Sciences (e.g. British Educational Research Association, 1992; British Sociological Association, 1992), of researchers always trying to gain the informed consent of participants to be involved in any research they are proposing to undertake and always trying to protect the anonymity and confidentiality of their participants, whatever information they give. However notions of informed consent are problematic, as is discussed later.

The pursuit of truth is also a problematic notion. It assumes that an increase of accurate information is beneficial to society (Chadwick, 2001). Bridges (1999) argues that it is essential to educational research, even if it is only to try to uncover what people understand to be truth through the interconnectedness of their beliefs (Bridges, 2001), but other authors (e.g. Hufton, 2001) disagree. Other motives which might drive research, such as gaining a doctorate, or a large research contract, or an impressive list of publications focus only on the consequence of individuals' (researchers') actions, and may be in tension with basic principles of professional practice.

Like any discussion of ethical principles and moral guidelines the views presented here have to be located within their contemporary and historical social, political, cultural and epistemological frameworks. As Simons and Usher (2000) argue, the application of ethics in research is situated in particular circumstances. It is these with which each researcher has to engage when making and declaring her/his moral decisions for action.

That is not to argue that ethics and morality are merely relative to their socio-political contexts. Usher, P. (2000) explores how particular moral voices can be distinguished from their contexts. However researchers' moral decisions are influenced by the personhood of the researcher and of the researched. Pring (2000: 141) distinguishes between general principles for guiding action in research and 'those which relate to the dispositions and character of the researcher' — and by the personhood, i.e. the right to individuality and autonomy (United Nations Convention on the Rights of the Child, 1989) of the researched (Aubrey *et al.*, 2000) for which researchers are said to have a duty of care (Glenn, 2000) to avoid harm to them.

Carrying out ethical educational research, then, involves researchers in a dialogue that is informed by social moral frameworks, whether codified or not, as well as by their own moral predilections and views. Implementing such research involves avoiding contravening the rights of the researchers and participants involved, which may be in tension, while not denying society the value of the information and conceptualisation that can be gained from the research (Cohen *et al.*, 2000). Usher, R. (2000: 162) sees this as an emergent or immanent ethical moment that 'is not purely a function of the application of ethical codes of practice' when a researcher has to consider the research sponsors and participants and her/himself in their contexts and how to meet their competing needs through a variety of ethical frameworks, ontological and epistemological perspectives, and research methods and techniques.

This raises issues about how research might be designed to meet the needs of a variety of participants and stakeholders without privileging the needs of some over others.

Kelly (1989) suggests researchers have to weigh up the balance of harm that might occur if they do not intervene at all, including considering the consequences of depriving people of opportunities or information from which they might benefit if the research was not carried out.

Ethical principles and moral practices for carrying out educational research

Definitions of professional ethical practice are often enshrined in codes to guide the decisions of researchers. Sammons (1989) discusses the creation of a draft code of ethics for statisticians in 1983. It was drawn up as a guide for action, to inform the moral judgements of researchers. Similar codes have been developed by the British Psychological Society (1993), the British Sociological Association (1992), the British Educational Research Association (1992), the British Association for Applied Linguistics (1994), and many others. Moral and ethical codes apply equally to quantitative research methods as to research based on qualitative data. Jones (2000) points out the importance of the code devised by the American Statistical Association (1998). University ethics committees police such codes to ensure that research carried out under their auspices does not breach them.

Making values and ethical frameworks explicit in research does not reduce its validity and reliability, as Kelly (1989) points out, because it underscores the contextual complexities within which research is carried out and of which researchers have to take account. Ethical issues that can arise at any stage of a research project are related to:

- the nature of the project itself;
- the context of the research;
- procedures adopted;
- methods of data collection;
- nature of the participants;
- the type of data collected; and
- what is done with the data and how it is disseminated.
  (Cohen *et al.*, 2000: 49)

The contexts of the research

The contexts in which educational research is carried out have an impact on the ways in which researchers engage with other participants. Such contexts include:

- the nature of the institutions within which research is carried out;
- the nature of the people with whom the research is carried out; and
- the socio-political contexts within which the research is carried out.

Foucault (1990) points out how membership of institutions of every type constrains the actions of individuals, distorting the views that they may be allowed to give or feel able to give to people researching the processes of those institutions. Such distortions affect the validity of a study. Senior staff, who control access to institutions for researchers, may, for example, restrict or select the range of participants with whom researchers can work. Particular categories of people may limit the research design that it is possible to implement and the nature of participation that is possible. For example, research carried out in primary schools raises issues about the nature of the consent gained from the children (David *et al.*, 2001).

Socio-political contexts frame research studies in various ways. Existing cultures shape how research and researchers are perceived (Weber and Mitchell, 1999) and so how participants respond to invitations to take part in research. Hammersley and Atkinson (1983: 83) point out how teachers altered their attitudes towards a researcher when they realised that he/she had been an experienced and successful teacher before becoming an academic researcher. One of the unintended consequences of inspections and of the National Curriculum on schools in England and Wales since the early 1990s has been to make teachers reluctant to get involved in any research projects that might add to their already daunting workload.

Legislation affects how research can be carried out. In many countries researchers have to gain permission from regional or national government authorities to carry out research in state schools and colleges. The purpose of some of this legislation is to protect participants against the misuse of information given to researchers or other people who request it. For example, in the UK the Data Protection Act (1984) only allows information on individuals to be held for lawful reasons and stipulates that appropriate security measures must be taken to guard against people gaining access to it without the permission of the participants. Government codes of practice limit how statistical data collected for government departments can be used (Raffe *et al.*, 1989).

Research sponsors, too, influence the framing of research projects. Major funding bodies for social science research in the UK, such as the ESRC, and the Nuffield and Rowntree foundations, define how projects funded by them may spend money and on what projects may focus their research. As part of their conditions of funding research, such bodies may demand control over the outcomes of the research, even demanding the right to read reports before they are published to ensure that there is no material in them that may be detrimental to the interests of the sponsors. BERA guidelines (1992) argue that researchers should be very careful about accepting sponsorship from bodies that might restrict publications of findings but, as Raffe *et al.* (1989) point out, relationships between researchers and gatekeepers are often determined more by bargaining power than by lofty ethical ideals, and if researchers need funding to investigate problems, they may have to accept funding from whatever source is available, whatever strings are attached to it.

Case study

Some of these problems, as well as other ethical issues which are discussed later, are exemplified in the following case study.

The purpose of the project was to explore the leadership of educational organisations in sensitive socio-political contexts. The project was sponsored by the School of Education, University of Leicester. The researchers, Hugh Busher, Bernard Barker and Angela Wortley, are grateful for its support.

In the late 1990s in England Busher, Barker and Wortley (2001) wanted to find out what impact headteachers had on change processes in schools. This involved exploring how headteachers perceived the external and internal environments in which they worked, how they responded to and interacted with these environments, how they tried to implement change, and how staff, parents and governors responded to and interacted with change processes. The focus of the study, the research design and methods used, and the publication of the findings raised a number of complex ethical issues.

The two schools chosen for this study formed an opportunistic sample. They were both secondary schools located within the same region of England, but in different sized towns and in different types of LEA. They had both experienced an Ofsted (Office for Standards in Education) inspection which had had a major impact on their senior personnel. Both were faced with making extensive changes in their leadership and management and in their processes of teaching and learning. The research used a multiple case study method (Yin, 1989) to explore how participants in the two schools made sense of the processes of change they were experiencing and, in particular, how they experienced the leadership of headteachers who were trying to cope with changing external environments. In addition to external researchers using open-ended interviews to explore how participants were experiencing the processes of change in their schools, there was an insider researcher, in each school, i.e. somebody who was an actor within the micropolitical organisational processes of each school. In one school the same person held both internal and external roles. The implications of insider-research are considered below.

In one school the insider researcher was a senior member of staff who had actually sought a post at the school to see if her/his ideas on improving schools worked in practice. In the other school the insider researcher had a visiting role as a school governor. To some extent, then, he/she was an out-sider — an observer of the complex world of the school. Nonetheless, he/she was also a player in the complexities of that school world, at least from the perspective of an engaged insider. Thus methodologically the study was complex, combining insider and outsider perspectives, within a double framework of action research by one researcher and ethnographic research by the others. It gave a great richness of insight. It also raised a number of ethical problems about data handling, let alone data gathering.

To sharpen the focus of the discussions in the interviews, the researchers asked participants to consider some critical incidents or issues in their working lives which might highlight the impact of the headteachers on changing the culture and teaching/learning practices of each school. Wragg (1984) suggested that it was in looking at critical incidents in schools and classrooms that the interactive processes of staff became most clearly visible. This, he argued, was because the differences in values between staff became most visible at such times. At both schools critical issues emerged around the experiences staff had had of Ofsted inspections, the action plans that emerged from them, and how the relevant LEAs engaged with them. However, such data raised an ethical minefield for the researchers because of their political sensitivity and the risk of causing harm to participants in those turbulent environments.

Ethical dilemmas of data collection: sampling, trustworthiness and voice

Choosing the people to participate in the research was ethically problematic. The number and identity of those invited to participate had to meet the requirements of the research design to strengthen the trustworthiness of the study but this number also was constrained by the resources available to record and transcribe interviews. Choice was further limited to those people who volunteered to take part, raising questions about the partial nature of the evidence that was collected (and not collected) and the extent to which it reflected (or did not reflect) the views, generally, of staff and governors in each school. Participants included teachers, heads of department, deputy heads, headteacher, governor, caretakers, and office staff. What is not clear is how far parent voices for each school emerged through the views of those staff participants who were also parents. Nor were students interviewed, largely because of time constraints. Some teachers portrayed what they claimed were students' responses to how headteachers led each school and tried to manage change. (Chapter 4 of this volume explores the concept of validity.)

To strengthen the trustworthiness of the data, three other sources of information were also used. Unstructured observation of each school's social milieu gave some indication of changes in the symbolism of the culture of each school. This was recorded in researchers' diaries.

Documentary and historical data gave some insights into the socio-political contexts with which the schools interacted. The documents included items from the local press and other documents such as Ofsted reports, local authority reports, internal school documents, a headteacher's diary, and local parents' association newsletters. These were in the public domain and easily accessible but there were no ethical guidelines about how such data should be used and interpreted.

In one school, it was not possible to interview staff and headteachers during the first year of the study period. So the views of what the school was like in this period could be gleaned only from retrospective interviews with participants. This use of oral historical data raised questions about the trustworthiness of those data, the range of perspectives gathered and, consequently, the trustworthiness of the findings and interpretation of the study. It raised issues about how accurately and in what ways participants recalled and recounted events (e.g. McCulloch *et al.*, 2000; Ben-Peretz, 1995). Although there is some evidence that particular high-profile events were recalled by participants, there were unanswered questions about whether other, possibly equally important, events were overlooked because participants did not consider them important, or thought that the researcher might consider them important. The use of a multiplicity of participants each telling their stories and versions of the events that happened tried to address this problem.

Wastage of witnesses was a problem in one of the schools. Out of a staff of 30, only five of the original ten participants, including the headteacher, remained with the project until it ended. To balance this one member of staff was brought into the project, a head of modern languages department replacing the co-ordinator of special educational needs (SENCO). However, doubt remained as to which perspectives of change were successfully represented through and throughout the project and what impact this wastage had on the authenticity of the outcomes of the project.

In a few cases the trustworthiness of the data was further undermined because participants did not want to engage in normal research processes of authenticating the record of research interviews. Some participants indicated that they did not want to see transcripts — they 'trusted the researcher's accuracy', they said. Others said it made them feel uncomfortable when they read their own words, particularly with all the hesitations retained in the transcript of their interviews. They thought the transcripts made them sound inarticulate. This unintentional causing of harm to some participants was addressed by one of the researchers talking with them about it.

Protecting the participants

In view of the particularly sensitive socio-political nature of the data gathered by this project the researchers thought it necessary to disguise not only the names of the participants but the dates of the action, too. Real dates were altered to protect the identity of the people and the sites concerned. To protect the anonymity of staff, parents and students, participants are referred to only by the initials of their formal roles in each school. Quotations from their interviews are similarly identified.

The need to sustain the confidentiality of participants' identities while allowing their voices to be heard was particularly acute. The outcomes of the Ofsted inspections and the natures of the local authorities in which the schools were located made it essential that participants' identities should be concealed to avoid loss of privacy and possible actual harm to some of their career prospects. It made it impossible to use participant reflection on early research outcomes to authenticate first draft researcher attempts to elaborate patterns of and explanations for actions that occurred, as these emerged from the participants' accounts.

Ethical dilemmas of being an insider researcher

The mixture of internal and external researchers was deliberately constructed to enhance the richness of data gathered, as Pring (2000) contended it would, and enabled internal and external perspectives on emerging interpretations of patterns of events to be cross-referenced. Membership of institutions gave privileged access to data that an external researcher may never have gained. This included not only minutes of meetings and internal school documents but accounts of conversations which occurred in non-public arena. It illustrates that negotiating access to research sites is as much a matter of bargaining power and social identification between researchers and participants as of ethical ideals.

However, insider research raised a number of ethical problems. One was how a researcher can use information which becomes available to her/him for one purpose, say, as a member of a governors' sub-committee, which he/she then needs or wants to use for other purposes such as research. It is not clear in this situation to what extent participants can be said to have given voluntarily their informed consent to supply information for research purposes. Second, it raised questions about whether or in what ways information gathered for research purposes might be used within the micro-political (management) processes of a school.

Having an insider researcher in the team raised personal ethical dilemmas for the external researchers about what information, gathered under normal research rubrics of confidentiality and trust, could be made available to the insider researcher. We doubted whether some participants would have been willing to express the views and thoughts they had, had they known the data would be made available to an active member of their institution. It led to the researchers setting boundaries around some data that effectively denied some of their research team colleagues access to it in certain forms and for certain lengths of time. This problem was compounded by one of the internal researchers being a senior member of staff in one of the schools and part of the focus of the research — trying to understand how change was brought about. As a participant in the school as well as a researcher he/she wanted part-ownership of both the processes and the outcomes of the research. In part this was because he/she was already engaged in research on her/his own behalf about leadership effects.

The perceived organisational status and power of the internal researchers raised issues about the extent to which this influenced participants' decisions on what information to give for organisational and research purposes and how they presented it. In turn, this challenged the trustworthiness of the data given since some participants might have been more willing to talk to the researcher, perhaps because they perceived her/him as understanding their school situation, and others less, because they feared what the researcher might do with any information given. It also raised different questions about the quality of data gathered, as well as the ethical position of the researcher, since some participants might have tried to use the researcher as a channel to pursue other political/managerial agendas in the school.

Ethics are problematic in all research methods and methodologies

To be ethical, a research project needs to be designed to create trustworthy (valid) outcomes if it is to be believed to be pursuing truth. Ethical problems emerge in all methodologies, although much of the discussion of ethics in educational research is focused on interpretative, critical, and feminist paradigms. In positivist research, ethical principles emerge frequently around the relationship of the researchers to the resource-providers for permission to carry out research; to the data providers (subjects); and to the public who want to know the outcomes (Raffe *et al.*, 1989: 16), as well as around statistical processes used to analyse data (Sammons, 1989; Jones, 2000).

Questionnaire surveys, like interviews, are intrusive, and their questions can be distressing for participants if they are asked to confront aspects of their work or their lives which they find uncomfortable. However, unlike their researcher counterparts using interviews, survey researchers are often unaware of the problem and not in a position to reduce levels of distress, as various ethical codes of research suggest they should, in order to leave the participants and the research field no worse off (not more harmed) at the end of a research intervention than when the research began.

The ethical principle not to cause harm faces researchers with questions about what data need to be gathered. Gathering unnecessary data is not only a waste of time for researcher and participants, so causing harm to the participants, but can also be regarded as an unnecessary invasion of participants' privacy.

The generalisability of findings from one situation to another is also dependent on research being carried out ethically. Attempting to answer questions from an inappropriate sample or data set, or choosing an inappropriate unit of analysis, may lead to misleading findings, undermining their transferability (Bassey, 1998). Although, such research boundaries may be arbitrary (Usher R., 2000), the more they are so, the more it is incumbent on a researcher to explore every possible meaning emerging from her/his research and present this to readers. Sammons (1989) argues the importance of choosing appropriate statistical techniques and not using them to over analyse or inappropriately analyse data. She also argues that statistical indicators chosen to represent the underlying concepts of a research project have to be appropriate (have construct validity). Jones (2000) points out that oversight of the ethical dimensions of quantitative research would be a significant weakness in a study.

Non-positivist approaches to research particularly raise ethical issues around the engaged role of the researcher. For example, in action research researchers are reflecting on their own practices (see e.g. Lomax, 1994) and seeking to bring about change. To do this ethically, researchers have to be morally committed to enacting declared values, which are participatory and emancipatory, by engaging other participants on an equal footing with the researcher in validating the research. This generates ethically informed practice in and through research since the findings of the researcher are moderated by the perceptions of other participants engaged in or related to the action under scrutiny.

Unsurprisingly, interviews, especially those carried out by insiders in an organisation, are fraught with ethical problems that are heightened when the researchers are formally powerful people in it. It raises questions about the nature of the consent that participants have really given when asked to take part in research, and the quality of the data they feel able to reveal without, in their eyes, harming themselves within the micro-political processes of their organisation. The problems are elaborated when the interviewer is a member of the opposite sex to the participants or of a different ethnic group, since such attributes may make some of the participants feel particularly uncomfortable and unwilling to share their views openly. Riddell (1989) argues that it raises questions about what sort of researcher (defined by characteristics of gender, ethnicity or socio-economic status) should discuss with what sorts of participants what sorts of issues in what sorts of ways.

Document-based research that writers such as Johnson (1994) regard as low-key or non-invasive itself contains a range of ethical dilemmas for researchers. These emerge particularly when documents written for one purpose or for a particular audience are used for other purposes by a researcher. In such cases it is not at all clear to what extent, if at all, a document writer has given informed consent for the documents to be used for research purposes. Certainly documents allow researchers to invade the lives of the participants in research, gaining insights into participants' views, values and attitudes which may not have been intended. It leaves researchers with a moral responsibility to protect the privacy and anonymity of the research participants. In the same way diary studies intrude on and reveal the private lives of research participants (Burgess, 1994) raising similar questions to other forms of document-based research.

Participating in research: choosing to be a participant

Researchers have a duty to avoid causing harm to participants and to the socio-political environments in which and with which they work, although feminist and critical researchers (e.g. Usher P., 2000) might argue the importance of intervention to raise consciousness of power differentials, whether or not gendered. Cohen *et al.*, (2000: 50) argue that this is a matter of protecting the rights of the participants: maintaining privacy, anonymity, confidentiality, and avoiding harm, betrayal, and deception. However, what counts as deception is problematic and debated later. In part this emphasis on avoiding harm is in the self-interest of the research community. If environments and participants have been harmed by some researchers, they may choose not to co-operate with future researchers.

In major part, however, this concern is altruistic. It leads researchers to seek those approaches that risk least harm to participants, although such choices are not absolute but dependent on the situations in which a study is being undertaken — including such factors as the location of the study, the age, gender, ethnic and socio-economic groups of the participants. Harm includes psychological pressure as well as physical danger. Questions that raise uncomfortable issues about the participant to themselves, or invite the participant to be revelatory about themselves to a stranger (the researcher), may raise the need for researchers to offer counselling to ensure any harm caused is dissipated when the discussion or observation ends.

Participating in any research involves risk to the individuals concerned (Chadwick, 2001). What is at issue then is how those risks can be minimised by researchers, and how participants can be helped to be fully aware of the risks involved so that they can freely choose whether or not they want to take part (Berger and Patchner, 1988). This emphasis on informed consent arises from fundamental democratic rights to freedom and self-determination (Cohen *et al.*, 2000). Explanatory letters and or pre-interview explanations are some of the means by which researchers try to gain informed consent from potential participants. The grounds on which informed consent may be established are:

- participants must be in a position, or old enough, to understand the choice that they are making — children need to have parental or guardian consent to participate;
- disclosure of purposes of research;
- disclosure of any risks to participants; and
- a provision allowing participants to withdraw at any time.
  (Cohen *et al.*, 2000:51)

Researchers sometimes have to take uncomfortable decisions about what might constitute informed consent in particular circumstances, e.g. in various types of restrictive institutions, such as hospitals, or when participants do not speak fluently the same language as the researchers, or when participants are members of organisations who have been nominated to take part in the research by senior staff whom they view as influential on their lives. In education, researching with children is problematic since children may not understand the consequences of taking part in research for them or significant others in their lives (David *et al.*, 2001; Aubrey *et al.*, 2000); i.e. it may be difficult to establish what constitutes reasonably informed consent by children. The test is whether participants understand sufficiently well the purposes, processes and intended outcomes of the research to be able to give a consent that reflects their reasoned judgement to participate. Although asking proxies for the participants — for example asking parents or teachers for permission for children to participate is sometimes perceived as a means of addressing this problem, it only serves more effectively to disempower the participants. Not least there is the risk that the participants will be unwilling to openly disagree with their proxies, even if they actually do, because the latter usually stand in powerful social positions compared to the former.

There are also particular problems for avoiding harm to participants when working in certain environments or with specific research methods, such as video recordings. The environments that raise most difficulty are those that are sensitive policy contexts, those which use or require insider researchers, and those which use elements of deception or covert research. Undercover research in organisations raises ethical problems (Beynon, 1988). Deception covers a wide range of activities, from deliberately misleading participants as to the nature of the researcher or the research, to unintentionally giving participants sufficient information about the research for them to realise in what they are participating, sometimes due to the oversight of a sponsor rather than a researcher her/himself, as Burgess (1989) illustrates. In such research the privacy of participants has to be protected perhaps by fictionalising or codifying names and places, and even dates. Beynon (1988) suggests that one approach is to always maintain the anonymity of the organisation, but small groups of people within an organisation may still be able to guess at the identities of participants or of the organisation.

Observation-based research, especially when video based is especially problematic since the people whose images are captured are forever revealed — the privacy and anonymity of participants is compromised — unless some very sophisticated and expensive techniques are used (Busher and Clark, 1990). There is also a problem about the authenticity of the actions which the images claim to reveal — the extent to which participants are acting up for the camera (Busher and Clark, 1990) or whether their actions are reconstructed by the researcher (Prosser, 2000). Further still, film and video image often only partially capture action because of the nature of the technology, thereby giving an unethical because incomplete view of that action.

Storing and disseminating research findings and outcomes

An underlying ethical principle is that participants have a right to know some of the outcomes of a study. It is founded on their knowledge product, be that questionnaire answers or observed actions. Sammons (1989: 55) suggests that participants should always be given an account of the findings of the research.

Other stakeholders also have an interest in the intellectual property rights of the research outcomes, for example researchers who have invested time, effort and thought in them, and sponsors who have invested funds or permitted access to research sites. Such rights cause tension, particularly where research sponsors are concerned to have particular points of view conveyed through the research, whatever the findings, as Osler *et al.*, (2000) discovered in a year-long wrangle with the DfEE as to whether their research on managing school exclusions showed evidence of institutionalised racism. Bulmer (1988) argues that it is important for researchers to protect their right to publish, so long as the identity of other stakeholders is protected by anonymity, and so should beware of giving organisations the right of veto over what is published about them, even if they have been a willing host to a study.

Writing up research also has to be carried out so that the presentation of the data both respects participants' right to privacy and sustains the right of society to know about the research (Burgess, 1989; Cohen *et al.*, 2000). This raises questions about what research outcome readers need to know about participants and about their contexts if they are fully to understand the outcomes of the research. It implies that all the results from a study should be published, whether positive or negative. Further, research reports should be explicit about the underlying ethical, social and political values held by researchers, participants and sponsors in a study, if they are to be as truthful as possible in presenting their findings (Usher R., 2000).

Statistical outcomes, Sammons (1989) argues, should be presented in such a way that they are not misleading and are comprehensible to lay people who do not understand statistics. The publication of raw score data on school performance is probably unethical since it is open to misinterpretation when not set in the contexts of other performance indicators of a school, and so is likely to cause harm to a school as an institution and to its members. Statistical outcomes to research should consider the impact of:

- sampling error;
- alternative interpretations to and discrepancies between interpretations of findings;
- the impact of other variables on the findings (internal validity);
- the appropriateness of the sample to the interpretations made (external validity); and
- the appropriateness of the level of analysis to the questions researched.

The storage of data after the end of a research project, particularly when linked to the personal data of participants, at least raises the possibility of harm being done to the participants (Raffe *et al.*, 1989), especially if those data are used for purposes other than the original research, and perhaps without the express permission of the original participants. Where those data are recorded in video form the problem is particularly acute and raises questions as to whether the data should be retained at all. It makes problematic ethically the holding of large data sets in the public domain, such as those requested by the DfES in England and Wales.

Coda

There is no solution (Burgess, 1989: 8). Fully ethical research is impossible to achieve (Busher and Clarke, 1990). Marlene de Laine (2000: 205) argues that 'fieldwork is inherently problematic by virtue of the conditions that make knowledge production possible ... where personal relations and social interactions are the context for unearthing meaning'. In the end researchers have to take decisions about how to carry out research that makes the process as ethical as possible within the frameworks of the project, including budgets of time and finance which they have available to them. These decisions include considering whether it is worthwhile undertaking a piece of research by weighing up the harm and benefit to participants and to society that may arise if the research is or is not carried out. Researchers are not always 'autonomous self-directing actors'; they may be mediators between two or more audiences (de Laine, 2000: 205).

It is in the process of mediation and the interstices of research life that researchers have to use ethical principles to guide their decisions in particular circumstances. The application of ethics to research is situated in and depends on how each situation is deconstructed to understand the needs of all the participants in it, including the researchers and the research sponsors. Research codes of practice are heuristics that remind researchers of the norms which powerful bodies in particular fields claim are appropriate within certain epistemological frameworks. But ultimately it is the researcher who has to decide how to carry out research as ethically as possible to minimise the intrusion to other people's working and social lives that social and education research implies. This emphasises the importance of a researcher's knowledge of the range and applications of research techniques available; of her/his ability to use these appropriately; of her/his ability to present the findings from a study in the fullness of their complexity; and of her/his ability to work sensitively with all participants in a research project within an explicit framework of values and ethics made visible at the start of a project.

References

American Statistical Association (1998) *Ethical Guidelines for Statistical Practice*, (revised edn.) Alexandria, VA: American Statistical Association.

Aubrey, C., David, T., Godfrey, R. and Thompson, L. (2000) *Early Childhood Educational Research: Issues in Methodology and Ethics*, London: Routledge/Falmer Press.

Bassey, M. (1998) 'Fuzzy generalisation: an approach to building educational theory', Paper given at *the British Educational Research Association Annual Conference*, Belfast: The Queen's University, 1998.

Ben-Peretz, M. (1995) *Learning from Experience: Memory and Teachers' Accounts of Teaching*, Albany: SUNY Press.

Berger, R. M. and Patchner, M. A. (1988) 'Research ethics', in Bennett, N., Glatter, R. and Levačić, R (eds.)(1994) *Improving Educational Management through Research and Consultancy*, London: Paul Chapman for the Open University.

Beynon, H. (1988) 'Regulating research: politics and decision making in industrial organisations', in Bryman, A. (ed.) *Doing Research in Organisations*, London: Routledge.

Bridges, D. (1999) 'Educational research: pursuit of truth or flight into fancy?' *British Educational Research Journal*, 25(5): 597–616.

Bridges, D. (2001) 'Still in pursuit of truth? A reply to Neil Hufton', *British Educational Research Journal*, 27(1): 83–84.

British Association of Applied Linguistics (1994) *Recommendations on Good Practice in Applied Linguistics*, London: BAAL.

British Educational Research Association (1992) *Ethical guidelines for educational research*, Edinburgh: BERA/SCRE.

British Psychological Society (1993) 'Ethical principles for conducting research with human participants', *Psychologist*, 6(1).

British Sociological Association (1992) 'Statement of ethical practice', *Sociology*, 26(4): 703–707

Bulmer, H. (1988) 'Some reflections on research in organisations', in Bryman, A. (ed.) *Doing Research in Organisations*, London: Routledge.

Burgess, R. (1989) 'Ethics and educational research: an introduction', in Burgess, R.G. (ed.), *The ethics of Educational Research*, London: Falmer Press.

Burgess, R. (1994) *Research Methods*, London: Nelson.

Burgess, R. (1994) 'On diaries and diary keeping', in Bennett, N. Glatter, R. and Levačić, R (eds.), *Improving Educational Management through Research and Consultancy*, London: Paul Chapman for the Open University.

Busher, H., Barker, B. and Wortley, A. (2001) *School leaders and Organisational Change in Turbulent Times*, Leicester: School of Education, University of Leicester.

Busher, H. and Clarke, S. (1990) 'The ethics of using video in educational research', in Anning, A., Broadhead, P., Busher, H., Clarke, S., Dodgson, H., Taggart, L., White, S. and Wilson, R (eds.), *Using Video Recordings for Teacher Professional Development* Leeds: University of Leeds, School of Education.

Chadwick, R. (2001) 'Ethical assessment and the human genome issues', in Shipley, P. and Moir, D. (eds.) 'Ethics in practice in the 21st century', *Proceedings of the Interdisciplinary Conference of the Society for the Furtherance of Critical Philosophy*, Eynsham Hall, Oxfordshire, October 1999.

Cohen, L., Manion, L. and Morrison, K. (2000) *Research methods in Education* (5th edn.) London: Routledge/Falmer Press.

David, M., Edwards, R. and Alldred, P. (2001) 'Children and school-based research: 'informed consent' or 'educated consent'?', *British Educational Research Journal*, 27(3): 347–365.

de Laine, M. (2000) *Fieldwork, Participation and Practice: Ethics and Dilemmas in Qualitative Research*, London: Sage.

Foucault, M. (1990) 'Foucault on education', in Ball, S. (ed.) *Foucault on Education*, London: Routledge.

Glenn, S. (2000) 'The dark side of purity or the virtues of double-mindedness', in Simons, H. and Usher, R. (eds.) *Situated Ethics in Educational Research*, London: Routledge/Falmer Press.

Hammersley, M. and Atkinson, P. (1983) *Ethnography: Principles in practice*, London: Tavistock Publications.

Hufton, N. (2001) 'Truth and inquiry: a reply to David Bridges', *British Educational Research Journal*, 27(1): 79–82.

Johnson, D. (1994) *Research Methods in Educational Management*, Harlow: Longman.

Jones, K. (2000) 'A regrettable oversight or a significant omission? Ethical considerations in quantitative research in education', in Simons, H. and Usher, R. (eds.) *Situated ethics in educational research*, London: Routledge/Falmer Press.

Kelly, A. (1989) 'The ethics of school based action research', in Burgess, R.G. (ed.) *The Ethics of Educational Research*, London: Falmer Press.

Lomax, P. (1994) 'Action research for managing change', in Bennett, N., Glatter, R. and Levačić, R. (eds.) *Improving Educational Management through Research and*

Consultancy, London: Paul Chapman for the Open University.

McCulloch, G., Helsby, G. and Knight, P. (2000) *The Politics of Professionalism*, London: Continuum.

Osler, A., Watling, R. and Busher, H. (2000) *Reasons for Exclusion from School: Report to the DfEE*, London: DfEE.

Pring, R. (2000) *Philosophy of Educational Research*, London: Continuum.

Prosser, J. (2000) 'The moral maze of image ethics', in Simons, H. and Usher, R. (eds.) *Situated Ethics in Educational Research*, London: Routledge/Falmer Press.

Raffe, D., Blundell, I. and Bibby, J. (1989) 'Issues arising from an educational survey.' in Burgess, R. G. (ed.) *The Ethics of Educational Research*, London: Falmer Press.

Riddell, S. (1989) 'Exploiting the exploited? The ethics of feminist educational research', in Burgess, R. G. (ed.) *The Ethics of Educational Research*, London: Falmer Press.

Sammons, P. (1989) 'Ethical issues and statistical work', in Burgess, R. G. (ed.) *The Ethics of Educational Research*, London: Falmer Press.

Shipley, P. and Moir, D. (2001) 'Editorial', in Shipley, P. and Moir, D. (eds.) 'Ethics in Practice in the 21st Century', *Proceedings of the Interdisciplinary Conference of the Society for the Furtherance of Critical Philosophy*, Eynsham Hall, Oxfordshire, October 1999.

Simons, H. (1995) 'The politics and ethics of educational research in England: Contemporary issues', *British Educational Research Journal*, 21(4): 435–449.

Simons, H. and Usher, R. (2000) 'Introduction: ethics in the practice of research', in Simons, H. and Usher, R. (eds.) *Situated Ethics in Educational Research*, London: Routledge/Falmer Press.

United Nations (1989) *Convention on the Rights of the Child*, New York: United Nations.

Usher, P. (2000) 'Feminist approaches to situated ethics', in Simons, H. and Usher, R. (eds.) *Situated Ethics in Educational Research*, London: Routledge/Falmer Press.

Usher, R. (2000) 'Deconstructive happening, ethical moment', in Simons, H. and Usher, R. (eds.) *Situated Ethics in Educational Research*, London: Routledge/Falmer Press.

Weber, S. and Mitchell, C. (1999) 'Teacher identity in popular culture', in Prosser, J. (ed.) *School Culture*, London: Paul Chapman.

Wragg, E. (1984) *Classroom Teaching Skills*, London: Heineman.

Yin, R. K. (1989) 'Designing single and multiple case studies', in Bennett, N., Glatter, R. and Levačić, R (eds.)(1994) *Improving Educational Management through Research and Consultancy*, London: Paul Chapman for the Open University.

Zimbardo, P. (1984) 'On the ethics of intervention in human psychological research with specific reference to the 'Stanford Prison Experiment'', in Cohen, L., Manion, L. and Morrison, K. (2000) *Research methods in Education* (5th edn.), London: Routledge/Falmer Press.

Part B
Approaches to Research

6

Surveys and sampling

Ken Fogelman

Introduction

It is commonplace for discussions of survey research in education to start by describing it as the most frequently used research method. A rapid review of the contents of the journal *Educational Management and Administration* over a two-year period confirms that this is equally true of research related to educational management or leadership. Of the 33 papers published in the journal in that period that were based on original empirical work, 19 reported on a survey of some kind, although for several this research method was combined with another method. By contrast, the second most popular method, the case study method, featured in 12 of these articles.

But these figures conceal a great variety in the research activities being carried out under the heading of 'survey'. Indeed in some cases it is not clear whether a particular piece of research is more appropriately described as a survey or as a small number of individual case studies, when, for example, the research consists of interviews with a number of headteachers.

It is therefore extremely difficult to arrive at a straightforward definition of what exactly a survey is. Some have tried. Hutton (1990), for example, wrote:

> Survey research is the method of collecting information by asking a set of preformulated questions in a predetermined sequence in a structured questionnaire to a sample of individuals drawn so as to be representative of a defined population. (1990: 8)

Whilst this accurately describes a common form of survey, most would feel that as a definition it is far too narrow. Many surveys use methods of data collection other than questionnaires, including interviews, which may be semi-structured or unstructured, and which therefore may include questions which are neither preformulated nor in a predefined sequence. Again some surveys, such as a national census, are carried out on an entire population rather than a sample. Nor, as discussed further below, would one want to exclude from a definition surveys based on a sample which may not be able to demonstrate representativeness. For such reasons more tentative state-ments are preferable. Cohen *et al.* (2000), for example, wrote:

> Typically, surveys gather data at a particular point in time with the intention of describing the nature of existing conditions, or identify-ing standards against which existing conditions can be compared, or determining the relationships that exist between specific events. (2000: 169)

Even here, one would want to interpret some of the terms used, such as 'conditions' and 'events', as broadly as possible; and note the writer's use of the word 'typically', which allows for exceptions.

Denscombe (1998) is even more inclusive, and his discussion is replete with terms such as 'generally' and 'in principle'. He writes of the typical characteristics of surveys and that they are about 'an approach in which there is empirical research pertaining to a given point in time which aims to incor-porate as wide and as inclusive data as possible'. As he rightly goes on to emphasise, 'The survey approach is a research strategy, not a research method'.

Varieties of surveys

As the above is beginning to illustrate, surveys can vary on several dimen-sions. They can vary in size or scope, instrumentation, structure and purpose.

Size or scope

At one extreme are surveys in which the number of respondents is extremely small. This might be where, for example, a questionnaire is being used as just one source of data within a case study of a single institution and is dis-tributed only to staff (or students or governors) within that institution. Equally, small numbers of respondents may arise where data are to be obtained through, for example, unstructured interviews and the balance that has to be struck between depth and richness of data and the resources avail-able imposes practical constraints on the number of interviews that can take place. At the other extreme, the number of respondents can be very large indeed. A national census involves many millions of respondents but the most dramatic examples in the field of educational research are probably those international comparative studies of educational achievement that study several thousand students in each of many countries (e.g. Elley, 1994).

Instrumentation

The questionnaire, the most common method of data collection in a survey, is used to obtain factual information, attitudinal information or a mixture of both. However, also common are interviews, which in turn can vary as to how structured they are and whether they are carried out face-to-face or by other means such as telephone or, increasingly, email. As mentioned above in relation to the international surveys of achievement, standardised tests can be used and the term 'survey' is occasionally applied to studies which obtain data through observation.

Structure

Most surveys, and certainly those carried out by an individual researcher, are cross-sectional, obtaining data at a single point in time, and use just one questionnaire or other means of data collection. However, more complex designs are possible. Most obviously there are longitudinal studies (or panel studies as they are more commonly called in the American literature) which follow up individuals over a period of time. These too can range from small studies of the growth and development of individuals to major projects such as national cohort studies that follow several thousand individuals over a long period ('from cradle to grave' in some cases) and draw upon many different sources of data (see, for example, Ferri, 1993). Longitudinal studies provide opportunities for particular kinds of analysis and therefore for answering some particular kinds of research questions (Fogelman, 1985) but they can also give rise to additional issues of sample attrition, response rates (Shepherd, 1993) and expense.

More complex survey designs are also possible by, for example, combining cross-sectional surveys of part of a sample with longitudinal surveys of the remainder. Time series, or trend, studies, which obtain data at several points in time but usually drawing a new sample on each occasion rather than following up the same individuals, are also possible.

Purpose

Given the variety found in survey research, in terms of scale, methods of data collection and complexity of design, it is not surprising that surveys can be used for many different purposes and to answer many different kinds of research question. Most of the issues of fitness of purpose — of whether a survey, of whatever kind — is appropriate, relate to the choice of the method of data collection. Such issues are discussed in other chapters. However, some more general points relate to the nature of the analysis to be carried out once the data have been collected. At the simplest level, a survey may have been carried out to do no more than head counts: to discover, for example, what proportion of headteachers have a certain qualification; or what proportion of heads of departments agree with a particular statement. At the next level are questions which can be addressed by two-way tables or simple correlations such as: Do the attitudes of heads of departments vary according to how long they have been in post? or What is the relationship between size of school and examination results? In exploring such relationships, the researcher often hopes to identify, at least as closely as possible, cause and effect relationships. Then more complex, multi-variate analysis (see Chapter 14) may be required to take account of intervening or confounding variables; for example: What is the relationship between size of school and examination results after the socio-economic characteristics of schools' student intakes have been taken into account?

Thus, because of the variety of methods and design that the survey as a research method encompasses, it is an approach which can be used to investigate a wide range of research questions. In broad terms, it is the appropriate method when systematic and comparable data are needed, and can be obtained directly from a relatively large number of individuals.

Practical and ethical issues

The early stages of preparation for a survey are just as for any other approach. Paramount is the need to identify clear, relevant, researchable and manageable research questions and then to decide on the most appropriate strategy and method(s) for obtaining answers to those questions.

Appropriateness for answering the research question(s) is the most important criterion for deciding which method to use, but resource issues should also be considered at this stage. What direct costs such as postage, stationery or travel, for example, will be incurred? How much of the researcher's own time (and skills) will be needed for the methods being considered — for interviewing, coding, transcription and analysis?

Other issues which can be particularly relevant to surveys are those relating to access. Is it necessary to obtain permission to distribute questionnaires or conduct interviews; for example from a local authority, the head of an institution or from parents? Where and when will people be available for interview? What time of year will be least disruptive when asking teachers to give time to complete a questionnaire or to be interviewed?

Such practical concerns can also have an ethical component. For any research strategy or method it is the researcher's responsibility to ensure that their instruments or methods of data collection are of as high a quality as possible, and as unobtrusive and inoffensive as possible. Similarly, as with any educational research, the concept of the informed consent of respondents is crucial (see Chapter 5). This can arise for the survey researcher in a particularly acute form in relation to anonymity and/or confidentiality.

In surveys in education, it is rarely possible to ensure the anonymity of the respondent. If questionnaires are used, the researcher will usually want to maximise their response rate by following up and sending reminders to those who have not returned them. This can only be done if you can identify who has and has not returned the questionnaire. Researchers are some-times tempted to get round this problem by telling respondents that the infor-mation they provide will be provided anonymously, since their name does not appear on the questionnaire even though the researcher uses a number-ing system to link a response to the respondent's identity. Not only is this dishonest but it won't fool the respondent. On the contrary, it may well irri-tate them and result in a reduction in the survey response rate or in the qual-ity of information obtained from the survey.

On the other hand, it is usually possible to guarantee confidentiality — that individual answers will be seen by no one other than the researcher (though if quotations from interviews are likely to be included in a thesis or report, even if they are anonymised, respondents should be made aware of this). The golden rule is to tell the truth and to explain the reasons for the procedures adopted.

Equally important is to ensure that whatever is promised does actually happen. Some years ago the author was involved in a study which distrib-uted questionnaires to school students together with a sealable envelope into which students were to put their completed questionnaire before handing it to their teacher for return to us. However, when these envelopes were returned they frequently also contained a second questionnaire which we had asked the teacher to complete. Thus, contary to what had been intended, there clearly had been an opportunity for the teacher to see the student's questionnaire. Such lapses are entirely the fault of the researcher and, in this case, could presumably have been avoided by greater clarity in the instruc-tions given to respondents.

This example also illustrates the importance of piloting. Most researchers are well aware of the need to pilot their questionnaire or whatever research instrument they choose to use. Too often neglected is the equally important need to pilot administrative procedures, to ensure that these too work effi-ciently and in the way intended by the researcher.

Sampling

Issues of, and decisions about, sampling need to be considered in a number of stages. The first crucial concept is that of *generalisation*. In a survey, as in any research, a particular set of subjects will be studied — most commonly indi-vidual people, though it may be schools or some other unit. However, the researcher will usually wish to argue that his/her findings have wider applica-tion and that they have relevance and implications beyond those particular individuals, i.e. they will want to generalise their research findings to some extent. This introduces the second important concept — the *population*.

In this context, the population is the set of individuals about which you the researcher want to be able to generalise — those people (or schools, etc.) to whom you want to claim that your findings apply. Thus identifying the relevant population is an important part of developing your research question. What you will need to decide is, about whom do you want to be able to draw conclusions at the end of your research? Is it, for example, all teachers (or heads or schools) in England or another country; those in a more limited geographical or administrative area; those in schools or colleges of a particular type; or is it those in a particular post or who teach a particular subject?

As already mentioned, there are examples of surveys where the answer to this question is the same as the answer to the question of who will actually be surveyed — a national census at one extreme, and a survey of the teachers in a single case study institution at the other. The purpose of a census is simply to provide information on the relevant population and not beyond. The case study researcher may or may not wish to generalise his/her results, but that is something which needs to be considered in the wider context of that case study (see Chapter 7). There are examples in the education management literature of surveys of entire populations. Harper (2000) reports a study of organisational structures in further education colleges in which he requested data, in the form of organisational charts, from all 452 institutions funded by the Further Education Funding Council in England and Wales. Wilson and McPake (2000), in a study of management styles in small (fewer than 120 pupils) Scottish primary schools, combined a small number of case studies with a postal questionnaire to all 863 such schools.

Much more commonly, resources and other practical constraints mean that we cannot study the entire population. Therefore we must study a *sample* of that population, preferably one that can be shown to be *representative* of the relevant population and which therefore allows us to be reasonably confident about the validity of whatever generalisations we make.

Methods of sampling

Samples can be created in one of two ways: *probability* sampling and *non-probability* sampling. Specific methods are described in more detail below, but what probability samples have in common is that they are created by a method in which the researcher controls and specifies the likelihood of any individual in the population appearing in the sample. With non-probability methods the researcher does not have this control and cannot state the likelihood of an individual being in the sample. In general, probability samples are much to be preferred, both because they are more likely to result in a sample which is representative of the population studied as a whole, but also because they are more likely to satisfy the mathematical assumptions which underlie many kinds of statistical analysis and inferential testing (see Chapter 14).

In reality, as we shall see, it may not be possible to create a true probability sample for various practical reasons, so this last statement may be seen as something of a counsel of perfection. What is important is that firstly, we should use the best sample we can within the resources and possibilities available; and secondly, where this sample falls short of what might have been ideal, then we should acknowledge this shortcoming and also recognise the implications it may have for the confidence with which we are able to generalise from our findings.

Probability sampling

Probability samples depend on the availability and accessibility of a *sampling frame*. This is a list of all the individual members of our population. The electoral register is an example of a sampling frame commonly used in social and market research. Possible examples in education would be a list of all the primary or secondary schools in a local authority or of the heads of those schools. However, this immediately demonstrates why probability sampling may be difficult or impossible, if an appropriate sampling frame does not exist or is not available to the researcher. This will often be the case if your population and your proposed sample is of teachers or students, for example.

However, if an appropriate sampling frame is available then it, and one of the following probabilistic methods of sampling, should be used.

Random sampling

This is where the sample members are selected literally at random from the sampling frame. Before this can be done another important decision has to be taken: that is, how big the sample will be. This determines the *sampling fraction*, i.e. what proportion of the population is to be selected in order to provide a sample of the desired size. The issue of sample size is discussed below, but for now we need to note that this is the point at which this decision has to be taken. Once the sampling fraction has been decided then we can proceed with the random selection. Of course, random selection does not entail any human action (such as sticking a pin in the list). Instead we must use a table of random numbers or a random number generator such as can be found in statistical packages such as SPSS.

Systematic sampling

This is very similar to random sampling, except that the sample members are selected systematically rather than randomly. Again, the sampling fraction has to be decided first and then names selected on a systematic basis. For example, if the sampling fraction is one in ten, then we select every tenth name from our list. Of course, the starting point, the first name, must be chosen randomly from the first ten names on the list — otherwise Mr Aardvark would be included in every survey. Generally, systematic sampling is equivalent to random sampling. Most population lists are organised in a way, for example alphabetically, where there is no danger of this being related to the other

characteristics of its members, and so systematic sampling should not introduce any bias and spoil the representativeness of the sample. However, it
should always be checked that this is the case for a particular sampling frame
which you intend to use in this way.

Stratified sampling

For some research questions there might be a reason to judge that some particular characteristic of your sample members is of such importance that you
want to impose further control over how it is distributed or represented in
your sample. For example, in a study carried out to compare female and
male heads, we might feel that there was a risk that random or systematic
sampling might not generate enough heads of one gender or the other, particularly if your sample is relatively small, to make possible the kind of analysis needed. In this case you should divide your sampling frame into males
and females (stratify by gender) before proceeding to draw separate random
or systematic samples from the two groups. This is stratified sampling, where
as the first stage we re-organise the sampling frame into groups whose members have a common characteristic and then sample separately from these
groups. Of course, this pre-supposes that we have the information that will
enable us to do this (i.e. that we know whether each of the heads is male
or female). If you do not, compromises may have to be made and you may
have to settle for a non-probability method of sampling.

Stratified sampling is most likely to be used for one of two reasons which,
interestingly, are opposed to each other. The first reason is where we are
convinced that a particular variable is of such importance that we want to
ensure that it is represented in the sample in the same way as it would be
in the total population. The second reason is the opposite one, where we
want to ensure that in a certain respect the sample contains different proportions to what would be found in the population. For example, if we
wished to compare the experiences of children with a relatively rare disability
with those of the general population of children, then we would probably
need to use different sampling fractions for the two groups. In this way we
could ensure that the minority group is large enough within our sample to
make that analysis possible. Another example is provided by Newcombe and
McCormick (2001) in their study of teachers' participation in financial decision making in schools. They distributed questionnaires to 141 government
schools in New South Wales, a sample which was stratified by school type,
i.e. primary, secondary and schools for specific purposes, making it possible
to compare results for these different types of school.

Cluster sampling

In order either to reduce time and costs, particularly if interviews are used,
or to increase the researcher's control over administrative procedures, it can

be helpful if the individuals or institutions in a sample are grouped together geographically. Cluster sampling achieves this. It entails a two-stage procedure. The first stage is to select a sample of geographical or administrative areas, such as local authority areas for example. The second stage is to select a final sample, for example schools, from within those areas (sometimes the entire population within those areas might be included). Strictly speaking, random, systematic or stratified sampling should be used at both stages, but it is common for the first stage to use purposive or judgemental methods (see below).

Cluster sampling can also be helpful when a sampling frame for the relevant population is not readily available but can be obtained at the lower level. For example, a list of all schools in a country might not be readily available but a list of schools for each area might be more easily obtainable.

Cluster samples are very common in survey research in education. Wilson (2001), for example, surveyed special needs provision in 203 comprehensive schools in five LEAs in the North of England. Similarly, Wise (2001), studying middle managers, sent questionnaires to heads and middle managers in all 94 schools in three authorities in the Midlands.

Stage sampling

Stage sampling is simply an extension of cluster sampling, where more than two stages are involved. For example, to create a national sample of school students we might first sample geographical areas, then schools within those, then classes within those schools, and finally students within those classes.

Non-probability sampling

Convenience sampling

This method is sometimes also known as accidental or opportunity sampling. All describe a practice which should be avoided if at all possible if sound claims for generalisation are to be made. A convenience sample is one composed of members most easily available to the researcher who does not attempt to make them representative of a wider population. This may be because there is no alternative, but in such cases it is essential that as much information as possible is reported about the sample and how it was selected. Was it composed of the researcher's friends, or people who were geographically convenient or teachers who were on a course, for example? Armed with this information, readers can form their own judgement as to how this may affect any conclusions that may be drawn from the research.

Purposive or judgemental sampling

Purposive or judgemental sampling is an improvement on convenience sampling in that the researcher applies his/her experience and judgement to select cases which are representative or typical. Again, of course, this must be clearly explained and justified to the reader by the researcher. As already mentioned, this can be a reasonable approach in the course of cluster or stage sampling, particularly if the number of cases at an early stage is small. Blandford and Squire (2000), for example, report a study of training provision for newly appointed heads, in which they approached a sample of LEAs which was 'representative of LEAs nationwide', geographically, in terms of 'whether [they are] county, metropolitan or London boroughs and in size'.

Quota sampling

Quota sampling attempts to impose greater control and can be seen as a non-probability equivalent of stratified sampling. As with stratified sampling, the first stage is to identify a particular variable of importance. Once the sample size has been determined, then quotas can be set for the numbers to be included in the final sample for each category of that variable. This might be of males and females or of schools of different types, for example. Usually, the researcher's intention is to ensure that members of category groups are represented in the final sample in the same proportions as they would be in the population as a whole. Quota sampling is frequently used in commercial research. For example, an interviewer might be told to interview certain numbers of people from particular occupational groups. The interviewer would then use convenience sampling (knocking on doors or stopping people in the street) to identify relevant individuals and fill those quotas.

There is a lively debate within the research community as to the merits of quota sampling, with the battle lines mainly drawn up at the academic–commercial frontier (see, for example, Marsh and Scarborough, 1990). What is beyond doubt is that quota sampling is an improvement on convenience sampling.

Dimensional sampling

This is an extension of quota sampling, but where the quotas are set in relation to a combination of two or more variables. So rather than quotas being selected on the basis of occupational group alone, an interviewer might be set a quota consisting of a pre-determined number for each possible combination of occupational group, gender and age group.

Snowball sampling

This technique can be used to generate a sample where potential sample members are particularly difficult to identify. Examples are rare in the field of educational research but in other areas of social research it can be used in, for example, studies of drug cultures or football hooliganism. Here, a researcher first has to identify and interview one or two people with relevant characteristics. Those people are then asked to identify others with the same characteristic whom the researcher could contact. They in turn would be asked to identify further sample members. In this way the sample is built up, like a rolling snowball.

Sample size

Almost always, one of the first questions a student researcher embarking on a survey asks is, 'How big should my sample be?' (By this they usually mean, 'What size of sample will be acceptable to my examiners?') There is no single, straightforward answer to this question but guidance can be given at several levels.

The first point is that while sample size does matter, of at least equal importance is the way that the sample is drawn. A small probability sample free of bias is preferable to a large sample that is biased and unrepresentative or whose lack of bias cannot be proved.

The next answer is that your sample should be as big as you can manage within the practical constraints and the resources available to you. In common sense terms, if your sample is well drawn, then the larger it is the more confidence you can have in generalising the results of your research.

Some writers on survey research rather arbitrarily suggest that 30 is the minimum acceptable size for any survey and this is generally acceptable for a small-scale, exploratory study. However, this also assumes that the intended statistical analysis of survey results will be simple. If the research questions entail making comparisons between sub-groups, then each of the groups must be large enough to give reasonable confidence in the findings. Thus the more complex the proposed analysis, the larger the study sample will need to be.

The final answer is a longer and more technical version of the statement that the larger the sample is, the more confidence we can have in generalising the findings. For this, we first need to imagine a situation where we draw a very large number of probability samples from a particular population. If we then selected a variable of particular interest (for this example, a continuous variable) and calculated the mean on that variable for each of those samples and plotted those graphically, we would get the distribution shown in Figure 6.1. This is the familiar normal or bell-shaped curve.

What this distribution shows is that we would obtain a large number of sample means that are close to the population mean, reducing numbers of means which are more distant from the population mean, and a very small number of means which are very different to the population mean. Just as a normal distribution of individual values can be described by the standard deviation, so can this distribution of means be described by a closely related statistic, the *standard error* of the mean. The formula for the standard error is:

Standard deviation divided by the square root of *n* (i.e., the sample size)
In Figure 6.1, the numbers on the horizontal axis represent the distance from

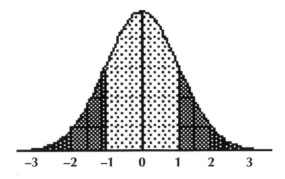

Figure 6.1 Hypothetical distribution of sample means

the mean in terms of the number of standard errors. Exactly as for the standard deviation in relation to the normal distribution of individual scores, we know the proportion of sample means which can be expected to fall within certain ranges, i.e. two-thirds of the means will fall within one standard error either side of the population mean and 95 percent of them will fall within two standard errors either side of the population mean. We now have moved a little closer to the answer to our original question, in that for a given result, for which we know the standard deviation and the sample size, we can say that we are 95 percent confident that the true population mean is within the range two standard errors either side of the sample mean (and this range is known as the 95 percent *confidence interval* around the mean).

Where the variable of interest is categorical rather than continuous, when we would report the result as a percentage or proportion rather than a mean (e.g. 40 percent of those interviewed say they will vote Labour in the next election), exactly comparable calculations are possible, except that the formula for the standard error of a proportion is:

Square root of (the proportion multiplied by one minus the proportion) divided by the square root of *n*.

In theory, we can use these concepts to help us decide in advance our desired sample size, in that we can decide on the level of uncertainty we are willing to live with, what range of possible difference from the true population result we can tolerate. Provided we know the likely standard deviation or proportion for the population we can then use the above formulae to calculate the desired sample size. In reality, this is rarely done in educational research (mainly because the relevant information is not available in advance). It is more frequently encountered in commercial research, where a survey company may well say to a potential customer something like: 'Give me this much money and we will be able to carry out this many interviews and you will be able to be 95 percent confident that the result we give you will be no more than this amount different from the figure for the total population. Give us this much more money and we will be able to carry out this larger number of interviews and provide a result which is more precise — 95 percent certain to be within this smaller range of the population figure'.

What we can do in educational research, and should do more frequently than we do, is make these calculations once we have our data. In this case we have to use the standard deviation (or proportion) from our sample as our best estimate of the population figure. We can then enter this, and our value for *n*, into the appropriate formula, calculate the standard error of the sample mean or proportion, and report the resultant confidence intervals for our results. In this way the researcher, and others interested in the findings, can see and evaluate the level of precision with which the results can be interpreted.

These concepts also relate very directly to those which underlie inferential statistical tests (see Chapter 14).

Response

So far, the discussion in the latter part of this chapter has focused on the *intended* sample — those to whom we decide to send our questionnaire or want to interview. However, we must also consider our *achieved* sample, those who actually complete and return the questionnaire or agree to be interviewed. Obviously we hope that the number of those invited to respond will equal the number of those who do so but that will rarely be the case. There is little point in our having taken great care to have drawn as large and representative a sample as possible, if the actual number of respondents is small or if they form a very biased sub-group of the intended sample.

Therefore we must take every possible step to maximise our response rate. The first requirement, as always, is to ensure that our research instruments are of high quality, as clear, simple and easy to complete as possible and seen as relevant by potential respondents. Instructions to potential respondents must also be clear. Seemingly obvious, but frequently overlooked, is that instructions as to what to do with a questionnaire should be on the questionnaire itself — not only in a covering letter which may become separated from it and lost. The contents of a covering letter, or any other means of contacting potential respondents, are also important. Again this should be clear and engage the interest of the potential responder but the researcher should also use it to introduce himself/herself and the purpose of his/her research as well as describing the uses to which data will be put and any relevant information relating to confidentiality. These and other research-based guidance on improving response are discussed more fully in Lewis-Beck (1994). You should also consider what is the best time to carry out your fieldwork. In England, do not expect a good response from primary teachers to a questionnaire sent to them during or close to an Ofsted inspection, at SATs time or shortly before Christmas.

However hard we try we will rarely achieve a response rate that appoaches 100 percent. Because of increasing pressures on schools and teachers, a 60 percent response rate to a postal survey is now considered to be quite acceptable. However, with any response rate of less than 100 percent there is still the possibility that respondents will be unrepresentative of our intended sample (and therefore of our population). Experience suggests that non-respondents may well be atypical in some way — teachers working in more pressured circumstances, individuals with more negative attitudes, students who are more frequently absent from school are just some of the possibilities.

It is therefore important to check, if possible, the characteristics of the achieved sample, either against those of the intended sample or of the population. Here is where longitudinal studies can have an advantage as they have the possibility of comparing the characteristics of those included and those omitted at one stage of the study using data from an earlier stage. For more common cross-sectional studies this is not possible but it is often the case that something can be known about the expected characteristics of the sample or population, even if this is only for one or two basic demographic variables such as gender, geographical distribution and/or type of school. These may be available from published national or regional statistics or from previous research.

Wherever possible, this should be explored and some simple checking analysis carried out. If this shows that your sample is close to representing what it was expected to represent, then you will have that much more confidence in any conclusions you draw from your survey. If the results of this analysis are more disappointing, at least you now know that and can be properly cautious in your discussion. Alternatively, if resources allow, you might consider a further reminder or some replacement sampling.

No researcher will be penalised for having had to accept the inevitable limitations and practical problems which arise in studying real life situations. What will be frowned upon is if you have not taken reasonable steps to avoid these as far as possible and can be shown to have failed to take sensible decisions; or if you do not recognise any limitations in your research; or if you do not take these into account in your discussion of your findings and any claims you may make as to their generalisability.

References

Blandford, S. and Squire, L. (2000) 'An evaluation of the Teacher Training Agency headteacher leadership and management programme (HEADLAMP)' *Educational Management and Administration*, 28(1): 21–32.

Cohen, L., Manion, L. and Morrison, K. (2000) *Research Methods in Education*, London: Routledge.

Denscombe, M. (1998) *The Good Research Guide*, Buckingham: Open University Press.

Elley, W. (1994) *The IEA Study of Reading Literacy: Achievement and Instruction in Thirty-two School Systems*, Oxford: Pergamon.

Ferri, E. (1993) *Life at 33: the Fifth Follow-up of the National Child Development Study*, London: National Children's Bureau.

Fogelman, K. (1985) 'Exploiting longitudinal data: examples from the National Child Development Study' in Nicol, A. R. (ed.) *Longitudinal Studies in Child Psychology and Psychiatry*, Chichester: Wiley.

Harper, H. (2000) 'New college hierarchies? Towards an examination of organisational structures in further education in England and Wales', *Educational Management and Administration*, 28(4): 433–435.

Hutton, P. (1990) *Survey Research for Managers: How to Use Surveys in Management Decision Making*, Basingstoke: Macmillan.

Lewis-Beck, M. S. (ed.) (1994) *Research Practice* (International Handbooks of Quantitative Applications in the Social Sciences, volume 6), London: Sage Publications.

Marsh, C. and Scarbrough, E. (1990) 'Testing nine hypotheses about quota sampling', *Journal of the Market Research Society*, 32(4).

Newcombe, B. and McCormick, J. (2001) 'Trust and teacher participation in school-based financial decision making', *Educational Management and Administration*, 29(2): 181–195.

Shepherd, P. (1993) 'Analysis of response bias' in Ferri, E. *Life at 33: the Fifth Follow-up of the National Child Development Study*, London: National Children's Bureau.

Wilson, M. (2001) 'Comprehensive School Governance and Special Educational Needs Provision: Policy, Practice and Future Priorities' *Educational Management and Administration*, Vol 29(1): 49–62.

Wilson, V. and McPake, J. (2000) 'Managing change in small Scottish primary school: is there a small school management style?', *Educational Management and Administration*, 28(2): 119–132.

Wise, C. (2001) 'The monitoring role of the academic middle manager in secondary schools', *Educational Management and Administration*, 29(3): 333–341.

7

Case study research

Michael Bassey

Recently I heard an American educational researcher start a lecture by saying, 'There are three kinds of researcher: those that count things and those that don't'. She paused, we waited. She continued, 'I do not belong to the first kind': laughter slowly moved around the hall. Her lecture was based on qualitative research. Case study is usually a form of qualitative research — and so doesn't involve counting!

Because this book is for educational managers and students I must make clear that I am writing about case study as a form of enquiry, as exploration of the unknown, and not as a learning tool in the form that often features in management classes. It is of course true that cases as used in classes have arisen from systematic and thorough enquiry, but they are usually written up with pedagogic intentions rather than with research criteria in mind.

A prescriptive definition of research case study

It may seem pedantic, but I am one who believes in starting from definitions. Several years ago I had the opportunity of examining carefully the concept of case study as a research approach (Bassey 1999), and I came to the conclusion that it needed pulling into shape! Figure 7.1 presents a definition that I believe gives a useful prescriptive account of what constitutes a worthwhile educational case study. Others provide different definitions: Yin (1994), Stake (1995) and Gillham (2000); see also Stake in Denzin and Lincoln (2000).

The terms in this box in italics inevitably entail value judgements being made by the researcher. It is worth elaborating on some of these and other terms contained in this statement.

An educational case study . . .

'Educational' locates this definition in the field of educational research (including educational management research), as opposed to discipline research in educational settings. I define educational research as critical enquiry aimed at informing educational judgements and decisions in order to improve educational action, whereas discipline research in education I see

---

An educational case study is an empirical enquiry which is:

- conducted within a localised boundary of space and time (ie a singularity),
- into *interesting* aspects of an educational activity, or programme, or institution, or system,
- mainly in its natural context and within an ethic of respect for persons,
- in order to inform the judgements and decisions of practitioners or policy-makers,
- or of theoreticians who are working to these ends, and
- such that sufficient data are collected for the researcher to be able:
  - (a) to explore *significant* features of the case,
  - (b) to create *plausible* interpretations of what is found,
  - (c) to test for the trustworthiness of these interpretations,
  - (d) to construct a *worthwhile* argument or story,
  - (e) to relate the argument or story to any relevant research in the literature,
  - (f) to convey *convincingly* to an audience this argument or story, and
  - (g) to provide an audit trail by which other researchers may validate or challenge the findings, or construct alternative arguments.

(Bassey, 1999: 58)

Figure 7.1. Prescriptive definition of research case study

as critical enquiry aimed at informing understandings of phenomena (in educational settings) which are pertinent to the discipline. (The term 'discipline' includes psychology, sociology, history, economics, philosophy, etc.) Educational research is more concerned with improving action through theoretical understanding, and discipline research with increasing theoretical knowledge of the discipline. The boundary between them is not clear-cut.

... an empirical enquiry ...
This means that the starting point is the collection of data — usually by asking questions, observing actions or extracting evidence from documents.

... conducted within a localised boundary of space and time ...
Most writers agree about this. When the report of the case study is written it focuses on a location and a defined period of time.

... (i.e., a singularity) ...
This is a term meaning that a particular set of events, or programme, institution, classroom, etc. is the focus of the case study research.

... into interesting aspects ...
Why spend time on it if the subject is not interesting? There should be something about the set of events, or programme, institution, classroom, etc. that is judged worth systematically describing to others, or there should be some feature or issue of it that deserves to be explored in order to try to understand what is happening.

. . . mainly in its natural context . . .

This is one of the strengths of case study research, and again is something on which most writers agree. Case study research entails being where the action is, taking testimony from and observing the actors first hand.

. . . and within an ethic of respect for persons . . .

Research bodies such as the British Educational Research Association (BERA) insist that all educational research should be conducted within an ethic of respect for persons (and of respect for truth and of democratic values). The closer one comes to the people being studied the more important it is to ensure that they are willing to be studied and that what they say or do is reported in such a way that it is not prejudicial to their best interests (see Chapter 5).

. . . in order to inform the judgements and decisions of practitioners or policy makers

Case study is arduous and demanding of both researchers and researched. It should not be wasted on trivial pursuits but should aim to contribute to some aspect of what educationalists (in the widest sense) actually do.

. . . or of theoreticians who are working to these ends . . .

We should not expect that all educational research will immediately inform the concerns of practitioners or policy makers. It is essential that researchers also build scaffolds for other researchers to climb — with the hope that ultimately the climbers will be able to inform those who follow them. Case study research can contribute to this.

. . . in such a way that sufficient data are collected . . .

Case study means that the researcher needs to collect sufficient data to allow him/her to explore features, create interpretations and test for trustworthiness. But 'sufficient' is a two-edged word meaning 'not too little, not too much'. There is no point in the case study researcher collecting more data than can be handled successfully in the time available — and that entails exercising considerable insight and judgement.

. . . to explore significant features of the case and to create plausible interpretations of what is found . . .

It is only of limited value for a researcher to conclude 'if teachers do x then y may happen'. It is much better to go beyond this and try to discover why this may happen for this may contribute to a theoretical understanding that illuminates other events.

. . . to test for the trustworthiness of these interpretations . . .

The critical approach should be ubiquitous in research. The question 'Does this really mean what we claim it means?' should always be in mind. Some tests of trustworthiness are given at the end of this chapter. In common with some other writers on case study I prefer the term 'trustworthiness' to the terms 'validity' and 'reliability' (for an elaboration of this concept see Lincoln and Guba (1985: 218)). 'Reliability' is an impractical concept for case study since by its nature a case study is a one-off event and therefore not open to exact replication.

... to relate the argument or story to any relevant research in the literature ...
If research is compared to a giant jigsaw puzzle then finding a new piece of the puzzle is of limited value unless it can be fitted into an area of the picture or at least stored with related pieces of the picture, ready to be slotted into it. The 'conceptual background' is an important section of most research papers, but the literature cited should be rigorously restricted to items judged pertinent to the enquiry.

... to construct a worthwhile argument or story and to convey convincingly to an audience this argument or story
Unless research outcomes are expressed in a readable way for the intended audience they are likely to be ignored and the enterprise wasted. This is a particular problem for case study researchers for their accounts, in trying to do justice to their data, tend to be lengthy. Some answers to this are given later.

... to provide an audit trail by which other researchers may validate or challenge the findings, or construct alternative arguments
This idea is not widely practised today but I commend it. The audit trail is a flow chart of the data, and of its analysis and interpretation, that enables others to examine the evidence for the trustworthiness of the study and also enables them to exercise their own creativity in finding alternative interpretations. The idea is to invite a colleague to conduct an audit of one's research and to comment on its perceived trustworthiness.

Different end-points for research case study

The comedian Peter Cook, playing a clergyman in the pulpit, told how he left the railway station by 'the way you're meant to go in and was hailed by a railwayman, "Hey, mate! Where do you think you are going?" — or at least that was the gist of his remark.' He went on: 'But I was grateful to that man, for he put me in mind of the kind of question that I want to ask you, "Where do you think you are going?" ' As researchers, you must ask yourselves the same question.

In my attempt to reconstruct the concept of case study (Bassey, 1999), I identified at least three different end-points (see Figure 7.2).

Story-telling and picture-drawing case studies
Story-telling and picture-drawing case studies are both analytical accounts of

---

- Story-telling and picture-drawing case study
- Evaluative case study
- Theory-seeking/theory-testing case study linked to fuzzy general predictions

---

Figure 7.2. Three different end-points for case study research

educational events, projects, programmes or systems aimed at illuminating theory. Story-telling is predominantly a *narrative account* of the exploration and analysis of the case, with a strong sense of a time line. For example, a story-telling case study might be an account of how a particular school responded over a period of time to the introduction of school development planning. Picture-drawing is predominantly a descriptive account, drawing together the results of the exploration and analysis of the case. For example, a picture-drawing case study might be an account of the system of school development planning operating in a particular school at a point in time. In both of these examples the research expectation would be that a case study attempted to contribute to theoretical ideas about school development planning. Often this entails the bringing together of a number of case studies as will shortly be illustrated.

An example of a story-telling case study is one that I wrote recently about events that took place over ten years earlier: 'The Nottinghamshire staff development project 1985–1987' (Bassey, 1999: Ch. 8). It is a 21-page account that draws on the 250-page case record prepared at the time. Drawing on interviews, questionnaires, documents and transcripts of group discussions, it describes how the project started and what steps I took to find out what was happening in my role as an illuminative evaluator to the project. It shows how I tried to tease out the ideology of the project, then tested it (I later found that the project sponsors did not accept that that they had an ideology!). I interviewed people who were heavily involved in the project and others who only knew of it at second or third-hand. Eventually I was able to describe the enthusiasm for it that the project generated in its key participants but also to show that the less people were involved in it the more they were inclined to treat it with cynicism. I finished this story-telling case study with this somewhat polemical statement:

> Perhaps the story has not ended yet. There are important messages for the national government . . . classrooms are being seen as units of production and teachers as technicians carrying out tightly defined functions. I believe it is time that the banner be raised again to assert the essentiality of teachers being recognised as professionals, fundamentally working for the effective education of young people, and striving to

enhance their practice through the shared process of structured reflective action. Only when they are free to exercise their own judgements
and make their own decisions can they provide that enthusiasm, insight
and enlightenment [that] young people need from their teachers if they
are to grow up responding creatively and happily to a changing and
challenging world. (Bassey, 1999: 115)

McMahon *et al.* (1997) provide an example of a picture-drawing case study:

This is a study of a primary school in Bristol, a school which has a
vibrant, exciting atmosphere, where pupils and teachers work hard and
effectively. A school described by governors, parents and teachers as
'marvellous', 'absolutely brilliant', 'exciting', 'inviting' and about which
the chair of governors said 'it's all buzzing in the school now'. The
classrooms and corridors are filled with displays of children's work,
there is a school choir which has sung in Bristol Cathedral, children
study the violin, participate in workshops with artists in residence,
enter and win competitions, put on excellent, high-standard perform-
ances for their parents at Christmas, look after an area of woodland
as part of an environmental project, enjoy and experience success with
their academic work and above all are valued as individuals. . . .
Teachers in schools like this can be justifiably proud of their work, but
the achievements here are greater, since this is a school that can accurately be described as one which is succeeding against the odds. (1997:
271)

This case study is based on interviews with governors, headteacher, teachers
and parents, observation and study of school documents. The case study is
largely descriptive, but clearly throughout the data collection, the researchers
have kept asking the question: 'How has this school been transformed from
one that was struggling?' They offer this explanation:

. . . hard work must be seen as a major explanatory variable. However,
it is also important to note that this work and effort has had a clear
focus and has been carefully planned by the headteacher in consultation with her staff. . . . The headteacher has been able to build her staff
into a strong team, help them develop a clear sense of direction and
purpose, and together they have turned the school around. It is for
these reasons that the school is succeeding against the odds. (1997:
280)

Theory-seeking and theory-testing case studies leading to fuzzy general predictions

This type of case study is best described by an example. MacGilchrist *et al.* (1997) carried out nine picture-drawing case studies in primary schools in England in the mid-1990s of systems of school development planning. They looked at questions such as: 'Who participates in preparing the plan?', 'Who acts on it?', and 'How is its success monitored?' Analysis of this data led them to ask further questions such as: 'Who has ownership of the plan, and how broad are its purposes?' They were seeking a theoretical structure and they discovered that their findings could be interpreted in terms of four types of school development planning which they termed the rhetorical plan, the singular plan, the co-operative plan and the corporate plan. Using their data they put to the test the 'assumption, made particularly by policy makers, that school development planners (SDPs) will improve schools, [that] they are the answer to self-management and as such will make schools more effective'. We can categorise their work in the nine schools as a multi-site theory-testing case study. They expressed the outcome as what I have called a 'fuzzy prediction'. It is 'fuzzy' (Bassey, 2001) because, instead of trying to state 'what works', it states 'what may work': in other words it has built in tentativeness or fuzziness (for an account of the concept of fuzziness in logical systems see Kosko, (1994)). MacGilchrist *et al.* said:

> This study . . . has shown that school development planning can be used as a school improvement strategy . . . Of the four types identified, only one [the corporate plan] was found to have a positive impact on student, teacher and school-wide improvements. (1997: 246)

Evaluative case studies

These are enquiries which set out to explore some educational programme, system, project or event in order to focus on its worthwhileness. The case may be tightly structured as an examination of the extent to which the programme's stated objectives have been achieved, or it may be illuminative in the phrase coined by Parlett and Hamilton (1977). It may be formative (in helping the development of the programme) or summative (in assessing it after the event). It draws on theoretical notions but is not necessarily intended to contribute to the development of theory — and in that sense is different from the other kinds of educational case study described above.

Multiple-site case studies

As noted, the study described above by MacGilchrist *et al.* (1997) illustrates the idea of multiple-site case studies. According to how the study is viewed this was either nine case studies in nine primary schools (each conducted along the same lines of enquiry into their development planning), or one case study into school development planning, carried out on nine sites. The distinction is, of course, unimportant. But the reason for the nine studies is very significant. These researchers were trying to say something significant about development planning and in order to do this they cast their net widely. As a result they came up with a four-fold typology. Perhaps they might have added to their typology had they studied more schools — but there is always a limit to what is possible. It is important to realise that in such a study there is an attempt to include as many varieties of practice as can be found, but no attempt to quantify them. If we wanted to know how prevalent these types of planning are, survey techniques would be needed. In this way sometimes case study and survey methods work in tandem, the case study informing the design of the survey.

Stages in conducting case study research

It is helpful to see the conduct of case study research as a stage-by-stage process, but the reader must recognise that the procedures described here will only rarely be in complete accord with the processes of actual studies. Research is a creative activity and every enquiry has its own unique character.

Stage 1: Identifying the research purpose
Stage 2: Asking research questions
Stage 3: Drawing up ethical guidelines
Stage 4: Collecting and storing data
Stage 5: Generating and testing analytical statements
Stage 6: Interpreting or explaining the analytical statements
Stage 7: Deciding on the outcome and writing the case report (publishing)

Figure 7.3. Possible stages in conducting case study

Stage 1: Identifying the research purpose

Going back to first principles, the purpose of research is trying to make a claim to knowledge, or wisdom, on the basis of systematic, creative and critical enquiry. It is about trying to discover something that was not known before and then communicating that finding to others. A helpful way of thinking about that 'something' is to see it as a research hypothesis to be tested, or as a research problem to be tackled, or as a research issue to be explored. Deciding initially on one of these provides a platform for asking research questions.

This is not a rigid classification. Often a research purpose can be expressed under more than one of these headings. Although one of the three may be judged to be the most suitable way of describing the research at a particular stage of enquiry, this may change and another of the three headings may be seen as a more apt way of describing the purpose of the research.

A *research hypothesis* is a tentative statement or conjecture that is in a form which can be tested. For example:

> That the introduction of performance management in this school will within three years have made a step change in our examination results.

It enables clear research questions to be asked which should provide evidence which either supports the hypothesis or refutes it. The research purpose is to test the hypothesis.

A *research problem* identifies a difficulty which often can be expressed as a contradiction between what is happening and what someone would like to happen. For example:

> The introduction of performance management in this school is welcomed by the senior management team (SMT) as a means of raising standards in examinations, but most staff believe it will damage senior/junior staff relationships and hence have a deleterious effect on results.

The popular idea that where there is a problem the job of the researcher is to find a solution, is usually unrealistic. The research is more likely to formulate and try out ways in which the problem may be better understood and so be alleviated or the difficulty reduced, and it is to this end that appropriate research questions need to be asked.

A *research issue* is the least defined purpose of research. It describes an area for enquiry where no problems or hypotheses have yet been clearly expressed that can direct the enquiry. For example:

> How will the introduction of performance management affect our school?

The research in this case will strive to focus the issue through asking pertinent research questions. Later the research can be reformulated as a problem or a hypothesis.

Early on in a research programme the question should be asked: 'What kind of report is it envisaged will eventually be written?' Will it, for example, be a story-telling or picture-drawing study, or an evaluative study, or a theory-seeking/theory-testing study? The last of these obviously links with the idea of a hypothesis, while story-telling, picture-drawing and evaluation tend to be linked to either issues or problems.

As an example, consider an investigation pursuing the above research *issue*. Suppose that it is refocused as an over-arching question:

'What are the current perceptions of performance management of school staff?'

This is the question that defines the claim to knowledge that the enquiry is intended to make when the first stage of the research is done, and hopefully will lead to a more focused enquiry that endeavours to move the school forward. It is not a research question in a technical sense because it does not set the agenda for data collection and analysis. The end point of this stage of the research is likely to be a picture-drawing case study.

Stage 2: Asking research questions

Research questions drive enquiry. They should be formulated in such a way that:

- sets the immediate agenda for research;
- establishes how data are to be collected;
- limits the boundaries of space and time within which it will operate;
- facilitates the drawing up of ethical guidelines; and
- suggests how analysis can start.

Thus, in terms of the above example these might be posed as research questions:

- What documents have come into school that influence staff perceptions? (Collect documents and news cuttings.)
- What is the understanding and expectation of each member of the school management team (SMT) of performance management? (Conduct 10-minute interviews based on four main questions.)
- What is the understanding and expectation of a 10 percent sample of non-SMT teaching staff of performance management? (Conduct 10-minute interviews based on the same four main questions.)

It will next be necessary, of course, to decide what the 'four main questions' are. Interview time is limited in recognition of the fact that everybody concerned is very busy and may well see the conduct of this research as unnecessary.

Stage 3: Drawing up ethical guidelines

Parallel to devising research questions should be the drawing up of ethical guidelines for the project. Ethical issues are discussed in Chapter 5. In the above example, the researcher and head (as senior member of the school) may agree the following guidelines:

- Interviews will not be tape-recorded but notes will be made and written up as brief reports. These will be shown to the interviewees as soon as possible after the events and will only be included in the case record in a form agreed by the interviewees, and with pseudonyms. Inclusion in the case record (see below) will mean that the researcher may cite the evidence in the case report.
- The case report will require the agreement of the head before it is made available to school staff.
- The case report will not be published outside the school unless permission is given by the head and chair of governors.

Stage 4: Collecting and storing data

Case study research has no methods of data collection or of analysis that are unique to it. In other chapters some data-collecting methods are discussed in detail; here it is worth stating two rules which, although superficially obvious, are ones that from time to time we all fail to observe. First, be systematic in recording data by, for example, noting date and time and place of collection, and keeping back-up files. Secondly, don't collect more data than you have the time and energy to analyse. You may want to consider analysing data as they come in, rather than waiting until they are all collected.

As part of a systematic approach, it can be valuable to number each piece of data as it is stored, for ease of future reference. For example, each interview report may be given a reference number, with decimal points for answers to each of the key questions.

I commend the following terminology for data storage and data processing. The *archive* is the total collection of rough notes, tidied-up notes, draft reports and final reports. It needs a running index and probably resides in cardboard boxes or the drawer of a filing cabinet. The *case record* includes agreed interview transcripts and agreed observation reports, the final versions of analytical statements, the interpretive writings, and the day-by-day journal of the research, and other documents. (It is a sub-set of the archive). These are the papers, polished in format, that will eventually be approved for public access, but which are likely to be too voluminous for the sustained attention of all but the most dedicated reader. They are the researcher's source for the writing of the case report and are likely to be stored as a set of files on the researcher's computer. The *case report* — the endpoint (perhaps one of several) of the case study — is written in one of the formats described earlier, drawing on the case record and citing it systematically as the source of data.

One essential feature of sound research is the application of a system for ensuring that in terms of data taken from people, only those which have been agreed in terms of the ethical guidelines are transferred from the archive to the case record.

The idea of *annotations* to data as they are stored can be helpful. Ideas often begin to develop during data handling and it is worthwhile having a systematic procedure for recording these changes — perhaps by using a different font on the computer.

It is helpful to keep on the computer a day-by-day *journal* of the researcher's activities — with entries showing who was seen, when, where and why, and recording when analytical work was done, etc.

Stage 5: Generating and testing analytical statements

Case-study work usually produces a great deal of data and analysis is needed to condense them into meaningful statements. These analytical statements need to be firmly based on the data and indeed may suggest the need for more specific data to be collected.

For example, a concise answer to the research question:

> What is the understanding and expectation of a 10 percent sample of non-SMT teaching staff of performance management?

will require careful re-reading of the interview notes, the formulation of draft statements (i.e., hypotheses), and the systematic testing of these (and amendment where necessary) against the data. The outcome should be one or more statements which are in accord with the data.

When this has been done for the other research questions it may be appropriate to look for deeper analytical statements. They will arise from reading and reflecting on the first round of statements, and going back to the data: they may be stimulated by the annotations that have been made. For example it could be that this analytical statement is posited:

> In this school the less staff know about how performance management will operate the stronger are their objections to it.

The result of testing analytical statements is that some of them stand and some need modifying, while others lack verity and are rejected. Analysis and data testing is an iterative process which continues until the researcher feels confident that the analytical statements he/she produces are trustworthy.

It is quite possible that the first round of enquiry will stop at this point and the central purpose of the research be refocused. Thus, if the analytical statement above is thought to be trustworthy the next move should be a management imperative, such as:

> Spend a training day briefing everybody about management performance.

In a large school this might be a useful outcome from a research case study — but we might hope that not too much time has been invested in producing it. What would be much more deserving of time would be a case study investigation into how performance management could enhance student achievements — an enquiry that might need research on a departmental basis.

Stage 6: Interpreting or explaining the analytical statements

This is where 'How?' and 'Why?' questions are brought to bear on the analytical statements in an attempt to provide understanding of the way things are. Interpretations tend to be associated with particular individuals or groups of people, while explanations tend to be attempts at expressing cause-and-effect relationships, within the boundary of the study.

Stage 7: Deciding on the outcome and writing the case report (publishing)

Before deciding that work on a case study is finished it is worth getting a colleague, as a critical friend, to conduct an audit; in other words, ask your

---

Tests of trustworthiness

1. Has there been prolonged engagement with data sources?
2. Has there been persistent observation of emerging issues?
3. Have data been adequately checked with its sources?
4. Has there been sufficient triangulation of data leading to analytical statements?
5. Has the working hypothesis, or evaluation, or emerging story been systematically tested against the analytical statements?
6. Has a critical friend tried to challenge your findings throughly?
7. Is the account of the research sufficiently detailed to give the reader confidence?
8. Does the case record provide an adequate audit trail?

Tests of respect for persons

1. Initially has permission been given to you by an appropriate manager to conduct the research in terms of the identification of an issue, problem, or hypothesis, in this particular setting?
2. What arrangements have been agreed for transferring the ownership of the record of utterances and actions to the researcher, thus enabling the latter to use them in compiling the case record?
3. What arrangements have been agreed for either identifying or concealing the contributing individuals and the particular setting of the research in the case report?
4. What arrangements have been agreed for giving permission to publish the case report and in what form?

Figure 7.4. Tests of probity in case study research

colleague to read through the data and its analysis and judge whether your understanding of what has been found is reasonable.

It may be that publication amounts to no more than distributing a few sheets of report reproduced on a photocopier, or speaking about the case at a staff meeting. If your research seems to have wider implications it may be appropriate to submit it for publication in a printed journal; in this case it may be possible to link the case report in the form of a narrative story or descriptive picture with a fuzzy prediction of what may be found elsewhere.

Tests of probity

There is not space here to elaborate on tests of probity but it is worth drawing attention to the questions of probity listed in Figure 7.4 (see Bassey 1999: Ch. 7). They make an appropriate end to this chapter.

References

Bassey, M. (1999) *Case Study Research in Educational Settings*, Buckingham: Open University Press.

Bassey, M. (2001) 'A solution to the problem of generalisation in educational research: fuzzy prediction', *Oxford Review of Education* 27(1): 5–22.

Denzin, N. K. and Lincoln, Y. S. (eds.) (2000) *Handbook of Qualitative Research* (2nd edn.), London: Sage.

Gillham, B. (2000) *Case Study Research Methods*, London: Continuum.

Hamilton, D., Jenkins, D., King, C., McDonald, B. and Parlett, M. (eds.) (1977) *Beyond the Numbers Game: a Reader in Educational Evaluation*, Basingstoke: Macmillan.

Harris, A., Bennett, N., and Preedy, M. (eds.) (1997) *Organisational Effectiveness and Improvement in Education*, Buckingham: Open University Press.

Kosko, B. (1994) *Fuzzy Thinking: The New Science of Fuzzy Logic*, London: Harper Collins.

Lincoln, Y. S. and Gub, E. G. (1985) *Naturalistic Inquiry*, Newbury Park, CA: Sage.

MacGilchrist, B., Mortimore, P., Savage, J., and Beresford, C. (1997) 'The impact of development planning in primary schools', in Preedy, M., Glatter, R. and Levačić, R. (eds.) *Educational Management: Strategy, Quality and Resources*, Buckingham: Open University Press.

McMahon, A., Bishop, J., Carroll, R. and McInally, B. (1997) 'Fair Furlong Primary School', in Harris, A., Bennett, N., and Preedy, M. (eds.) *Organisational Effectiveness and Improvement in Education*, Buckingham: Open University Press.

Parlett, M. and Hamilton, D. (1977) 'Evaluation as illumination: a new approach to the study of innovatory programmes', in Hamilton, D. *et al.* (eds.) *Beyond the Numbers Game: A Reader in Educational Evaluation*, London: Macmillan.

Stake, R. E. (1995) *The Art of Case Study Research*, London: Sage.

Stake, R. E. (2000) 'Case studies' in Denzin, N. K. and Lincoln, Y. S. (eds.) *Handbook of Qualitative Research* (2nd edn.), London: Sage.

Yin R. K. (1994) *Case Study Research*, London: Sage.

8
Action research
Pamela Lomax

Introduction

The linking of the terms 'action' and 'research' highlights the essential feature of action research: trying out ideas in practice as a means of improvement and as a means of increasing knowledge about educational management and leadership. Some writers have argued that action research is about improving practice rather than producing knowledge (Elliott, 1991), while others say that action research is a means of creating 'living educational theories' that contribute individual epistemologies of practice, which taken together contribute to knowledge more generally (Whitehead, 1993). What is clear is that action research, although rigorous, is a very eclectic form of research. It builds upon educational practitioners' existing skills and experiences as reflective practitioners (Middlewood *et al.*, 1999). It utilises many traditional research skills and most of the tools discussed elsewhere in this book have been used in action research.

I have adapted my preferred definition of action research from Carr and Kemmis (1986).

> Action research is a self-reflective, self-critical and critical enquiry undertaken by professionals to improve the rationality and justice of their own practices, their understanding of these practices and the wider contexts of practice.

This definition suggests the following approach to action research for educational managers:

- that managers are thoughtful and the enquiry intentional (self-reflective);
- that managers are willing to have their ideas challenged (self-critical);
- that managers will challenge existing knowledge and practice (critical);
- that managers start with open minds and not with prior knowledge of the results (enquiry);
- that managers see themselves as educational professionals;
- that managers seek to change practice in line with identified values (to improve);
- that managers are committed to effective practice (the rationality);

- that managers are committed to fairer practice (and justice);
- that managers are willing to change their current working practice if necessary (of their practices);
- that managers are willing to reframe their current knowledge if necessary (their understanding of these practices); and
- that managers are willing to attempt to influence other managers, institutional practices and policies (the contexts in which they operate).

This is a big task and the most important advice for the novice action-researching manager is to THINK SMALL. Put ambitious schemes on hold and identify a small aspect of practice as a beginning. It will grow.

This chapter is about establishing the principles of action research so that you can design your own enquiry to suit your particular aims and context. Action research is usually seen as a cyclical activity where you make a plan, carry it through, monitor what goes on, reflect on events critically (using the monitoring data) and move forward. This is an extremely simplistic idea and in my experience one that has never operated as smoothly as this description implies.

Establishing the principles of action research

It is important to be clear that educational action research is different from traditional educational research, because the latter was based on scientific premises that do not hold for action research. The most important difference is that in traditional research the researcher was required *not to influence the situation being studied*; in action research, the researcher intentionally sets out *to change the situation being studied*. This one difference means that the cultures of the two types of research activity are very different. It is important that researchers are comfortable with the culture of action research if they want to use it. It might be that researchers in some societies will find that action research is not for them. For example, there is a requirement to be clear about your value position because your values will be the yardsticks against which you can measure success. Another requirement is to draw upon a critical community (critical friends) to help move your thinking forward and this usually means exposing the more vulnerable sides of your practice. Both these requirements are incompatible with the image of the traditional manager from industry who would have been required to respond to market forces rather than values and who would have been expected to be a forceful decision maker rather than show hesitation about the best way forward. These requirements may also be more easily followed in specific cultural conditions such as the Western European and North American contexts (see Chapter 2 of this volume).

The following questions might be useful in deciding if a first project is manageable. If you are unable to answer these questions openly and honestly, you should choose a project that is less challenging to your status and self-esteem as a manager or less at odds with the culture within which you work.

Purpose

Action for improvement (to do with effectiveness and justice):

- Can I improve my practice so that it is more effective?
- Can I improve my understanding of this practice so as to make it more just?
- Can I use my knowledge and influence to improve the situation?

Focus

Participatory research (doing it oneself, on oneself):

- Can I take responsibility for my own action?
- Can I look objectively and critically at the part I play?
- Can I learn from my own practice and change if necessary?

Relations

Democratic (involving others as partners):

- Can I involve others in the action research process?
- Can I involve them in setting the agenda of the research and in interpreting the outcomes?
- Can I incorporate their (possibly different) perspectives into my explanation?

Method

Critical, rigorous and iterative:

- Can I monitor what is happening effectively?
- Can I collect rigorous data that provide evidence to support my claims about action?
- Can I make good professional judgements that will inform subsequent action?

Validation

Peer (testing outcomes with other professionals):

- Will the data provide evidence to support the claims?
- Will the data provide evidence that I have improved the practice?
- Can I convince my professional peers with my argument?

Action research by educational managers

I have drawn the following examples of action research from three educational leaders with whom I have worked in the UK. All the examples come from schools in the south of England, where the culture of education was conducive to the form of action research described in this chapter. The first two examples come from secondary schools and the third from a primary school. My purpose in describing this work is to show the centrality of the following ideas in the type of action research I am describing:

- educational values;
- educational professionalism; and
- reflection and critical community.

Educational values and a deputy headteachers's management of staff development

> Good quality educational research for me is practitioner research. It is about me changing as a result of my research and striving to live my values more consistently in my practice as an educational manager. This means that I need to identify and recognise these values, and to face up to contradictions in my practice, acting to overcome them. (Evans quoted in Lomax, Whitehead and Evans, 1996: 10)

Moyra Evans is a successful educational leader. Action research was the means through which, as deputy headteacher of a large comprehensive school, she improved staff development, which was one of her main leadership responsibilities. She began by monitoring her weekly meetings as she supported a group of teachers who wanted to improve the exam results of children in a particular subject. She planned the meetings and the subjects to be addressed, recorded what happened, discussed her data with her critical friends, and adapted her practice. In due course she could demonstrate that she had substantial and valid data about what had happened and how she had acted. She was able to offer some convincing explanations, drawing evidence from the data and refining her explanations as she shared her interpretations with critical audiences. She was able to develop theories about how to support teachers in school-based staff development and how to deal with the ethical issues that could arise (Evans, 1995).

I have used Evans's quotation to start this section because I think it gives a clue to the contribution that action research can make to the theory and practice of educational management and leadership. Much management knowledge has been taken directly from studies of industry and is viewed as business practice rather than educational practice. It is usually judged in terms of the scientific criteria of social science, in value-free terms. These criteria are insufficient for a full understanding of the issues involved in educational management and leadership and they mask important distinctions that exist between education and industry. For example, education is a value-based process whereas making computer components is not; educators have a responsibility for their student's development that is different from the treatment of customers in the retail trade.

Evans's opening statement points to an action research that incorporates a value dimension in its theory and method. She is guided by a moral commitment to appropriate educational action rather than to solely technical solutions (Wildman, 1995). Values are qualities that provide meaning and purpose; they can be used as the explanatory principles for why people make the judgements they do. This is why the clarification of values takes a high priority in action research. Values are questioned, modified, clarified and sometimes changed as the research proceeds. Where this kind of critical engagement with values is not possible for personal or cultural reasons, action research is pointless and if continued, the activity becomes a management tool for manipulating people rather than action research.

Moyra Evans's ideas about effective staff development changed drastically through her research. She changed her own practice as a school leader and was able to influence school policy and practice and teachers' expectations of staff development. One of the reasons why her understanding of the practice of staff development changed was that she was forced to reflect on her own values and how she put them into practice in her action. At the start of her research, Evans believed in the emancipatory potential of action research, yet it took some time for her to realise that some of the school's staff development initiatives were not emancipatory. Her action research led her to see this. At the end of her first year of supporting the staff development of teachers, she was confronted with some evaluation data that showed teachers' complicity in going along with the school's agenda for staff development although they did not see this as improving their teaching. She realised the ways she had seen as most appropriate for developing teachers' practice came from *her own* concerns as deputy headteacher. She had provided a hierarchical learning situation in a 'done to' model of in-service education in which the teachers felt no ownership. This was not what she had wanted to happen. She was clear about her values. She had wanted the teachers to be engaged in open access, self-identified, professional development rather than training to resolve needs identified elsewhere.

Her action altered radically from this point. She changed her model so that the professional development of teachers in her school was predicated on their perceived needs not those determined by her. The Denbigh Action Research Group set up by Evans is an example of a well-established successful group of teachers who identify themselves as collaborative action researchers.

Evans' formula for success included a number of factors: teachers connecting their knowledge to the communities they teach in terms of content and relationships (Belenkey *et al.*, 1986: 221); teachers being part of supportive networks; teachers empathising with other teachers' experiences in order to support them in their learning; teachers pushing the boundaries of what they know through the process of reframing (Schon, 1983: 140); teachers' excitement at seeing their students learning more effectively and being more successful; and teachers learning about themselves so they understand their own values and the forces that drive them to reflect and reconstruct their knowledge. The history of this group and the part played by the university to support its work is well documented in a recent paper (Evans *et al.*, 2000). The title of the paper 'Closing the circle' makes the point that a successful action research community permeates the whole school and includes students. The Denbigh Sixth Form Action Research Group was set up four years after the teachers group was formed showing that a form of research that took root in a community of teacher researchers can be transferred to the classroom with benefit for the teacher and the students.

Moyra Evans's approach to staff development has been maintained at Denbigh School although it is six years since she completed her PhD. She has continued to publish and disseminate her action research and to encourage other teachers in the school to do the same (Evans, 1998; 1999; Morgan, 1996; 1997). For example, two teachers from Denbigh, Tracy Wade and Clayton Hughes, presented their research at the 1999 British Education Reesearch Association (BERA) annual conference. The teachers gave a clear account of what they did in their classrooms, they outlined their success criteria and they gave evidence and examples of children learning something important. Hughes (1999) showed markedly improved scores for the GCSE results of the modern language students in his class; Wade (1999) showed some amazingly creative work produced by her students for the information and communication technology curriculum.

At the beginning of this chapter I suggested that cultural difference is an important variable in achieving success through action research. Evans was clearly aware of the risk that she took in conducting her research. It involved a senior member of the school giving up her control over teachers' learning. Leaders in such schools are often seen as knowing the answers to problems, and to be responsible for directing teachers in pursuit of the solutions (Evans, 1997). This is a factor in Western European and North American cultures that needs to be overcome if action research is to flourish. Moyra Evans was able to change the culture of her school and so move it towards being the school it is today through an action research process that took five years initially and has been supported for another six years subsequently. Where action research has significant impact, it clearly takes time for the impact to be made.

I believe that it is possible for very different cultures and societies to adopt an action research approach. Hong Kong is a case in point. There, action research is supported by a number of initiatives at Department of Education and University level but has not taken root in schools in the way it has in the UK. Wai Shing Lee *et al.* (1999), writing about the lack of action research in Hong Kong, suggest a number of factors at the professional level that militate against its adoption. These factors — the isolated culture of teaching; the 'deskilled' nature of teaching; and the dichotomy between theory and practice — work in a similar fashion in both Hong Kong and the UK. They are factors that discourage the open communication and discussion necessary for successful action research. Wai Shing Lee *et al.* (1999) argue that:

> a special system with its own culture and characteristics survives and blossoms hindering the development of professionals, teacher reflectivity, action research, school improvement, educational innovation and democratisation of the workplace.

The reasons given for this is the cultural heritage associated with paternalism (from both Chinese and colonial sources) that has led to a cluster of phenomena that is counter productive to action research. Wai Shing Lee *et al.* (1999) list these as the professional-bureaucratic divide, the 'we (administrators) know what's best for them (teachers)' and the practice of supervising to ensure standardisation. These factors exist also in the UK. It is arguable that it is global characteristics of education systems such as these that prevent action research in Hong Kong rather than more personal cultural values.

I maintain that educational values are not absolute qualities that necessarily remain unchanged. Clarifying personal educational values is crucial in Western Europe and North America today, because single prescribed ways of thinking and acting no longer exist. Clarifying personal educational values across cultures is even more important. It is one of the strengths of action research as a cross-cultural tool that the research starts with the researcher's own values. It is the task of the action researcher to clarify these educational values so that they can be used as clear yardsticks for measuring the success of the action. It is the responsibility of the action researcher's professional peers, people from the same cultural milieu, to judge whether the desired outcome is achieved.

Educational professionalism and a teacher-governor's management of teacher-governor relations

> ... time for research is always limited, since the primary responsibilities of the action researcher are those of a working practitioner. ... It is precisely for these reasons that I believe that those who engage in

action research demonstrate the ultimate expression of professionalism. (Linter, 2001)

There has been a general trend in recent years in the UK for the autonomy of educational managers and leaders to be reduced as quality has become identified with bureaucratic procedures and institutional practices for monitoring the effectiveness of schools and colleges. Educational managers throughout the world will recognise this scenario. In the UK it has been associated with the changing role of the headteacher towards a more narrowly administrative role, the prescriptions resulting from the national curriculum and assessment and the narrowing of the syllabus in teacher education.

Educational action research demands a critical approach, in which the leader is expected to challenge educationally inappropriate ends as well as inefficient means. I recognise that this is difficult in many contexts. In Hong Kong, for example, the Chinese community values conformity and hierarchy and individuals would expect to adapt their action to the community to which they belonged (Wai Shing Li *et al.*, 1999). This might pose less of a problem than that faced by teachers in the UK who may have little control over the issues that concern themselves most. In most situations there is a choice between passively implementing directives and being more innovative and adapting them to suit local conditions. Rod Linter is a good example of an educational leader who decided to be proactive when faced with what he saw as the damaging effects of too much change imposed on schools. He says he became a teacher governor as a personal and political response to the de-professionalisation of the teaching profession. His action research was undertaken as a practitioner response to the 1988 Education Act and is set against a background of the local management of schools (LMS), formula funding, open enrolment, league tables, Ofsted inspections and an emerging educational market place. He saw the reforms as forcing schools to accept the idea that they should operate as successful business enterprises and this was contrary to his social and educational values.

Linter spent six years researching his practice. He used action research as an independent and critical form of enquiry to confront the value contradictions that he faced. He says that his thesis is an evidence-based, generative response, which is an authentic expression of his professionalism (Linter, 2001). At the start, his action research was aimed at influencing the school's governors who had been given increased powers over the school's practice by the recent legislation. He determined that governors needed to be better informed, more visible and active within the school if the new powers were to be used to the benefit of the school and in line with 'educational' rather than 'market' values. When he started his research, there was no interaction between governors and teachers and he determined to change this.

His success in generating meaningful interaction between staff and governors is reported in three action cycles. In the first cycle he persuaded individual governors to spend time in school and visit classrooms and observe lessons. He found that enabling governors to experience the daily workings of the school early in their term of office capitalised on their enthusiasm as new governors. The new governors also benefited because they could talk about their classroom experiences in the governors meetings, where otherwise they would have remained silent.

A second cycle was the result of being asked to deliver school-based in-service training (INSET). Linter encouraged the governors to attend and even repeated the session for ten governors who could not attend the initial meeting. The INSET session was set up with the aim of getting the staff and governors to work together. Linter wanted to ensure that the governors were seen and saw themselves on the side of local practice; he wanted their support to interpret national policy so as to best fit the local context. The title of the session, 'Setting our own agenda', was intended to spell out the message that the development agenda was one for the whole school to decide and that staff and governors were partners in the enterprise.

His last cycle described his work chairing a working party that was set up by the headteacher to examine the nature of the changes that had taken place within the school over the previous five years and make practical recommendations which would bring about a better working ethos within the school. He determined to involve governors in this and set about designing and conducting a survey of teachers, students' and governors' views on the matter. This widened the scope of professional dialogue and secured a whole-school mandate for change. The working party process revealed a school that desired to learn and to seek change. It provided evidence that the separation of teachers and governors was historical and that the broad foundations for a collaborative learning culture that included school governors had been laid. Linter believes that the generative outcome of the three cycles of research enabled the school to undertake changes that would not have been possible at the beginning.

Rod Linter argued that researching one's practice is the ultimate expression of what it is to be professional. This is in line with those ideas that see action research as a social process and not simply a research method. I think his work demonstrates a new professionalism in education, which rests on a democratic knowledge-base that includes educators' theories, which have been generated through relevant experience and validated through systematic research (Lomax, 1999). This is different from the old idea that educational knowledge is an objective body of facts, which should be interpreted and managed by a small group of experts. The new professionalism is premised on a process of continuous professional development. It would be an evidence-based profession, but with an open mind about what could constitute evidence. It would recognise that evidence may reflect situational differences embodied in the different ways in which particular communities work. I believe that this view of professionalism and the role of action research is a global alternative to global materialism.

Reflection, critical community and an infant headteacher's attempt to make sense of her practice

> We need to create a 'collective professional confidence that can help teachers resist the tendency to become dependent on false scientific certainties . . . by replacing them . . . with the situated certainties of collective professional wisdom among particular communities of teachers'. (Hargreaves,1995: 153)

Action research adds a self-conscious discipline to good reflective professional practice. There are two important aspects of this discipline. The first, an inward looking dimension, puts emphasis on the researcher as a learner, committed to personal development through improving their understanding of their own practice (*reflection*). The second, an outward looking dimension, puts emphasis on the researcher as a collaborator, actively seeking the validation of their practice and knowledge (*reflexivity*). Both elements depend on the fact that we are able to represent meaning in a concrete, objective form.

Margaret Follows was a headteacher of an infant school for ten years. Now no longer in post, she is engaged in an action research enquiry which uses her previous school experience as a focus for developing ideas about a fair(er) assessment. Her intention is to explore, critically, some of her own tacit knowledge by focusing on her past practice, which she represents in a fictionalised form. To do this she has involved professional colleagues to help her to deconstruct and reconstruct the past events so that they can learn from them together.

As part of her enquiry she constructed a story book, '*All About Ourselves*' by Polly and Robert. (Follows, 2000). The story book was based on the work of two children who had very different achievements, abilities, learning styles, personalities, interests and life experiences, and whose routes to learning and the implications for teaching would also have been different. The story book was based on data taken from: school learning and assessment policies; assessment records; children's personal portfolios of work; class teachers' formative assessment records; individual records of achievement and baseline assessment; curriculum plans; and annual and mid-term topic planners which provided a framework for teaching over time. Follows's aim was to provide a picture of the children's learning, development and attainment during the three-year period, 1994–7. The story book was a means of representing the concrete data to provide a picture of the whole child in a form that was in tune with the reality of infant classrooms; the story book was also *her own* construction, containing *her tacit* knowledge about infant education.

Because Follows was using action research to look at historical events, she needed to adapt the methodology to suit its purpose. She used what Van Manen (1995) has called *retrospective* reflection (done after the act) which is different to *contemporaneous* reflection (done during the act) and *anticipatory* reflection (done before the act). Van Manen argues that contemporaneous reflection or reflection in action is not possible because 'the active practice of teaching is too busy to be truly reflective' (1995: 35). Margaret used a form of retrospective reflection called *memory work* that has been developed as a critical group activity to deconstruct events from the past in order to promote a better understanding of them (Haug (1987); Scratz and Scratz-Hadwich (1995); Lomax and Evans (1996)). Memory work enabled her to put in place the critical debate necessary to promote reflexivity, where the affirming or questioning response of others to our communicated meaning challenges us to see something else. In action research, critical community is encouraged through the formation of critical friendships and co-researching practices (Lomax, 1994a), and through the requirement that the claims emerging from the research must be critically validated against evidence, and that the research should go into the public domain.

Sharing action research with 'critical' others also demands a subtle use of representation. Margaret used the story book as a representation of her past practice. It became the focus for a number of group sessions in which she hoped that others could help her to deconstruct and reconstruct her past practice *vis-à-vis* assessment. Following these sessions she re-edited the story book so that its final form emerged from the critical research process in which she was engaged. Before each session she thought long and hard about her purpose in presenting the material. When she presented the children's drawings and their emergent writing, she intended to present their learning and attainment through showing their developing language skills. In this way she believed that she was demonstrating the children's ongoing learning and development without reference to their attainment in national curriculum assessment. She wanted to generate discussion about the developmental and conceptual stages of learning, as seen through the drawings and not about what she defined as the narrow and linear measurement of numerical scores.

In the first session she learned that she had not taken account of how much her considerable experience and knowledge of events had structured her understanding of the story book material. This tacit knowledge was not available to the other members of the group.

She decided to rewrite the story book and to try to clarify the essential knowledge that teachers possess about the children they teach. She was able to involve two teacher colleagues who had a personal knowledge of the research context. The two teachers had been members of the school staff when Follows was headteacher. They agreed to act as her research collaborators. They had first-hand knowledge of the two children, having been their class teachers for two out of the children's four years at the school. They could help Follows to explore this insider knowledge and its relation to the judgements that they had made about Polly's and Robert's work and the criteria and standards of assessment they had used at the time. They had three meetings. They used the technique of memory work to focus back together. They had concrete examples of the children's work before them and they addressed the questions, 'What, when, how and why did we do this?' so that they could triangulate their memories.

Follows has used the results of these meetings in the most recent editing of the story book. Now it provides a fuller description and explanation of the children's learning, development and attainment in relation to curriculum planning, classroom organisation, the context of each activity related to each child's piece of work, assessment records and the possible next steps in the learning for each child. It includes a series of pictures and writing done by two children over a three-year period with captions written by her. Following each pair of pictures she has answered three questions about the children's work: 'What is there to see?' 'How best can we understand what we see?' and 'How can we put our understanding to good use?' There is an introduction, which sets the context and provides background information about the children, and a conclusion which draws together the analysis provided after each picture. The footnotes that support this analysis show the evidential source of her conclusions, clearly distinguishing between objective data and constructed data. A more holistic picture is beginning to emerge.

I have included an account of Follows's research because it clearly demonstrates the importance of different forms of representation in supporting reflection and critical community. The more usual forms of representation used in action research have been through reflective journal writing or capturing action on video. The former has been used quite widely across different cultures. Moyra Evans used fictionalised story in order to share her perceptions of staff development with the teachers in a less threatening way than the use of video might have been. At Denbigh School most of the teachers found this method acceptable and began writing fictionalised accounts themselves for the purpose of sharing with the group. Writing and discussing these fictionalised accounts frequently led to the teachers seeing connections that had previously been invisible to them. Rod Linter also used a more unusual form to represent his work in a series of 'rich' pictures. He says that the act of constructing the pictures revealed new connections within the data that were previously invisible to him and also enabled him to generate pur-

poseful statements in which he could share his feelings with others. It facil-
itated an understanding of the painful and emotional conditions he had experienced and allowed an exploration of possibilities in a humorous vein. It
was no accident, he says, that the rich picture, 'You saw us waving but we
were drowning', which depicted the issue of teacher redundancy, was presented in the form of classic seaside postcard humour. For Linter, it triggered
the tragic comedy of the educational condition.

Eisner (1993; 1997) has argued that new forms of representation 'are
rooted in an expanding conception of the nature of knowledge' and can lead
to new ways of seeing things. He says they encourage empathy and recognition of the place of human feeling in understanding. They provide a sense
of particularity that suggests authenticity and are evocative in that they
encourage multiple interpretations. Finally, they support the exploitation of
individual aptitudes that have tended to be ignored as research skills. New
forms of representation may also be a way of encouraging cross-cultural ideas
to flow more easily.

Conclusion

> The new categories of scholarly activity must take the form of action
> research. What else could they be? They will not consist in laboratory
> experimentation or statistical analysis of variance, nor will they con-
> sist only or primarily in the reflective criticism and speculation famil-
> iar to the humanities. (Schon, 1995: 31)

I like the definition of action research provided by Carr and Kemmis (1986)
in which they describe a self-reflective enquiry undertaken by practitioners
to improve the rationality and justice of their educational practices, their
understanding of these practices and the situations in which these practices
occurred. I particularly like their emphasis on the social justice of practice
and I think this parallels the emphasis that I have put on values. My dispute
with them might be that they seem to imply that social justice is an absolute
principle whereas I prefer the more tentative construction of working
towards implementing personal and professional values.

Jack Whitehead is an exponent of the value of recognising the creative
and critical capacities of each individual to create their own theories from
within their own personal and professional perspectives. Alongside its theoretical implications, Whitehead's approach stresses the importance of sustaining enquiry by being open to the possibilities, which our values and life
itself permits. This means valuing the humanity of others in ones relations
with them (Whitehead, 1999a; 1999b). In this context he cites the writing
of Fukuyama (1992), who wrote about the quality of valuing the humanity
of the other (*isothymia*), and the destructive quality in which individuals seek

to demonstrate that they are superior to others (*megalothymia*). Whitehead sees action research as a value-laden form of enquiry, which we use in giving some meaning and purpose to our lives as educators. In this sense the imagined solution, the practical outcome, the improved practice, the contribution to a better life, lead both methodology and theory (Whitehead, 1993).

Whitehead's ideas strongly support my view that research should be done by educational managers themselves and not by so-called experts. I like the way that Gurney (1989) argues that the researcher should be both innovator and implementer; the one who poses the questions and the one who investigates the solutions. I value this way of empowering professionals. This also relates to what I see as an ethical–professional dimension. I think educational research has to include in its doing an educational outcome; it has to address the issue of its own motives and explain what is meant by improvement in immediate professional terms (Lomax and Whitehead, 1998). This is one reason why I characterise educational research as insider research. It implies that the manager-researcher will engage in a continuing critique of her own educational management values as part of the research process as she seeks answers to the questions that her management practices pose.

Being an insider to the research is crucially significant if one accepts the existence of 'situational' rather than 'scientific' certainty (Hargreaves, 1995). As insiders, we have the opportunity to transform our own understanding through self-reflective strategies that recognise other dimensions of the human condition besides the scientific, rational ones. This opens up the possibility of using moral, spiritual, political, aesthetic, emotional, affective or practical criteria. Follows's (2000) attempt to use her tacit knowledge of children's learning in order to identify a fair(er) form of assessment is an area that begs the use of criteria that can access the somatic, nonverbal quality of attention that is based on a recognition of kinship, which Heshusius (1994) called a participatory mode of consciousness.

I think educational management research should be practical. I think that intervention in my own management practice to bring about improvement is extremely practical. This does not mean that my research is concerned merely with technical matters. I view practical research in terms of the practical ethic discussed by Adelman (1989) where educational purposes and means are addressed together making for informed, committed action (*praxis*). For me, practical does not exclude theoretical, but locates theoretical in a practical context of ongoing professional evaluation and action.

I want my research to be authentic so that other educational managers are able to recognise it for what it is and empathise with my underpinning values. I dislike deception and manipulation of others. I see my emphasis on the importance of co-researching rather than treating others as respondents or informants as related to my wish to empower others in the research relationship. I like to enable others to speak for themselves rather than interpreting their positions for them, although I am happy to facilitate their understanding where I can.

I think research should be rigorous. I think it is more difficult to work with 'subjective' data than with 'objective' data and therefore educational management research, with its emphasis on values and action, demands high-level research skills (Lomax, 1994b). This has important implications for the idea of validity, which is about being able to make a plausible case for one's research claims before an 'educated' audience of peers. But we can get too obsessed with the notion of validity and there is a danger in attempting to codify the grounds or criteria for validity too closely because we are likely to lose a sense of our own tentativeness. However, I have included some criteria for judging action research at the end of this chapter that you might like to apply to your own research; you may also look at *You and Your Action Research Project* (McNiff *et al.*, 1996), a blow by blow guide to doing action research.

Most important for me is that research should be holistic. As a teacher-educator investigating my own practice, I do not separate my intent to motivate my students, from my intent to help them develop their technical competence, from my intent to help them refine their professional judgement. I value respect for the whole person, which I think means treating professional knowledge holistically. I object to the way in which particular practices are separated into higher order skills and lower order skills, and to the way in which certain powerful interest groups lay claim to the former, like Fenstermacher's (1992) idea that schools are places where teachers can learn technical competence (the systemics of schooling) but universities are places where they might learn to acquire knowledge of the educative purposes of schooling. His 'elitist' views make me feel ashamed when I read what Holley (1995) says of academics:

> Teachers are seduced by academics who simultaneously include and exclude us in their writing about teaching. Our presence is taken for granted and yet denied and we are enticed into narratives which reduce us by exalting us. (1995)

Finally I believe that educational research should be influential. I want educators' voices to be heard and I want them to share their values and persuade others about the significance of their work.

Table 8.1 Criteria for judging action research

Attribute	Outcome	Criteria for judging
Purpose	Action for improvement	• Have I improved my practice so that it is more effective? • Have I improved my understanding of this practice so that it is more just? • Have I used my knowledge and influence to improve the situation — at local, institutional and policy levels?
Focus	Doing it oneself, on one's own practice	• Have I taken responsibility for my own action? • Have I looked objectively and critically at the part I played? • Have I learned from my own practice and made changes where necessary?
Relations	Democratic	• Have I incorporated others' perspectives on the action into my explanation? • Have I involved others in setting the agenda of the research and in interpreting the outcomes? • Have I shared ownership of the action research with others?
Aim	To generate theory	• Have I explained my own educational practice in terms of an evaluation of past practice and an intention to create an improvement, which is not yet in existence? • Have I described and explained my learning and educational development that is part of the process of answering the question? • Have I integrated my values with the theories of others as explanatory principles?
Method	Critical, iterative	• Have I monitored what was happening? • Have I found sound evidence to support my claims about action? • Have I made good professional judgements that will inform subsequent action?
Validation	Peer	• Have I tested the strength of my evidence and the validity of my judgements with other teachers and academic peers?
Audience	Professionals, policy makers, users, academics	• Have I influenced the situation?

References

Adelman, C. (1989) 'The practical ethic takes priority over methodology', in Carr, W. (ed.) *Quality in Teaching*, London: Falmer Press.

Belenkey, M. F., Clinchy, B. M., Goldberger, N. R. and Tarule, J. M. (1986) *Women's Ways of Knowing*, New York, Basic Books.

Carr, W. and Kemmis, S. (1986) *Becoming Critical: Education, Knowledge and Action Research*, Lewes: Falmer Press.

Eisner, E. (1997) 'The promises and perils of alternative forms of data representation', *Educational Researcher* 24(2): 4–10.

Eisner, E. W. (1993) 'Forms of understanding and the future of educational research', *Educational Researcher*, 22(7): 5–11.

Elliott, J. (1991) *Action Research for Educational Change*, Milton Keynes: Open University Press.

Evans, M. (1995) 'An action research enquiry into reflection in action as part of my role as a deputy headteacher', Ph.D. thesis, Kingston: Kingston University.

Evans, M. (1997) 'Shifting the leadership focus from control to empowerment — a case study', *School Leadership and Management*, 17(2): 273-283.

Evans, M. (1998) 'Using story to promote the continuing professional development of teachers', *British Journal of In-service Education*, 24(1).

Evans, M. (1999) 'Using fictional story in teacher research', *Educational Action Research Journal*, 16(3).

Evans, M., Lomax, P. and Morgan, H. (2000) 'Transferring the excitement of what is learned in a community of teacher researchers to classroom communities of pupils', *Cambridge Journal of Education*, 30(3): 405–419.

Fenstermacher, G. G. (1992) 'Where are we going? who will lead us there?' Address to the Annual Meeting of the American Association of Colleges of Teacher Education.

Follows, M. (2000) 'Looking for a fair(er) assessment of children's learning, development and attainment', *CARN Newsletter*, No. 2, June 2000.

Fukuyama, F. (1992) *The End of History and the Last Man*, London: Penguin.

Gurney, M. (1989) 'Implementer or innovator? A teacher's challenge to the restrictive paradigm of traditional research', in Lomax, P. (ed.) *The Management of Change*, Clevedon: *Multi-Lingual Matters*, 13–28.

Hargreaves, A. (1995) 'Beyond collaboration: critical teacher development in the post modern age', in Smyth, J. (ed.) *Critical Discourse on Teacher Development*, London: Cassell.

Haug, F. (1987) *Female Sexualisation: A Collective Work on Memory*, London: Verso.

Heshusius, L. (1994) 'Freeing ourselves from objectivity: managing subjectivity or turning towards a participatory mode of consciousness', *Educational Researcher* 23(3): 15–22.

Holley, E. (1995) 'What is good quality educational research?', Unpublished paper, School of Education, University of Bath.

Hughes, C. (1999) 'The impact on GCSE students' learning of my action research project', paper presented in the symposium, School-University Partnership in Teacher Action Research at the Annual Conference of the British Educational Research Association, Sussex 1999.

Linter, R. (2001) 'Research at the policy and practice interface: the experience of a teacher governor', Ph.D thesis, Kingston: Kingston University.

Lomax, P. (1994a) 'Action research for managing change', in Bennett, N., Glatter R. and Levačić, R. (eds.), *Improving Educational Management through Research and Consultancy*, London: Paul Chapman.

Lomax, P. (1994b) 'Standards, criteria and the problematic of action research', *Educational Action Research: an International journal*, 2(1): 113–125.

Lomax, P. (1999) 'Working together for educative community through research: towards evidence based professionalism', *Research Intelligence*, 68: 11-16.

Lomax, P. and Evans, M. (1996) 'Working in partnership to implement teacher research', in Lomax, P. (ed.) *Quality Management in Education: Sustaining the Vision through Action Research*, London and New York: Routledge/Hyde.

Lomax, P. and Whitehead, J. (1998) 'The process of improving learning in schools and universities through developing research-based professionalism and a dialectic of collaboration in teaching and teacher education 1977–1978', *Journal of In-Service Education*, 24(3): 447–467.

Lomax, P., Whitehead, J. and Evans, M. (1996) 'Towards an epistemology of quality management practice', in Lomax, P. (ed.) *Quality Management in Education: Sustaining the Vision through Action Research*, London and New York: Routledge.

McNiff, J., Lomax, P. and Whitehead, J. (1996) You and Your Action Research Project, London and New York: Routledge/Hyde Publications.

Middlewood, D., Coleman, M. and Lumby, J. (1999) *Practitioner Research in Education*, London: Paul Chapman.

Morgan, H. (1996) *Motivation of Sixth Form Students*, Teacher Training Agency (TTA) pamphlet, Teacher Research Grant Scheme, London: TTA.

Morgan, H. (1997) *Students Talking to Teachers — the Role of the Form Tutor in Helping to Support and Motivate Students*, TTA pamphlet, Teacher Research Grant Scheme, London: TTA.

Schon, D. A. (1983) *The Reflective Practitioner: How Professionals Think in Action*, New York: Basic Books.

Schon, D. A. (1995) 'The new scholarship requires a new epistemology', *Change*, November/December 1995.

Scratz, M. and Scratz-Hadwich, B. (1995) 'Collective memory work: the self as a re/source for re/search', in Scratz, M. and Walker, R (eds.) *Research as Social Change*, London: Routledge.

Van Manen, M. (1995) 'On the epistemology of reflective practice', *Teachers and Teaching: Theory and Practice*, 1(1): 33–50.

Wade, T. (1999) 'Using action research to enhance the learning experience of pupils in information and communication technology', paper presented in the symposium, School-University Partnership in Teacher Action Research at the Annual Conference of the British Educational Research Association, Sussex 1999.

Wai Shing Li, Wai Ming Yu, Tak Shing Lam and Ping Kwan Fok, (1999) 'The lack of action research: the case for Hong Kong', *Educational Action Research Journal*, 7(1): 33–49.

Whitehead, J. (1993) *The Growth of Educational Knowledge*, Bournemouth: Hyde Publications.

Whitehead, J. (1999a) 'Educative relations in a new era', *Curriculum Studies*, 7(1): 73–90.

Whitehead, J. (1999b) 'How do I help you to improve your learning? Spiritual, aesthetic and ethical contradictions in my discipline of education', in 'My discipline of education', Ph.D. thesis, University of Bath. See also the Living Theory Section of http://www.actionresearch.net

Wildman, P. (1995) 'Research by looking backwards: reflective praxis as an action research model', *ARCS Newsletter* 13(1): 20–38.

Part C
Research Tools

9
Interviewing
Ted Wragg

Introduction

Interviewing is one of the oldest and most widely used of social science research techniques. Suppose Person A wishes to find out information, while Person B has a point of view, is in possession of relevant facts or has undergone certain experiences. What could be more straightforward, on the surface at any rate, than Person A simply seeking out Person B, asking direct face-to-face questions and noting down the answers?

Interviewing is a particularly useful tool for managers engaged in research and study, allowing the investigator to enquire into such matters as the development and support of teaching competence, relationships between insider and outsider groups and individuals, the impact of decisions on members of institutions, factors influencing the outcomes of teaching and learning. A number of useful texts have been written on the subject, many pointing out the caveats as well as the advantages, such as Briggs (1986), Powney and Watts (1987), Oppenheim (1992), Holstein (1995), Kvale (1996) and there are numerous web sites offering on-line courses.

Research interviews, although apparently a perfectly natural means of communication and enquiry, are in practice riddled with numerous pitfalls for the unwary. For example, the questions asked may turn out to be loaded ones, if the interviewer merely seeks to confirm a prejudice. Respondents may not tell the truth, particularly if they believe their answers may show them in a bad light or reach the ears of their superiors. Consider the following hazards, describing but six out of countless opportunities for inaccuracy or distortion, which could render interviewing worthless if it were undertaken without forethought.

Interviewer bias

Questions may be worded so as to lead the respondent towards the expression of certain beliefs endorsed by the investigator: e.g., 'Is there too much bureaucracy in this school, and what are you going to do about it?'.

Sample bias

An investigator interviews people in a shopping centre, an unrepresentative sample of the population at large, but still concludes that 'few parents understand much about their children's education'.

Hired interviewers

Some studies of people hired to conduct interviews have shown that they may fake answers when subjects are unco-operative or for other reasons.

Ethnic issues

People may respond differently to interviewers from their own and to those from a different ethnic background, an especially sensitive issue when adults interview children. In one of our research projects pupils in a school were interviewed by two people, one white the other black. On certain issues children gave different answers to the two researchers.

Straitjacket interview

Some tightly structured interview schedules permit little latitude, so respondents may not be able to reveal their true feelings, or explain what lies beneath their answer: e.g., 'Are you in favour of paying good teachers more money?' Answer 'Yes' or 'No'.

Interviewer's or respondent's image

Interviewers' own status, purpose and function may distort, leading to answers that are more a public relations exercise than an accurate response, particularly if a senior manager responsible for liaison between staff and parents were to ask a question such as: 'What are relationships like between teachers and parents in this school?'. Managers interviewing other managers in the same or a different institution are in a particularly difficult position, for people become especially apprehensive, however disarming the interviewer may be, at the possibility of being judged by someone familiar with their type of work.

Why interview?

Despite the potential hazards, interviews are still a fruitful source of information when handled skilfully, either as the sole means of enquiry, or in conjunction with observations, diary analysis, or questionnaires. As with all research methodology it is important to start with research questions, rather than focusing on a particular technique. In some cases questionnaires will be better than interviews. If studying improvements in achievement, a standardised test of proficiency might be a more appropriate tool than an interview asking subjects how capable they think they are, or whether they believe they have improved.

If an investigator wanted to study teachers' use of praise, hypothesising that higher achieving pupils receive more praise than lower achievers, then a sample of teachers might be interviewed to elicit if this were believed to be true. A more effective strategy, however, would be to use scores derived from an objective test to identify the highest and lowest achievers, to obtain classroom behaviour descriptions obtained from lesson observations or transcripts, and then to conduct interviews to supplement this information.

If you wish to ask numerous simple questions requiring short answers, or ratings on a five or six point scale, a questionnaire might reach a wider audience and produce more information. If your questions are such as to require a great deal of careful thought rather than a spontaneous reply you might in any case prefer a written response. On the other hand, if the target population consisted of very young children, poorly educated people, or those who had difficulty with writing for some reason, then you would probably obtain better results from talking to them, rather than asking them to write.

Where to interview?

It may seem a small matter but the setting for interviews can be important. Most of us feel more at ease in one location than another. Even professional people, used to meeting officials, attending meetings and using telephones, feel on their guard when interviewed in a formal setting as can happen in a crisis or during an encounter with the Inland Revenue.

Sometimes interviewer and interviewee do not even meet as interviews by telephone and by email are commonly used by marketing and public relations firms. In education, the face-to-face interview is still the most frequent form of discourse, as both parties often want to see each other when talking about human affairs and there is some unease about the veracity of replies given via the somewhat detached medium of email.

Conducting an interview in comfortable chairs, perhaps in someone's own room or home, may be more conducive to a relaxed atmosphere than the office of the interviewer. Not that this is always perfect, as people may be over-confident when on familiar territory and give false information. The key question is: 'Given the nature of the interview, what location makes most sense?'.

One important element is *confidentiality*. Interviews may cover sensitive ground and without privacy few people will be frank. If you interview parents in a school, for example, it should be away from other parents, teachers and their own children, unless their presence is desirable. When interviewing children or teachers, it may be necessary to do this away from their peers, in whose company they often feel they must act in a certain way. Investigators studying students, especially adolescent boys, often find that in a group interview they strike a strong 'anti-education' note, whereas in individual interviews they may admit to being interested in their work and resenting their colleagues' attempts to disrupt classes. Young children, however, may not communicate at all unless in the company of their parents or friends.

Whom to interview?

The selection of an appropriate sample is a problem throughout educational research. A single or a few respondents may be atypical, and a cast of thousands may be equally unrepresentative, if badly selected. More information can be found about this question in Chapter 6.

The first-order choice is between a *random sample* and an *opportunity sample*. An opportunity sample consists of those whom it is convenient to interview, either because they are willing to talk or because they come your way. The group of parents out shopping referred to above comprised an opportunity sample. The investigator was wrong, therefore, to make inferences about 'parents' when the sample may have been predominantly of mothers from one social class or background, depending on the location of the centre and time of day, while few fathers may have been interviewed.

A random sample gives everyone an equal chance of being interviewed. However, your final sample could, by chance, contain more female than male respondents. You might prefer, therefore, a stratified random sample. To obtain a *stratified random sample* you specify in advance, as part of your research design, which sub-groups of the whole sample are important. This is usually decided on the basis of previous research findings or professional judgement.

You can then match sample numbers to overall numbers, say two-thirds of one group to one-third of another if this is the overall mix. Beware, however, of too many stratifications. Male-female is an easy, two-category split, but the more dimensions you add, the more rapidly your sample expectations expand. If you added colour of eyes, social class, achievement and personality, for example, you could find yourself with a survey design consisting of 200 or 300 cells and either have empty cells (e.g., no responses in the 'female, first year, blue-eyed, middle-class, low achieving, introvert' category) or several thousand people to interview.

When a random sample is selected it is customary to have a 'reserve list' in case anyone drops out of the sample or refuses to be interviewed. Interviewing in some areas invades well-defended privacy, and on topics to do with taboo subjects the refusal rate might be high. Consequently, if many people drop out or refuse to be interviewed, and are replaced by others, one has an opportunity sample of people willing to be interviewed, rather than a genuinely random sample. There is nothing wrong with an opportunity sample provided that (a) the investigator states clearly that this is what it is, and (b) over-bold claims, inferences or generalisations are not made from the interview data. Many interesting pieces of research based on interviews have used opportunity samples.

When to interview?

The timing of interviews may not seem important, yet it can be a quite critical issue, particularly if the interview is part of a battery of data-gathering devices. Suppose one is interested in knowing something about how teachers react to certain pay proposals. Any preliminary interviews designed to elicit information about their attitudes, experience or behaviour would need to take place immediately before or at the very beginning of the pay cycle. If the interviews were left too late people may simply forget how they once felt. Views about pay bonuses, for example, will eventually be coloured by whether or not somebody received one.

Attitudes and behaviour may transform dramatically over time, a phenomenon which researchers into personality call 'function fluctuation'. Human memory can also be very frail, especially about emotive issues. When respondents are being asked to describe or evaluate events, they should be interviewed as close to those events as feasible.

A good example of this occurs in research into classroom interaction. If you record a lesson and plays it back to a teacher for discussion, this interview should take place within a very short time of the lesson. On your return several days later you will often be surprised at how little teachers can recall of the lessons in question. Teaching is a busy job and many thousands of incidents occur every day.

The interview itself may exert an influence on events. People subsequently observed in classrooms may behave differently if they have made the judgement, during a preliminary interview, that the researcher holds certain beliefs or expectations. Nor should they be interviewed when markedly upset or euphoric, unless this emotional condition is the subject of, or central to, the enquiry. In a study of teachers alleged to be incompetent we once carried out (Wragg *et al.*, 2000), some had great difficulty talking about events they had found traumatic.

Other aspects of timing are self-evident. Late evening is a time when both investigator and respondent may be fatigued. People who work evenings are not always accessible at times when other workers can be found at home. Students in rural areas may not be available after classes because of their transport. One experienced interviewer made the mistake of interviewing a group of teachers after they had been to a meeting. He found that many used identical phrases in their replies, as these were fresh in their minds from the meeting they had just attended. This actually led to a change in the research approach.

Using interviews in pilot studies

One common use of interviews is at the early stage of an enquiry that may or may not go on to use interviews in its main phase. Three typical examples are given below.

Example A

An investigator intends to study teachers' attitudes to a new curriculum using an attitude questionnaire. In the first instance teachers known to be either hostile or particularly receptive to new ideas are interviewed, with actual phrases used in conversation being noted down. Eventually these are used as part of a pool of possible items for the attitude inventory.

Example B

The heads of two linked institutions, where students transfer from one to the other at the end of a phase, are interested in an experimental programme to make the transition as smooth and trouble-free as possible. Prior to this they interview a number of pupils, parents and teachers from each institution to help them discover more about anxieties, communication or lack of it, teachers' ideas, parents' and pupils' perspectives. The experimental programme is influenced by what was discovered in the interviews.

Example C

A senior manager responsible for staff development, wishing to observe and study teachers at work, interviews several experienced teachers, getting them to keep diaries describing their job. A checklist is then drawn up, with items like 'assessing', 'preparing', 'asking questions', 'dealing with misbehaviour', 'ordering equipment'. These are then used in lesson observation to categorise the types of job teachers find themselves doing in a day.

Types of interview

Three kinds of face-to-face interview are commonly distinguished: the structured, semi-structured and unstructured interview.

Structured interviews

Based on a carefully worded interview schedule these usually require short answers or the ticking of a category by the investigator, as in a written questionnaire. Indeed it is common for a sub-sample of people who have been given a questionnaire to be interviewed, partly to amplify and partly to check their written answers. The structured interview is useful when a lot of questions are to be asked which are not particularly contentious or deeply thought-provoking. If the area under investigation requires more profound deliberation the respondent may become irritated at being forced into one word or one category answers. In such a case the semi-structured interview would be far better. Typical items in a structured interview schedule require yes/no answers, or some quantification of time such as 'always, often, sometimes, rarely, never'. Since this sort of information can so easily be collected by questionnaire method there is no reason to interview unless face-to-face questioning really is a superior method.

Semi-structured interviews

Again, a carefully worded interview schedule is assembled, but in this case much more latitude is permitted. Often there is an initial question followed by probes. The schedule may contain spaces for the interviewer to record notes, or the interview may be taped. A semi-structured interview schedule tends to be the one most favoured by educational researchers as it allows respondents to express themselves at length, but offers enough shape to prevent aimless rambling. An extract from a semi-structured schedule used during an enquiry into home/school liaison is shown in Figure 9.1 below.

Since last September, have you helped _____ at home with English or other subjects? (Circle code as appropriate)

        Yes, often
        Yes, occasionally
        No, or hardly ever

If YES

What sort of things do you do?

MOTHER

FATHER

Probe   How does _____ feel about it?

If NO

Why is this?

Figure 9.1 Extract from semi-structured interview schedule

Unstructured interviews

In-depth interviews roam freely and require great skill. They are often, though not always, used by researchers working in an interpretive paradigm, while the more structured style of interview tends to be favoured by those enquiring along more positivist lines. Some researchers use more than one type of interview. In fields such as psychotherapy, practitioners receive extensive training in interview techniques. Sensitively and skilfully handled, the unstructured interview, lasting maybe two or three hours, can produce information which might not otherwise emerge. A manufacturer of baby buggies once engaged a group of psychologists to do in-depth interviews with mothers. Whereas conventional market research might be concerned with price, shape, colour and convenience, for example, the unstructured interviews produced information of a different kind. Some young mothers eventually talked about their fears of babies suffocating, conflicts with grandparents who wanted to buy traditional prams: deep-rooted attitudes or anxieties such as would only emerge during skilful questioning. In general, novice interviewers are best advised not to embark on this kind of interview until they can confidently handle a more structured situation, and not before they are fairly clear about their own value system. For more information and discussion of narrative and its analysis, see Chapter 12.

Group and team interviewing

The most common format in educational research is the one-to-one interview, but it is sometimes useful for two people to be involved as interviewers, provided this does not over-awe the subjects. It is perfectly possible for students taking higher degree courses to work collaboratively on an interview project, provided it is absolutely clear who did what and that their work can be judged individually as well as collectively.

Group interviews

Group interviews involve several respondents and one interviewer. Indeed the *focus group* has become a means widely used by political parties to elicit views about their policies or the state of the nation. Despite the problem of undue prominence being given to the statements of the very articulate or vociferous, an interview with a small group of perhaps three or four people can be quite useful. If, for example, an investigator wishes to construct a picture of life in a school, as perceived by its students, this can be assembled quite accurately with a group, whose members often correct each other on points of detail until a consensus is established. Nevertheless caution must be exercised. The consensus might still be fiction.

Team interviews

Team interviews normally involve two interviewers working in partnership, provided, of course, subjects are not over-awed by the pair. In some contexts, say a study of sex roles in adolescence, it might be useful to have a man and a woman present. Similarly, in a multicultural context a white and black interviewer might work in tandem. The advantage of the team interview is threefold. Firstly, it may facilitate responses from some subjects; secondly, it allows one person to ask questions and the other to make notes, or to observe certain aspects of the respondent's behaviour; thirdly, since interviewing can be such a subjective process, it allows two people to make separate records of the event and then compare their two versions.

Using several interviewers

Sometimes, usually in funded research or as part of their coursework for a higher degree, a group of interviewers might embark on an interviewing programme. This occasionally happens in small-scale research where the investigator has friends or colleagues — fellow students on their course, a spouse, a group of student teachers — who are willing to help out and increase the sample being studied.

It is most important that training should be given to such collaborators, otherwise both validity and reliability will suffer: validity, because different interviewers may address different issues, and reliability because they may address the same issues, but record and interpret answers in a different way. Ideally they should be given an explanation of the purposes of the research, told how to use the schedule and be supervised whilst conducting a pilot interview. All should use whatever form of words is agreed for each question and not improvise. Alternatively, a video of an interview can be shown, with trainees filling in the schedule as if they are the interviewer.

Careful scrutiny of the responses should show if different interviewers are misusing the schedule or not recording accurately. Differences between interviewers cannot be entirely obliterated, but they can be minimised. If there are preliminary and follow-up interviews, lists can be exchanged so that interviewers do not see the same respondent on both occasions, unless this is desirable on other grounds.

Devising an interview schedule and choosing language register

Many interview schedules are assembled hastily, the assumption being that the questions are self-evident and the process unproblematic. It is a highly skilled job to devise an interview schedule which elicits relevant information, contains no redundant items and eliminates questioner bias. Even a watertight schedule cannot totally excise the kind of bias inherent in tone of voice, gesture and facial expression, for example.

The investigator needs first of all to make a list of areas in which information is required. These should then be translated into actual questions and probes, bearing in mind the age and background of the respondent. Language register is vital here and professional jargon should be left out unless the person being interviewed is fully familiar with it.

Language is an especially important issue in a multicultural setting where several different mother tongues might be spoken. If possible, especially with people whose proficiency in English may be limited, the interview should be conducted in the presence of someone able to translate, should there be any problems of comprehension and interpretation. In some of our projects in the Middle East and Hong Kong we used and are using speakers of Arabic and Cantonese in this way, (see Chapters 2 and 12).

Suppose an investigator is studying the extent to which parents participate in events arranged by the school or college prior to enrolment. Meetings have been held for parents or potential students to demonstrate and explain courses and teaching methods, and the interviewer wants to know about these.

The obvious question to ask is: 'What did you think of the meetings?', but this might merely elicit non-committal answers such as 'Not bad' or 'Quite interesting'. An over fussy question like: 'How do you evaluate our attempts to communicate the attainment targets of the curriculum to parents?' might be the wrong language register for many respondents. 'Presumably you went . . .' suggests the person must reply in the affirmative. A better strategy would be to build up an item until it meets the requirements, bearing in mind the following:

- Some parents might not have attended the meetings because they did not receive an invitation.
- In some cases only one parent might have attended, in others none or both. Why do people not go? Is it job demands, child-care problems, lack of interest?
- Some parents might say they were present because it looks negligent not to have attended, so they should be asked to describe what happened. Often people who say 'Yes' in the first instance, retract when asked about the event.
- If a great deal of information is to be collected then a code might be built in for easy circling and subsequent data analysis, e.g.:

Yes	1
No	2
Don't know	3
No response	0

Consequently the final item, with question and probes, would be as shown in Figure 9.2.

Question 8

Last October parents were invited to a meeting where teachers explained their teaching methods. Were you invited to it?

       Yes
       No
       Don't know

If YES

Did either of you go?

       Mother only went
       Father only went
       Both went
       Someone else (e.g., grandparent) went (state who)
       Neither went
       Don't know

If YES

(a)   What can you remember of it?

(b)   How did you feel about the meeting?

(c)   What did you learn from it?

If NO

Why did you not go?

Figure 9.2 Example of an interview item with question and probes

Pilot interviews

Once you have assembled a schedule two points are worth remembering:

- *Pass it on to experienced people for comment.* What is straightforward to you as the investigator may be baffling to another person. Sometimes you are too close to your research and others can be more objective.
- *Carry out one or more pilot interviews.* Try out your completed schedule with one or two typical respondents. Do not make the mistake of trying it out on a sophisticated colleague or friend and then using it with children or less well educated people. Be prepared to modify it, considerably if necessary, in the light of informed comment. Pilot the modified version

again. There are many instances of investigators committed to a round of interviews who only discover the ambiguity or other inadequacy of their instrument after the first few subjects have responded. By then it is too late to modify it.

Organising time and travel

Pilot interviews can give a rough idea about the amount of time needed but many investigators, even experienced ones, are hopelessly unrealistic about the time required for interviews. Suppose someone decides to interview 100 people. This would be over-ambitious for a higher degree assignment, though it might be feasible for a thesis, since it is fairly difficult to conduct certain kinds of interview properly in less than an hour, especially semi-structured and unstructured interviews. A thorough interview can take as long as two or three hours, so perhaps between 45 minutes and one-and-a-half hours should be allowed on average. One then needs to add travelling time and make an allowance for 'abortive visit' time, when arrangements fall through.

It is difficult, particularly for part-time investigators who usually have to do their research evenings and weekends, to do more than one interview a day. A full-time researcher might manage three or four. Clearly, therefore, assuming a part-time investigator can give up to three evenings a week, a proposed 100-interview programme would need several months. In some enquiries it might be undesirable to aggregate data collected in September with that assembled the following March. The intention to conduct 100 interviews might be unrealistic in this context. A better plan would be to select a smaller number of people for intensive interview, perhaps those representative of certain salient points of view, and collect the rest of the data in other ways.

Travel time and costs are also a consideration. Funded research usually has travel costs built in, but independent investigators pay their own bills. Travel by public transport can be very inefficient and time can easily be wasted, so it is well worth planning the interview visits carefully. If one is travelling, for example, a local map should be used with places to be visited marked on it in red. If someone is not available there may be another person nearby. Interviewing in a school or college requires the same sort of careful advance planning. Find out when teachers are free if they are to be interviewed, or make sure you know where students can be found. Check that your visits do not coincide with events or holidays. Then if meetings are cancelled unexpectedly if there's a sudden outbreak of Lassa fever, for example, at least you did your best.

Analysing interviews

Analysis time is also frequently underestimated, even by experienced investigators. Even quantitative data have to be added up or transferred to data-processing packages and qualitative analysis is immensely time-consuming. If one records a one-hour interview, playback time alone will be one hour while transcription will take several hours more.

Even using computer software to transcribe from sound would be time consuming, as few tapes are sharp enough for problem-free transcription. The investigator can easily compile a transcript containing perhaps 5,000 words and running to 15 or 20 pages. These have to be read and inferences drawn from them. Thus our optimist who earlier embarked on 100 interviews may have 700 hours of transcribing and analysis time.

It is not essential to transcribe taped interviews, and many interviewers rely on handwritten notes assembled during the interview, with the tapes for backup. These need to be subjected to content analysis, a matter discussed more fully in Chapter 15. Suffice it to say that it is important for subjective content analysis and the selection of illustrative quotations for the report to be double-checked, wherever possible. The first reader might deduce from reading interview transcripts that certain points are being stressed by subjects. A second reader should independently make a list of salient points. Areas of disagreement can then be discussed and analysed further.

It is also useful to think of content analysis as being a two- or three-stage operation. Usually the investigator knows why certain questions are asked, but when all interviews have been completed other matters of importance often emerge. A first rapid reading of all transcripts by two independent readers can be used to decide how the main analysis should be conducted, or a 'sandwich' model may be employed, whereby this analysis is followed by a final rapid re-read to see if anything has been missed or become distorted.

Validity and reliability

These concepts apply to interviews as much as to any other data-gathering device. Chapter 4 deals with this topic in greater detail, but a few issues are raised briefly below.

Validity

Does the interview measure or describe what it purports to measure or describe? How does the evidence collected compare with other sources of evidence such as written self-reports and diaries, questionnaires, test scores, or observation data? Are the constructs employed meaningful ones (i.e., would experienced practitioners regard them as important and are they rooted in previous investigations)? Is the evidence collected in any way predictive of future behaviour or events?

Reliability

Test-retest and split-half types of reliability are not always feasible or relevant with interview schedules. Nevertheless one should ask whether two interviewers using the schedule or procedure would get similar results and whether an interviewer would obtain a similar picture using the procedures on different occasions. This point can be checked by asking interviewers to code and report on the same videotape after intervals in time.

Conducting the interview

A great deal of common sense needs to be employed when interviewing people. Establishing a good rapport with your subject is essential, but not to such an extent that he/she merely wants to please the interrogator. The style should be a balance between friendliness and objectivity. The tight-lipped interviewer with a sphinx-like expression can alienate just as readily as the affable interviewer, too eager to signal agreement with respondents, can distort.

The beginning of an interview is very important. When interviewing strangers or lay people you should carry some kind of credentials, especially as door-to-door salesmen such as encyclopaedia and magazine reps, for example, now frequently use the 'I'm doing a piece of research' gambit to gain entry to homes and institutions. A letter on headed paper or from a supervisor explaining that you are a bona fide investigator will usually be sufficient.

Make sure all the preparation has been done. There is nothing worse than arriving to interview someone and finding they have a different expectation from the one you thought. Do not commence interviews until you know the ground is cleared and people understand the purpose and aftermath of the interview. It is easy to explain this briefly, should there be doubt: 'I'm interviewing several people to try to find out what they think about the appraisal of teaching', or 'I'm talking to a lot of children in your class about boys' and girls' performance in exams'.

Avoid tendentious openings: 'Most young people are browned off with education nowadays, so I'd like to know how you feel' or 'There's been a lot of publicity about falling standards lately, so I want to know what you think about it'.

It is not a bad idea to start off with easier questions that arouse interest and do not alienate people, especially if they see you as an authority figure. Always remember to ask at the end of the interview if there is anything the subject would like to ask you. You have probably asked a lot of questions and it is the least you can do.

Finally, and most importantly, assure the subject that the interview is confidential. Do not under any circumstances break this promise. Some investigators' code of ethics requires that the interviewer's 'picture' should later be given to the respondent for comment. For example, a transcript of the conversation can be sent, or the interviewee can be asked to comment on a draft account, saying whether it faithfully reflects the views put forward. You need to use your judgement as to when this is an appropriate procedure, or what to do if people deny saying what your record shows they said.

Difficult topics

Some topics, particularly to do with sex, religion, politics or private lives, may be too difficult for you to handle unless you are an experienced interviewer. Sometimes one needs to use projective techniques or other devices to elicit an accurate picture. These can be complex, so below are three examples where the investigator uses a particular device to get round a difficult problem.

'Guess who' technique
A researcher investigates the use of illicit drugs. She suspects that few subjects will admit to using them, so she says, 'Guess who this describes. This person uses (name of drug). Without telling me the names look through this class list and tell me how many people it might be'. If a whole class come up with a number like 12, 13 or 14 the investigator would have a rough idea of how many were involved without anyone having given away the names of friends.

Illustrative event
When people talk about some issues their language is often vague. For example, teachers often talk about their classes being 'busy' or someone 'having a firm grip'. A clearer picture can emerge if the person is asked to describe a few illustrative events, i.e. things which happen during a class which indicate that the group was 'busy' or that a certain teacher did or did not have 'a firm grip'.

Projective techniques
People reluctant to talk about their own fears or desires, may find that projective techniques (appearing to talk about someone or something else) offer a device which may produce valuable information. Pictures are often used: 'This is a photograph of physical aggression between two pupils (tell the storyline behind it). What do you think the teacher should do?' Many respondents soon begin spontaneously to talk about themselves and their own beliefs and practices, some even switching to the first person. This needs skilful handling, both in administration and interpretation, and the advice of a good psychologist should be sought.

Stereotypes to avoid

Finally, these stereotypes may read like caricature, but they are alive and well. Try to avoid swelling their numbers.

- *The Squirrel.* Collects tapes of interviews as if they are nuts and does not know what to do with them other than stack them on shelves as 'pending'.
- *The Ego-tripper.* Knows in his heart that his hunch is right, but needs a few pieces of interview fodder to justify it. Carefully selected quotes will do just that, and one has no idea how much lies on the cutting room floor.
- *The Optimist.* Plans 200 interviews with a randomly selected group of senior managers by Christmas and is shortly to discover 200 synonyms for 'Get lost'.
- *The Amateur Therapist* ostensibly enquires into the research question but gets carried away during interview and tries to resolve every social/emotional problem encountered. Should stick to the research.
- *The Guillotine.* So intent on getting through the schedule that he/she pays no attention to the answers and chops respondents short in mid-sentence (actually does manage to do 200 interviews by Christmas).

References

Briggs, C. (1986) *Learning How to Ask: A Sociolinguistic Appraisal of the Role of the Interview in Social Science Research*, Cambridge: Cambridge University Press.

Holstein, J. A. (1995) *The active interview*, London: Sage.

Kvale, S. (1996) *Interviews: An Introduction to Qualitative Research Interviewing*, London: Sage.

Oppenheim, A. N. (1992) *Questionnaire Design, Interviewing and Attitude Measurement*, London: Pinter Publishers Ltd.

Powney, J. and Watts, M. (1987) *Interviewing in Educational Research*, London: Routledge.

Wragg, E. C., Haynes, G. S., Wragg C. M. and Chamberlin, P. (2000), *Failing Teachers?* London: Routledge.

10

Questionnaires

Judith Bell

Introduction

The trouble with questionnaires is that sometimes, they seem like a very easy way to get hold of a great deal of information quickly (no need to decide what to do with the responses until they arrive) and any fool can devise one in the time it takes to drink a cup of coffee. Wrong on all counts. They are fiendishly difficult to design and should never be considered by anyone who believes that: 'anyone who can write plain English and has a modicum of common sense can produce a good questionnaire' (Oppenheim, 1992: 1). Of course, the ability to write plain English is always a help and common sense is a commodity which is good to add to the research armoury, but before any method of data collecting can be considered, decisions have to be made about *precisely what it is you need to find out*. Sounds obvious, but that is the stage that is so often hurried or even overlooked completely; this omission can result in the selection of entirely inappropriate data-collecting instruments which produce useless responses. So, we'd better start at the beginning.

Let's say that you have recently taken over responsibility for the Diploma in Forestry Management in your college and though you are fairly confident that most aspects of the diploma programme are sound, you have reservations about others. You have just heard that in six months' time the college is to receive a visit from a team of external assessors who will require evidence of the college's claims for quality provision. The only evidence you have is examination results, and they have tended to be . . . well . . . variable. That's probably not surprising because college policy has always been that if employers are willing to release their employees for the three years of the part-time diploma, then students are accepted. Some want to come; others don't. Some want to work; others won't. You discover that there are no records of student feedback, nor of any curriculum discussions between college-based and forestry management placement staff. It was clear that the diploma course needed a thorough spring-clean.

Let's also say that you are half way through a Master's course and that your dissertation looms. Subject to the approval of the college principal and the dissertation supervisor, here is an opportunity to kill two birds with one stone by carrying out an investigation into the quality of the Diploma in Forestry Management.

It's easy to select a topic in general terms but the hard work begins when you move from the general to the specific. You'll have your own ideas about the particular aspects which should be considered but you also need to consult colleagues and students about what they consider to be vital elements in the programme. Their views might be different from yours. Your first-thoughts, top-of-the-head shot at identifying priorities might include:

- something on the curriculum;
- quality of teaching in the college and on placements;
- quality of student support;
- quality of supervision, particularly on placements;
- relevance of the college course to the work of forestry management;
- balance of theory and practice;
- relationship between college and placement staff;
- students' views about all the above — and anything else they consider important;
- college social and sports facilities;
- effectiveness of the tutorial system;
- library access;
- study facilities;
- assignment feedback to students;
- overall quality of the programme.

Some or none of these might be selected as being of prime importance but those that are selected will form the framework of your study. How much time will you have for this investigation? Which items are absolutely essential and which merely desirable? Time has to be spent on this stage of the research, but it's easy to lose sight of the key issues. Punch (1998) reminds us that at this crucial stage in the research planning, it's good to remember to ask the 'What are we trying to find out?' question. He warns us that:

> The focus on this question almost always shows that there is: 'much more here than meets the eye'. The topic expands, and many questions are generated. What perhaps seemed simple and straightforward becomes complicated, many-sided and full of possibilities. (1998: 36)

Quite so. But a word or warning: boundaries have to be set because if they aren't, you could go on expanding the topic for ever. External assessors would come and go; reports would be produced; blame and praise allocated in equal measure; courses closed and others opened and you would still be at the stage of deciding what the focus of your study should be. Not everything can be done, so decisions have to be made about what is essential, what is merely desirable and what can be done in the available time.

It would be impossible to include all the items on the first-thoughts list, so let's say you decide to consider students' views on the following priority areas:

- quality of teaching, support and supervision of students in college and on placements;
- relevance of the college diploma programme to the work of forestry management;
- balance of time spent on theory of forestry management and practice;
- students' overall satisfaction with the diploma programme.

What is the best way of obtaining students' views on these topics? You know what information you require and you now have to decide how best to obtain it. Only when you have considered *precisely* what you want to find out — and why — will you be able to decide on which data-collecting instrument will be best for your purposes. If you decide on a questionnaire, work can start on question wording — and that is not as easy as it sounds.

The importance of precise wording

From concepts to measurable indicators

All questionnaire items have to be worded in ways that will make their meaning absolutely clear to students and that are *measurable*. Let's start with the most difficult item in our list of priority areas: students' satisfaction with the diploma programme. If students are asked a question such as 'Are you satisfied with your course?' responses might well be on the lines of 'No', 'Yes', 'Sort of', 'It's all rubbish'. It might be argued that if all the researcher needed was information about the number of students who said they were satisfied, this question would be perfectly all right. But what does 'satisfied' actually mean? Might it mean: 'It's a darn sight better being warm and dry in college than working in a freezing forest in the pouring rain'? Or might it mean: 'This is the best course I've ever known, the teaching is excellent, the placements and the balance of theory to practice just right', etc? The Yes/No type of response is of no real value here because you need to know more and to discover what 'satisfactory' and 'satisfaction' actually mean to the students. Ways have to be found to overcome this dilemma.

Satisfaction is a concept and we can't actually observe or measure concepts but we can probably think of ways in which individuals indicate or demonstrate satisfaction. Take time to think about it. Talk about it to colleagues. Brainstorm it. Produce flow charts with ideas because somehow or another you will have to find ways to move from the unobservable to the observable.

Rose and Sullivan (1996) provide some useful examples of ways in which the concept of 'class' might be observable:

> If we wish to understand something about class (a concept and there-fore . . . not observable), what can we observe in the real world which manifests class? That is, what indicators can be used for class so that we can obtain data about class? This is the essence of the measurement problem and when we link an unobservable concept with an observ-able indicator we are producing *operationalizations*. (1996: 12/13)

They define 'measurement' as being simply a way of saying that, in respect of some variable, one case is *different* from another — not bigger or smaller, better or worse, but only different (1996: 17) and 'operationalization refers to the rules we use to link the language of theory (concepts) to the language of research (indicators)' (1996: 13). They suggest that 'employment' or 'social class' might serve as indicators of 'class', so what indicators might there be of 'satisfaction'? This is quite tricky and you may need several attempts at producing indicators, so once again, ask colleagues and friends for their views, build up a flow chart, focus the mind and get back to basics and the *'what do I need to know?'* question.

Ambiguity, imprecision and assumption

If you were to be asked what you meant by 'curriculum' you would, I'm sure be able to provide a clear, succinct and comprehensive definition but are you absolutely sure all your colleagues would give the same definition? Ask a room full of people, some concerned with education, some not, and in all probability you would get a variety of responses. If you ask students they might tell you it means 'syllabus', 'subjects' or something to do with the course. In other words, you cannot assume they will all have the same under-standing of 'curriculum' nor that their understanding is the same as yours. Other wording has to be found which will make it clear what is meant.

Leading and presuming questions

It's surprisingly difficult to avoid asking leading questions. If the wording is on the lines of: 'Do you not agree that there is insufficient time spent on forestry practical work?', then that's obviously a leading question, as well as one that is potentially confusing; but other questions such as: 'Does the col-lege make adequate provision for counselling?' may be harder. What is 'ade-quate'? There's a presumption here that respondents know that a counselling service exists, what it does and whether or not it is adequate. In its present form, therefore, the question is invalid; if you really want to know something about students' opinions of the service, you'll need to produce a more precise wording that will enable respondents to give a clear answer.

Double (and even triple) questions

Consider this question:

> 'Has the science component of the programme helped your understanding of pest control and planting techniques?'

Well, perhaps it helped my understanding of pest control but not planting techniques. If information is required about both, then separate questions are needed.

Here's another:

> 'Is the quality of teaching, support and supervision in college and on placements good?'

You wouldn't put a question like that of course; the wording here is just your reminder about what you want to find out. It's a very complex question and would need to be broken down into separate components, with explanations about the meaning of 'support' and 'supervision'. However, it's pretty common to come across questionnaires with double questions, particularly in hotel 'feedback' questionnaires such as:

The management is always looking for ways of improving the service to guests. We should be grateful if you would circle the appropriate number below and return the form to reception.

How would you rate the service and cleanliness of the hotel?

Excellent	Very good	Good	Satisfactory	Less than satisfactory
1	2	3	4	5

I found this in the bedroom of a large chain hotel and all the following questions followed a similar format. They certainly believed in stacking the odds to emphasise the positive with only one negative item, but that's the least of it. The double question is obvious but there are multiple features of both. You might consider that the service was good in parts. Perhaps the personnel at reception were pleasant and helpful and there was an efficient chamber maid who did a great job, but maybe the porter was surly and the waiters in the dining room were downright disagreeable. As far as cleanliness was concerned, the bedroom was spotless and most public areas were fairly clean except the toilet in the foyer which was filthy.

It's easy to mock, and far more difficult to produce flaw-free questions, but this example is poor in another way. You often see 'excellent' and 'very good' on questionnaires, but how exactly do you distinguish between the two? I've never seen an explanation of the difference. Usual practice is for hotels, travel companies and others to group responses. In this case, I don't have much doubt that 'excellent', 'very good' and 'good' would be grouped and the summary of guest comments would be that '80 percent of guests rated everything under the sun as good or better.'

Memory and knowledge

In our example above, your respondents are likely to have only about half-an-hour to complete the questionnaire and so your questions need to be worded in a way that will enable respondents to answer without much hesitation, but what about: 'What marks did you get for pest control in your first year?' Sounds straightforward enough, but respondents in their third year may not remember. They would need to check and there's no time to check so they'll either not answer or they'll guess. Similarly, you might ask: 'Do you think you will be able to obtain a sufficiently high mark for the final diploma examination to be awarded a pass?' But students may not remember, or even know, what the pass mark is, so what's the point of asking a question like this?

Finalising your questionnaire

The importance of question selection and precision wording means that a good many drafts may be required before your final version comes up to standard. Eliminate any item that doesn't comply with the 'what are we trying to find out?' rule. There's neither the time nor the space to fill the questionnaire with irrelevancies in case they come in handy. You want every single item to be worded in such a way as to ensure that all items are necessary, that respondents understand what you mean, are able to provide an answer on the spot and are not offended by your wording or assumptions. You may change your mind several times about the order of questions so it's probably a good idea to write questions on cards or separate pieces of paper. Cards are easier to handle and to sort but anything will do. As soon as the sorting and eliminating is done, you'll be ready to move on to issues of appearance and layout — apart from one last check. Go through each question or item and ask yourself once more:

- Are any of your questions ambiguous or imprecise, or do they contain any assumptions?
- Do any questions require memory or knowledge which respondents may not have before they can be answered?

- Does your questionnaire contain any double, leading, presuming, offensive or sensitive questions?

Questions or statements?

It's not all over yet because even though you know what you want to find out, the way the questions are worded will influence the usefulness of the responses you get. Go back to the item relating to the quality of students' supervision while on placements. It wouldn't really be enough to have responses like 'good', 'non-existent' or 'bad', would it? Wouldn't you want more detail? You might decide that ranked items would be likely to produce a greater degree of discrimination and that a Likert scale would be better than straight questions. It would be up to you to decide which approach is best, but let's look at what a Likert scale might look like.

Likert scales ask respondents to indicate rank order of agreement or disagreement with a statement which is generally on a three-, five- or seven-point range though researchers frequently prefer an even number of items, mainly to avoid the neutral central point. Note that we are now talking about statements where respondents are asked to rank responses by circling a number, so let's have a look at one possible example.

In my view, the supervision provided for forestry management practical work is good.

Circle the appropriate response.

Very strongly disagree	Strongly disagree	Disagree	Agree	Strongly agree	Very strongly agree
1	2	3	4	5	6

The statement order could equally well have begun with 'Very strongly agree': researchers will frequently change the order during the course of the questionnaire in order to make sure students are awake. Of course, that means that you also have to be awake and to remember what you are doing when you come to score the responses. That also means that you need to decide not only how you are going to score and but also what the scores will mean *before* questionnaires are distributed.

We need to be careful about what we can deduce from Likert scales. They certainly arrange responses, individuals or objects from the highest to the lowest but the intervals between each may not be the same (Cohen and Manion, 1994: 128). We can't assume that the highest rating (6 in the above case) is six times higher than the lowest (which is 1).

All that can be said is that 'data in each category can be compared with data in the other categories as being higher or lower than, more or less than etc. than those in the other categories' (Denscombe 1998: 178). In spite of these limitations, Likert scales can be helpful and as long as the instructions to respondents are clear, useful information can be obtained.

So, you take your pick. Questions or statements?

Question order and appearance

If you're satisfied you've done everything possible to ensure that the word-ing of questions is as clear as you can make it, it will be time to decide on the order in which they are to appear on the questionnaire. There shouldn't be any complex or sensitive questions, but if one or two have slipped in, it's best to place them well down in the order. The last thing you want is for potential respondents to take offence or decide it's too hard and to throw your questionnaire into the nearest bin.

Appearance is important. I've no doubt we've all received scruffy ques-tionnaires, particularly those which have been distributed to friendly house-holds as part of a school project, but this isn't a school project and it has to look good. Remember that in all probability you'll be the one who is required to carry out the analysis of responses and to produce a report of findings, so it becomes rather important to be able to see and record responses with-out having to search for them in irregularly positioned boxes or circled num-bers which are all over the place.

Respondents' rights

You are asking respondents to do you a favour when you ask them to par-ticipate in your survey, even if they are students and you are their boss. They are entitled to know why they are being asked to complete your question-naire and what you are going to do with their responses. Unless you or a colleague plan to distribute the questionnaires in person, and explain the 'Why?' and the 'What?' on the spot, a letter is required. Be honest and don't promise anything you can't deliver. Many investigations promise anonymity and confidentiality but occasionally both terms have been variously, and to my mind damagingly, interpreted. Sapsford and Abbott (1996) provide what is a helpful definition of anonymity and confidentiality. They write that:

> As we are using the term, confidentiality is a promise that you will not be identified or presented in identifiable form, while anonymity is a promise that even the researcher will not be able to tell which responses came from which respondent. (1996: 319)

So if anonymity is promised, there is no question of numbering questionnaires and keeping a record of which number applies to which respondent.
Nor tricks such as numbers or symbols on the back of the questionnaires.
But that also means there is no possibility of sending reminder letters if
respondents don't respond. If the forestry management questionnaires were
to be distributed in class, then any blank returns would mean that the students declined to participate and that would be that. If the questionnaires
are distributed via internal mail or by post, then you have to accept whatever returns you get.

There can be some difficulties over confidentiality. If in your report you
say that 'the Director of Resources was of the opinion that . . .', you are
revealing his/her identity if there's only one Director of Resources. If your
description of a school or department is very explicit, everyone who works
in that area may immediately know which school or department you are talking about. No one will mind being identified if the report is complimentary
but if a school happens to have poor examination results and high truancy
rates, it might be less joyful about the world knowing about it. Sapsford and
Abbott (1996) make their views perfectly clear when they write that:

> . . . a first principle of research ethics — to be found in all the various
> codes of conduct imposed by professional and academic organisations
> — is that the subjects of research should not be *harmed* by it. (1996:
> 318)

Sad to say, there have been cases where individuals and organisations have
been harmed. The subject of ethics in research has already been covered in
Chapter 5 of this book but the dangers of loose interpretation of 'anonymity'
and 'confidentiality' are worth reinforcing here (see Bell, 1999: 118–133).

Piloting the questionnaire

Sorry if by now you feel everything is now done and dusted and you're ready
to distribute the questionnaires, but there is another important step. No matter how busy you are, all data-collecting instruments have to be piloted. You
may have consulted everybody about everything, but it's only when a group
similar to your main population completes your questionnaire and provides
feedback that you know for sure that all is well. If you can't find a similar
group, then ask friends, colleagues or anyone you can get hold of. There's
another very good reason why you absolutely have to carry out a pilot exercise and that is that so far you have not considered how you will record and
analyse your returns: when the 'real' questionnaires are returned, you need
to know what to do with them. Even if yours is to be a straightforward
descriptive study which only requires frequencies (the number of items in
each category) and frequency distributions (how often each item occurs), trial

analyses need to be made and methods of presentation considered. As Youngman (1978) reminds us:

> At the risk of disillusioning many readers, the first truth of research analysis is that it does not start the day after the last item of data is collected ... the analytical strategies must be planned early in the research processes ... Deciding upon the actual research procedure will determine the precise nature of the practicable analyses. (1978: 3)

Right. It might be that for the purpose of the college study, frequencies and frequency distributions will be enough, but your dissertation may well require more sophisticated analysis and that would need to be tried out before questionnaires were distributed. If a computer statistical package were to be used for analysis, then you would need to be absolutely sure which package was appropriate, what would be involved in keying in the data and in understanding what the printout meant. So once again it's back to asking precisely what do I need to find out and which statistical strategies will be necessary in order to provide me with that information? It's best to find out before you have finally committed to the wording of your questionnaire.

Distributing the questionnaires

At last it's time to distribute the questionnaires to your respondent group. It would obviously be best if you or your colleagues were able to distribute and explain the purpose of the study in class time, but that's not always easy to achieve. For a start, not all colleagues will be overjoyed at losing their class time to your research project so that even if you have permission from the college management to conduct your survey, you may not be top of the popularity poll with your colleagues unless you ask them and obtain their agreement beforehand. If they say 'Definitely not — we need every minute we can get if these students are to pass the exam' you may be able to pull rank, but that approach would be generally unwise. For example, if you insisted and even showed the letter in which the principal gave permission, you could probably say goodbye to any possibility of collaboration, assistance or support from the protesting colleagues in future. Best not to rock the boat too much.

If the class completion method fails, you might be forced to distribute the questionnaires via the internal mail system, but the rate of return would inevitably be lower and you really do need as many completions as possible if the study is to mean anything. Whatever approach is selected, or forced on you, do your utmost to avoid postal distribution. In the first place, you or the college would have to provide a stamped addressed envelope, which is expensive. More seriously, the rate of return for postal questionnaires is generally poor, even if stamped addressed envelopes are provided. What to do then? Well, you could try being exceptionally nice to your colleagues before crisis time. You will already have consulted them about which topics are essential and will have asked their advice about questionnaire wording. They know why the study is being carried out and though they may think the entire quality exercise is a waste of time and an annoying additional task when there is already insufficient time to do their regular job, they are likely to be more responsive to a request for help with distribution if they have been participants in the exercise. Well, it's worth a thought.

Producing the report or dissertation

If you were carrying out this study as part of a Master's or doctoral dissertation, you would already have carried out a review of the literature. As you read, themes would have begun to emerge together with valuable insight as to how others planned their research. In any investigation, we are always looking for patterns and groupings. If all you did was to provide a list of every student's response to each question, you would be left with pages of lists which meant very little — few readers would be willing to spend the time necessary to make sense of them for themselves. All data need to be interpreted and if patterns do emerge, they will require particular comment, though you should take care not to make claims which cannot be substantiated. Decide which methods of presentation will best illustrate the data, tables, charts, histograms (see Bell, 1999: 173–195).

Your aim will be to produce a clear, informative report of the findings which, you hope, will contribute to the college understanding of students' perceptions of the diploma in forestry management and/or be one worth while component of your dissertation.

If your preparation was carefully carried out; your questionnaire clear and well designed; comments from your pilot exercise considered and any appropriate changes made; and possible methods of analysis tried out before distribution of the questionnaire, then all will be well. You will be able to congratulate yourself on a job well done.

Table 10.1 Action checklist

Action points	Comment
1) Select a topic which really interests you and that is likely to be worth all your time and commitment.	If you have no interest in the topic, you will quickly become bored and lose interest in it.
2) Spend time refining and focusing your topic and never lose sight of key issues.	Set boundaries. You can't do everything. Decide which aspects of your investigation are essential and which are merely desirable.

Table 10.1 *Continued*

Action points	Comment
3) Make sure you have permission to carry out the study.	Never assume it's bound to be all right to conduct your research — there might be regulations about research being carried out in your institution.
4) Consult colleagues about the topic. They may have good ideas and different points of view from you.	They may know about useful sources of information — and you may well need their help throughout the research so it's as well to recruit them as participants.
5) Are you sure a questionnaire is the best way to obtain the data you need?	Always refer back to the 'What am I trying to find out'? question.
6) Take time over question wording.	And remember that responses need to be measurable.
7) Concepts are abstractions and so can't be observed or measured.	Ways have to be found to link concepts to indicators.
8) Are any of your questions ambiguous or imprecise? Are you making any assumptions?	If so reword them.
9) Does your questionnaire contain any leading, double or presuming questions?	If you're not sure, ask colleagues what they think.
10) Are you asking respondents to remember something that happened some time ago? Are you assuming they have knowledge which they may not have?	If so reword your questions.
11) Are your questions in the right order?	If you have any complex or sensitive items, don't put them early on in the questionnaire.
12) Are the appearance and layout of the questionnaire good?	A scruffy appearance will do nothing to encourage responses.
13) Respondents have rights and they're entitled to know why they're being asked to complete your questionnaire and what you're going to do with the responses. Does your survey meet this requirement?	They're doing you a favour by completing the questionnaire, so they should be fully informed.
14) If you promise anonymity and/or confidentiality make sure your respondents know what you mean.	If you promise either or both, you must honour that promise.

15)	Always pilot questionnaires. You need to be absolutely sure the wording is clear to respondents.	Make any necessary wording changes and try out methods of analysis with the pilot returns.
16)	Decide on methods of questionnaire distribution.	Try to negotiate distribution and completion in class time if possible. Avoid a postal questionnaire unless you're desperate.
17)	If your trial recording and analysis has been well done, you should know beforehand exactly where and how you intend to record responses.	As you record, you will be looking for patterns and recurring themes.
18)	In an ideal world, it would be good to wait until all returns were in before beginning the recording process.	But we don't live in an ideal world and you will inevitably be short of time, so start recording as soon as returns start to come in.
19)	Make sure your report is clear, to the point and highlights key issues.	Don't make it hard for your readers to understand what you're saying or they may decide not to bother.
20)	Thank everyone who has assisted you with the research.	You may need their help again some time.

References

Bell, J. (1999) *Doing Your Research Project: A Guide for First-time Researchers* (3rd edn.), Buckingham: Open University Press.

Cohen, L. and Manion, L. (1994) *Research Methods in Education* (4th edn.), London: Routledge.

Denscombe, M. (1998) *The Good Research Guide*, Buckingham: Open University Press.

Oppenheim, A. N. (1992) *Questionnaire Design, Interviewing and Attitude Measurement* (New Edition). London: Pinter.

Punch, K. F. (1998) *Introduction to Social Research: Quantitative and Qualitative Approaches*, London: Sage.

Rose, D. and Sullivan, O. (1996) *Introducing Data Analysis for Social Scientists* (2nd edn.), Buckingham: Open University Press.

Sapsford, R. and Abbott, P. (1996) 'Ethics, Politics and Research', in Sapsford, R. and Jupp, V. *Data Collection and Analysis*, London: Sage.

Youngman, M. (1978) *Statistical Strategies*, University of Nottingham, Rediguide 20.

11

Observation as a research tool

Janet Moyles

Introduction

Observation as a tool for the researcher can be powerful, flexible and 'real'. It is not dependent, like questionnaires or interview methods, on respondents' personal views but seeks explicit evidence through the eyes of the observer either directly or through a camera lens. 'Because observed incidents are less predictable there is a certain freshness to this form of data collection . . .' (Cohen *et al.*, 2000: 305). Observation is normally part of ethnographic research and leads to a description of people, events and/or cultures: it is a holistic approach concerning the observation of 'everyday' events and the description and construction of meaning, rather than reproduction of events (Robson, 1993). As the teaching profession has been opened up to scrutiny, observation in school, particularly in classrooms, has become somewhat commonplace, albeit for different purposes (for example, school inspections, as we shall see later).

This chapter will examine a range of issues relating to our understanding of observation as a research process and tool. Using examples from my own educational research in early years settings and primary school classrooms and drawing on others' research in wider arenas, it will explore:

- observation as a 'natural' process and in educational research;
- two main forms of observation with brief ethical considerations;
- various ways of supporting observational research;
- some ways of analysing and interpreting observational data; and
- reliability and validity issues in relation to observational data.

Of necessity in such a short chapter, the subject of observation cannot be handled in any great depth and therefore additional references are given at the end for those who wish to delve deeper into the issues.

Observation as a 'natural' process

It is something of a natural instinct for many of us to be observers. Whether we are on a beach watching others enjoying the outdoors or scrutinising the weather through our windows, we look at, see and interpret what is happening. On the beach on a warm sunny day we expect to see sunbathers and children playing — we don't expect to see winter coats and gloves. When we look out of the window upon the weather, we may look optimistically for the kind of sky that will suit our purposes for that day. Our everyday observation skills function very much alongside our purposes for observation and are often determined by what we *think* or *hope* we are going to see. Whatever it is we observe and want to understand undergoes significant *interpretation*. However, in the process of interpretation, we cannot divorce our underpinning values and beliefs from the ways we ourselves perceive a situation or what we expect to occur. So it is in educational research, particularly from the perspective of those within education as teachers and managers who will have certain 'views' and expectations of schools and classrooms.

Herein lies a significant challenge for educational researchers, especially those stepping 'outside' a teaching or management role for a short period, who want objectively to observe educational phenomena. As Cohen and Manion (1994: 106) point out, the purpose of observational research is 'to probe deeply and to analyse intensively' sometimes 'with a view to estimating generalisations about the wider population' (1994: 106–7). Interpreting what is observed, from the potential wealth of data that are gathered especially in field work, is a key feature of observational research, although a majority of the interpretation, if we are trying to be objective, needs to occur directly from the data gathered (not always as easy as it sounds). It is difficult always to be wholly objective. King (1984) stated his intention in his seminal research into infant classrooms as being an 'interested, non-judgemental observer' (1984: 7) but then found himself drawn in by the children and his development of an empathy for the teachers' roles. What we can try to do is to acknowledge and overcome our personal interpretations by a variety of means, not the least of which is using our professional knowledge as educators and researchers to ensure clarity of concepts, purpose and method both before and after observational data collection.

When we make decisions about *what* to observe, we need first to be clear about what are our *purposes*. This means ensuring that our conceptualisation of the research question is a clear as it can possibly be (Robson, 1993). What is it we want to study and why? In order to try to make staff meetings more equitable and encourage participation in issues from a wider group, we may simply want a clear picture of, for example:

- How many teachers make a contribution to discussions in staff meetings?
- How many of these contributions last longer than five seconds?
- How many of these contributions are questions?
- How many of these questions added to the debate?

In classrooms, we may want to see how often individual (focus) children interact with the teacher and what is the basis of this interaction:

- How many times does a teacher interact with a particular child(ren)?
- How many of these interactions extend beyond one exchange?
- How many open-ended questions are posed within these exchanges?
- Does the response involved show evidence of children using thinking skills?

We can only really gain this information by observation (and through recording) — if we ask teachers and others for such information, they may find it difficult to divorce feelings from 'facts'. Their perceptions of events may be clouded, for example, by whether they felt more concerned about getting home before the rush hour than attending the staff meeting at that time, or concerns about the deleterious effects of the focus child's behaviour up on other children. To find out what actually happens it is necessary to observe (and, of course, to interpret knowledgeably from our reading and own understanding).

Observation is a very useful research tool because it can:

- give direct access and insights into complex social interactions and physical settings;
- give permanent and systematic records of interactions and settings;
- be 'context sensitive and ecologically valid' (Denscombe, 1998: 156);
- enrich and supplement data gathered by other techniques (allowing triangulation and thus increasing reliability);
- use very varied techniques, yielding different types of data and with the potential to be widely applied in different contexts; and
- be used to address a variety of types of research questions.

Those embarking upon educational research through observational methods need, however, to be aware of some of its challenges. For example, it places high demands on time, effort, resources and on the researcher's sustained commitment. The wealth of data gathered has to be categorised and analysed. There are often unknown effects upon the subject(s) of the observation which can impact upon the data gathered and it is susceptible, as we have seen, to observer bias and underlying assumptions. These can all affect the reliability of the data (see Chapter 4 in this book). Different forms of observation will be more or less susceptible to these factors as we shall see.

Forms of observation

We can observe using 'naturalistic' approaches (Guba and Lincoln, 1987) or more 'formal' approaches (Croll, 1986). In the former, the researcher is drawn in as a participant in specific events and contexts either overtly or covertly. It may involve becoming a 'complete participant' (LeCompte and Preissle, 1993: 93) — that is, one with an insider role within those being studied who may know (overt) or may not know (covert) they are being observed. Or it may involve being a 'participant-as-observer' — a more likely role in school and classroom-based research where educational researchers are likely to be witting or unwitting participants in classroom life when undertaking observations. (For more details on participant/non-participant observation see Cohen *et al.*, 2000, Chapter 17.)

In formal approaches, the researcher is non-participatory and often uses systematic observation tools as a means of data gathering. These pre-determine the focus of the observation and can be quantified, for example, by noting the number, frequency or timing of particular events. In the case of the questions in the previous section, we would be observing frequencies of events, event sampling and duration from a primary data source (Anderson with Arsenault, 1998).

Both participant and systematic observation are common in educational research, an example of the former being the research of Woods (1996). The well-known ORACLE research of Galton *et al.* (1980; 1999) gives useful examples of systematic observations of both teachers and children. The forerunner of most classroom observation instruments was that developed by Flanders (1970) which is known as the Flanders Interaction Analysis Category (FIAC) system. (For full information on FIAC see Wragg (1999); for examples of systematic observation of meetings, see Williams (1994).)

Systematic observation

The benefit of well-conceived systematic observation schedules, such as those within the ORACLE studies, is that they offer the opportunity for replication and comparison of data over time. The writer and colleagues have recently used the ORACLE teacher observation schedule, for example, to establish whether the type and level of teacher interaction in primary classrooms has changed since the advent of the National Literacy Strategy and the Literacy Hour approach to teaching and learning (Moyles *et al.*, 2002). The interesting results indicate that teachers have increased their levels of interaction with pupils but that variation exists between KS1 and KS2 teachers in the level and type of demands made of pupils through questioning. This would have been difficult to access without the opportunity for comparison which the ORACLE teacher observation schedule permitted.

The difficulty with systematic observation for the beginning researcher is the development of the observation instrument itself. Even if one utilises an established instrument there is the challenge of learning how to use it effectively, because, of course, if it is used in any way other than that for which it was designed, this will invalidate the findings. Clearly some relatively simple instruments can be designed which serve a useful purpose. For example, a simple tally, as shown in Figure 11.1, can usefully show the number of times two different teachers make a direct response to (a) boys and (b) girls during a 20-minute lesson.

	Boys	Girls
Teacher 1	‖‖ ‖‖ ‖‖ ‖‖ ‖‖ ⫼	‖‖ ‖‖ ‖‖ ⫽
Teacher 2	‖‖ ‖‖ ‖‖ ⫽	‖‖ ‖‖ ‖‖ ⫼⫽

Figure 11.1 Number of times two different teachers made direct response to (a) boys and (b) girls during a 20-minute lesson

What this cannot tell us is the duration or content of the observations but, for example, it is interesting to see that one teacher makes more direct responses to boys whilst the second teacher shows more balance in the responses. Finding out why this may be so could be established by either developing a much more sophisticated instrument or by, for example, video-recording and analysing the observed lessons or perhaps interviewing the teachers to gain their perceptions. Similarly, Figure 11.2 shows the interactions between participants in two minutes of a staff meeting. What this reveals, readers can decide for themselves.

These kinds of instrument can be made more sophisticated by adding layers of information related to the content of the interactions under investigation (who asked 'open' and 'closed' questions, about what area of interest

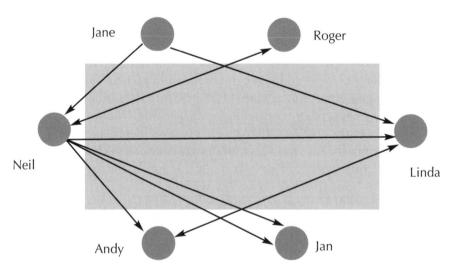

Figure 11.2 Two minutes of communication in a staff meeting. Who communicates with whom?

were the questions asked) or to the antecedents and precedents of any observed events (at the point of misbehaviour or disagreement, what was previously said and what followed). Another way is that used in the Exeter Schedule (see Wragg, 1994: 43–49) in which the researchers decided on a list of child behaviour characteristics (e.g., noisy or illicit talk, physical aggression to another pupil, defiance of teacher) and also on a list of how teachers might deal with that behaviour (e.g., order to cease, getting into close proximity to child, humour). All the categories had to be agreed in advance by the group of observers. These two lists (after piloting and inter-rater reliability measurement) then formed the basis of a series of schedules which were used on segments of lessons to monitor how teachers' manage pupil misbehaviour. (Some of my own examples of semi-structured observation schedules with explanation of purpose, are given at the end of this chapter).

Participant observation

Participant observation allows the researcher to be part of the 'natural' setting and to 'become' part of it (often with no pre-determined view about what findings will emerge or how they will be interpreted). Participant observation involves making field notes and/or recording events using audio-visual means in a relatively unstructured way. When the researcher is covertly engaged in research, it is unlikely that the participants will know — the researcher joins the group or subjects and acts and reacts as they do, recording observations at a later time. This kind of covert operation happens when, for example, researchers want to find out how particular groups live. Television and newspaper journalists occasionally use this method in developing work for documentary programmes by, for example, joining groups of homeless males or football hooligans and living life as they do. One of the classic examples of this is the participant observation recorded in Whyte (1981). Covert research of this type raises many ethical issues, particularly in relation to whether the ends justify the means (Foster, 1996; Hitchcock and Hughes, 1997). It is very unlikely to be tolerated in educational research because of the sensitivity associated with children as direct or indirect research participants and issues of informed consent and negotiation of access (Bell, 1993). You can read more about the ethics of such research in Chapter 5 of this book.

Non-participant and semi-participant observation

Non-participants usually enter the 'scene' of the research with knowledge of what they want to observe and why they want to observe that phenomenon. In many observations in educational research, it is probably true to say that whilst much of it is non-participant, the context of practitioner-based research, in which many researchers are themselves teachers, makes it very difficult for the researcher not to be an 'informed', semi-participant observer. This raises some difficulties (like getting too 'involved') but is also useful because the researcher already has 'insider' knowledge to bring both to recording important events and to analysing the data gathered through field notes. Being non-participant involves the researcher in aiming to be 'invisible, either in fact or in effect (i.e., by being ignored)' (Walliman, 2001: 241). It is possible, although difficult, to be a 'fly-on-the-wall' in classrooms. This is more likely if the researcher (a) spends considerable time in the classroom or in meetings with their research equipment (e.g., camera, tape-recorder); and (b) takes particular measures, such as avoiding eye-contact with subjects and wearing unobtrusive ('chameleon') clothing. As a non-participant it is also necessary to turn a 'blind eye' to occurrences in the classroom that are not part of the research (the child who is misbehaving can become an embarrassment to the teacher with an observer present), whereas a semi-participant can, if the teacher chooses, share the experience at the end of the observational session. Clearly there are challenges in this situation to retaining objectivity. Fortunately, combining and triangulating methods allows some reduction of this in interpreting findings.

Combining methods

Counting or monitoring observed events in the ways outlined above clearly falls short of giving a more holistic picture. Even with complex systematic observation schedules, the frequency or duration of observed events can only give a certain picture of what is happening and this often requires interpretation alongside further knowledge of the context. For this reason, many researchers combine the use of systematic observations with either other forms of observation, for example, with a classroom non- or semi-participant researcher taking field notes, with video/audio recordings or with interviews or prior surveys (see final section of this chapter).

Observer effects

It is difficult to realise the effects the researcher may have on a situation but these may include the following — and many others:

- Concern on the part of subjects at being observed and, therefore, not behaving normally (some people will admit to this in follow-up interviews as, for example, did the headteacher who said that he always provided wine for end-of-term staff meetings but felt he should not do so when the meeting was being observed).
- Particular focii, e.g., of the teaching or meeting, being avoided at the times of observation because they are not felt to be appropriate. (I had an experience in a nursery where the teacher felt it more appropriate to show herself in a direct instruction situation rather than in a play and learning

situation with children even though the project was focusing on play and learning).

- Wanting to be seen to be like others who may also be observed (e.g., perhaps wanting to be seen to be conforming with what is 'required', yet not necessarily having considered what that might be).
- Concern that those observed may respond adversely to being observed (e.g., children may 'play up' because there is a stranger in the classroom — a case to be made here for being a semi-participant).

See Delamont (1992) for other considerations.

Observer bias

Whilst all researchers will try to remain as objective as possible, observer bias is difficult to avoid totally (there is no such thing as value-free data gathering!) Observational biases occur because of:

- *Selective attention*. Our sensory mechanisms (as we saw above in relation to looking, seeing and interpreting) are themselves subject to bias. We both select what we 'want' to see and then interpret this from our own perceptions and values;
- *Selective encoding*. The observer will have certain expectations of what is likely to be seen and, in interpreting data, will make unconscious and subconscious judgements about them. Surfacing these whenever possible through discussion with others is vital to ensuring the validity of outcomes;
- *Selective memory*. Especially in observations using field notes, it is vital that, if not written contemporaneously, notes are written up as soon afterwards as possible. It is also necessary that all observations are clearly contextualised (see section on recording observations);
- *Interpersonal factors*. Whilst the non-participant researcher is trying to obtain a distance between her/himself and the subjects, being in the same room or setting as those observed inevitably raises relationship (and power) issues. The participant-observer may find that personal likes and dislikes can surface when getting a feel for the culture and ethos of the context.

Awareness of both effects and bias takes us part-way to generating countermeasures. For example, it is helpful and necessary wherever possible to have someone else's opinion on instruments or procedures. In fact, structured and semi-structured observation instruments should always undergo rigorous piloting so that any biases can be identified. It is also useful to check your own potential biases against what others have written in relation to research of a similar kind, hence the advisability of reading any research similar to your own as well as literature on research methodology.

Ethical issues

In recent years, Ofsted inspections in schools in England and Wales have made the task of the observational researcher somewhat more difficult, in that there is often an assumption in schools that the observer has similar purposes to inspectors in conducting observations; it is difficult to encourage practitioners out of this mind-set which can carry negative connotations about observation. This is where it is vital to ensure, both for ethical and objectivity purposes, that the subjects are absolutely clear about the right of subjects to an explanation of aims, procedures, purposes, publication possibilities, the consequences of the research and the right to refuse to take part or withdraw at any stage. The subjects need to be competent to make these decisions, acting voluntarily and making their decisions on the fullest possible information. The researcher needs to be clear that subjects fully comprehend the nature and outcomes of the research and that they will have anonymity and confidentiality assured (Burgess, 1989).

There is also the issue of turning a 'blind eye' in order to respond appropriately to incidents during observational research (Maykut and Morehouse, 1994). On one occasion whilst undertaking classroom-based research, I deliberately (and obviously) turned off the video and carefully studied a classroom display because of an 'incident' between a teacher and a child which was outside the research brief and where it was obvious that being observed might cause distress to both subjects.

Various ways of supporting observations

Various means of recording data can be used to support data collection as we have seen, from making relatively unstructured field notes through to using very defined and pre-determined structured and systematic observation schedules. The content of 'live' recording — that is, the field notes taken directly by the observer that have their origins in anthropological research — is, at the point of gathering, entirely the observer's choice. S/he decides what to gather and when to gather it, with an emphasis on meanings and explanations growing explicitly from the context. Both participant and non-participant observations must be contextualised and both can benefit from technological support through video and audio recordings, provided that both the observer and equipment effects are considered.

Contextualising observations

Observational data should always be contextualised; that is, details of the context and circumstances in which the observation took place must be collected alongside the observational data. This is vital because it is important to retain information about:

- the context of the observation — meeting, classroom, playground, staff development session;
- the overall environment of the observation (e.g., classroom, meeting room) — make an accurate plan of it to aid memory;
- how many subjects were involved at different points — subjects may come and go from view dependent on the context of the observation;
- the roles of the subjects involved — chairing the meeting, presenting papers, listening to the teacher;
- the time of day at which the observation occurred — this can be very significant in relation to the subjects' responses and behaviours;
- the seating arrangements — in classrooms, whether the children were in groups (and of what size); and in meetings who sat where;
- the timetable of events — what happened at the start, in the middle and at the end of the observation (time this for your own purposes later);
- the point at which any critical incidents occur as this may be useful information later.

Other information will depend on your purposes for the observation and the methods used.

Video recordings and photographs

While both will need to be sampled and coded, they are useful for highly focused study or examining fine-grained behaviours such as non-verbal interaction (see Prosser, 1998). They are particularly useful because moving and still images can be revisited to provide exact replicas of earlier data gathered or sequences of events which are being analysed. I have also used video in observational research to play back to teacher subjects a video sequence of a lesson or activity (pre-selected by them) for their comment and analysis, thus including the teacher as a research-partner in observational research. These 'video-stimulated reflective dialogues' appear to provide an effective means by which teachers can reflect on practice and consider potential and relevant changes to practice (Paterson and Moyles, 2001; Moyles *et al.*, 2001) — all as a result of observation! The use of such visual data allows practitioners to step outside their own practice whilst simultaneously providing an opportunity to review, draw awareness and reflect upon action as precursors to meaning-making methods (Fletcher and Whitehead, 2000; McNamara *et al.*, 2000). Whilst most observation is non-interventionist, this is an example where the outcomes of the observation (deriving both qualitative and quantitative data) could be used to develop further observations.

Videoing classroom events or meetings can be useful in capturing the essence of the whole context but there are downsides: the focus range of the camera or the particular 'fix' used by the person operating the camera can skew the data. As was indicated earlier, the mind-set of the observer can determine what is 'seen' and what is therefore video-recorded. For this reason, in my research, which focused directly upon the teacher's role, the camera was fixed almost exclusively on the teacher so as not to be drawn to child participants (Moyles *et al.*, 2001). One can argue that this does not then capture the whole pedagogic process but, as with any method, decisions have to be made as to what will give the best 'fitness for purpose' for required outcomes. In this case, a focus on children could mean that actions, reactions and other behaviours of the teacher would be missed whilst the camera pans to children.

Still photographs, particularly those taken in timed sequence, can be useful for recording the progression of events in a classroom or meeting. They can help to identify otherwise difficult aspects such as who is attending or who is apparently on task at any point within the sequence. They can also offer a record of several different contexts in which observations were conducted and be used as memory-joggers for follow-up interviews.

The images obtained from digital video and still cameras can also be manipulated, often to the benefit of research. For example, video recordings can be taken and sequenced still images extracted from them which can then be used as discussion points with research subjects. Digital video is also ideally suited to the processes of observational research in that it provides an immediacy that traditional photography does not (with the exception of Polaroid photographs). Images can be re-presented immediately following events. Digital video can provide individual or sequences of stills, which can readily be electronically forwarded to distant colleagues for further analysis. Digital images can also be anonymised by the blurring of faces in order to protect the subjects from identification and to encourage participants to make inferences or judgements about 'missing' information.

Audio recording

Audio taping is perhaps more user-friendly, especially with the very small and efficient recorders now available, but suffers from the loss of non-verbal cueing which might, under some circumstances, be very useful observational information. There is also the issue of 'hearing' what is said, particularly when several subjects may be talking at once or there is background noise which is likely to be the case during meeting or classroom observations. Ideally, radio microphones (which can be used for both audio and video recording) should be used but these can be off-putting for subjects in that they must carry around both the microphone and the battery box and it needs much practice before these are 'forgotten'. Similarly, having a large tape-recorder and microphone in evidence in the centre of the meeting table is unlikely to be forgotten easily by subjects, with a consequent risk of compromising the validity of data collected.

There is also the issue of transcribing audio recordings in order to analyse the responses of subjects or to examine the dialogue between them; transcription can be very time-consuming and may require significant clerical support. This can equally apply to video recordings (for ways around this problem see the final section on analysis).

However, audio and video transcriptions allow numerical aspects to be extracted with greater ease; for example word counts for particular concepts can be undertaken, the average length of utterances can be calculated, the number of words spoken by individual subjects can be determined and the length of silences can be noted.

Researchers need to remember that the processes of both video and audio recording can be intrusive for those being observed and may mean that the meeting or event may not be conducted in such a 'naturalistic' way as without such recording. In either circumstance, the subjects of the observation must give their full consent (in the case of children, parental consent) as described under 'ethics' above. Arguably, however, the benefits of having video and audio data, particularly when it comes to analysis, outweigh any disadvantages for the various reasons suggested. This equally applies to other ways of recording observations which will now be briefly mentioned.

Semi-structured observation

In many ways this is a misnomer: observation is either structured or unstructured. However, for a number of reasons, the researcher might wish partly to structure the observation but also leave opportunity for informal data gathering. For example, in research attempting to establish the roles in the classroom of teaching assistants (TAs), I found it helpful to track — using a semi-structured schedule — each TA's broad, overall tasks in classrooms (for example the areas of curriculum in which engaged, whether working with individuals or groups of children), whilst at the same time, making audio-recordings of conversations with children and taking field notes of the context of the work (another example of combined methods). No attempt was made in the semi-structured schedule to determine the finer points of the role as these were available through the other means.

Another example of semi-structuring observations might be in relation to the rating scales occasionally used by researchers. These are apparently objective measures but are subjectively determined. For example, the researcher engaged in observation of a staff development session might rate the overall setting according to a number of criteria which operate on a scale from excellent to poor in terms of content, presentation, audience participation and so on (Williams, 1994). Meetings can be observed and ranked on a Likert-type scale from business-like to dysfunctional, or classrooms ranked on a scale from well-organised to chaotic. Such scaling does need accurate measures of inter-rater reliability to be of value, however, and that reliability itself depends on the criteria previously determined for rankings such as 'business-like' or 'well-organised'. These measures (classed as high inference) require considerable subjective judgement to be made by the observer, where more structured schedules require 'low inference' judgements in that they require the observer merely to record whether or not something happened.

Shadowing procedures

Shadowing is not always thought of as observational research but to my mind, clearly stands in that category. It is often semi-participatory, requiring on-going field observations in very close proximity to the subject. For this reason it carries certain conditions which need to be met, not least of which is that the subject must feel wholly at ease with the researcher in constant attendance. Therefore the process needs careful setting up and considerable non-shadowing trial time so that the subject, as far as possible, both feels comfortable and is able to ignore the researcher if the outcomes are to be valid. The process can reap significant benefits, especially if repeated over time, because it can give a total picture of a particular role. I have used such methods on a number of occasions mainly in matching the expectations of a role with the actual daily fulfilment of that role, in one case in terms of the teaching assistant's role. The intention was to find a match (if one existed) between the TA's job description and the role actually undertaken. The potential disparity only became available visibly when the tasks undertaken over time and in proportions to the day were matched against the role as described and required by the school. This could equally apply to any role within the institution which carries a job role description. The kind of analysis undertaken from the results of shadowing was quite straightforward, but that is not always the case.

Analysing and interpreting observational data

It may be obvious to say that analysis has to be based on what it was the researcher wanted to find out in the first place but it is not always easy, especially in more informal approaches, to ensure that the research aims and objectives dominate. It is very easy, in fact, to get diverted by potential findings, which are interesting in themselves but do not necessarily contribute to the original hypotheses. That said, it does not mean that we cannot move beyond our objectives and add findings additional to the original intentions — these will frequently emerge in observational research, particularly when we begin to interpret the data gathered.

It will be necessary to consider the following when analysing and interpreting the two principal forms of observational data:

- *Structured observations.* These take longer to conceptualise and prepare and are behaviourist in origin. Structured observations allow comparison, are discrete, have little overlap and categories are (and must be) mutually exclusive.
- *Informal observations.* These are based on an interpretive paradigm and are quicker to prepare but are likely to take much longer to analyse outcomes. There can be much overlap and categories may evolve rather than be pre-determined.

As has been said previously, it is possible that one may inform and feed on the other. In the case of the Study of Primary Interactive Teaching (SPRINT) project (Moyles *et al.*, 1999–2001), the use of the ORACLE teacher schedule was combined with video observation and reflective dialogues with practitioners, to give a more robust outcome in terms of understanding interactive teaching within primary schools' literacy hour (DfEE, 1998).

This research in particular, shows that it is important to know what type and level of analysis you intend to employ *before* collecting your data. In the case of SPRINT, the researchers wanted to compare the pre-literacy hour period exemplified by 1996 (the period in time of ORACLE 2, see Galton *et al.*, 1999) with the first year of the literacy hour in practice (1999–2000) to find out whether teaching strategies had changed and, if so, to what extent. In addition, we wanted to establish primary teachers' understanding and use of interactive teaching, given that it was given such prominence in the 'new' strategies (i.e., for literacy, numeracy and ICT). Hence, video observation was used to develop both reflective dialogues, giving information about understanding, and classroom use with children. Observational methods predominate in this project as the researchers identified these as the most appropriate way of gaining the information required.

In this project, as in many others, the amount of transcription and analysis required was great. This is generally to be expected in research of this kind. A way around the problem of excessive transcription of audio and video tapes is (a) to consider prior to undertaking this approach what the researcher wants to get out of it; and (b) to re-run the tapes fairly soon after the event and make notes on the most salient points, determined earlier by the focus of the observational research. Another way is to limit the transcription to five-minute slots spread out across the tape (whether audio or video) so as to 'sample' within the timeframe.

It was mentioned above that video and photography provide the means by which body language and non-verbal communication variables can be fed into the observation equation. This is an area of great interest but also one that is fraught with interpretational challenges. If body language is the main focus of the study and a clear conceptualisation of it has been elicited, then it can provide a useful source of additional information to support other data gathering (see Neill and Caswell, 1993). Certainly it can give cues and clues but it is easily over-interpreted by novice researchers.

Tools for analysis and data presentation

Researchers should not underestimate the sheer quantity of data that they may gather during the course of informal observational research. It is exceedingly easy to find that you have collected so much data that you are not certain how to analyse or write it up. Somehow, gathering data seems more productive than analysing it and inexperienced researchers often use the process as a bulwark against potential failure. By far the best advice is that given by Silverman ('Analyse your own data as you gather them' (2000: 120). The first session of field observation, or the first batch of completed schedules, alongside your initial analysis of existing data and concepts through the literature, can provide sufficient data to allow analysis to begin. It also gives an indication of how much analysis and interpretation can occur from a relatively small amount of data. This is the point at which it is necessary to check your original analytical intentions and, having made a few forays into it, check that what you decided is still appropriate to your research requirements. For example, do your categories now seem to fit the data gathered? Which concepts look like being the most productive in terms of quantity of related data?

The analysis of transcriptions, as Silverman (2000) suggests, 'depends upon the generation of [the] research problem out of a particular theoretical orientation' (2000: 130), hence the need for having considered carefully and at the outset a clear conceptualisation of the problem under investigation.

There are straightforward, manual ways of categorising and ordering the data gathered: see Cortazzi (1993); Coffey and Atkinson (1996); Dey (1993); Huberman and Miles (1994) for both theoretical and practical examples. These entail various means by which the data are reviewed and main concepts highlighted (usually with a highlighter pen). In addition, a range of useful computer-based analytical tools such as Atlas TI, McShapa, Nud*Ist and Nvivo is now worthy of consideration (web sites for them are given in the references at the end of this chapter for those who wish to find out more). It is important to remember that these tools are only as good as the person who programmes in the categorisations, so an initial manual run-through is still desirable. The technique or computer programme chosen will depend on the skills of the researchers and their own views as to what will give the most effective and reliable outcomes. All these methods need the observations or field notes to be transcribed into text. Computer-based programmes require that data are imported in various structures into the program, usually by means of Word documents.

Excel and similar spreadsheet packages support the ultimate presentation of quantitative data through charts, tables and graphs to give ready visual access to data but the data must be input in coded format. Coding observation schedules at the point of data gathering is recommended if not vital. The power of SPSS in handling statistical data effectively and efficiently is well-known in the research world. It can provide a range of statistical tests which can be applied to data thus securing a range of reliability measures, e.g., analysis of variance across subjects or fields or correlations between items (for a straightforward guide see Coolican, 1999).

Electronic storage is neater and data more quickly retrieved, allowing potentially more time for analysis. It can also add rigour, for example, to counting frequencies, and can offer more confidence in the patterns that data analysis may reveal.

Observation and reliability/validity measures

As has been emphasised, observation is probably most effective when combined with other forms of data gathering, e.g., interviewing or questionnaire survey, because of the issues of the interpretation of what is observed and of potential observer bias, identified at the start of this chapter. Used in combination with other methods, it offers the opportunity for findings to be validated through triangulation (see Chapter 4 of this book). Validity is also concerned with the credibility of the means and tools by which the data is collected (Simpson and Tuson, 1995: 63) as we have seen.

Determining reliability is highly dependent upon the range of factors which were discussed earlier, namely (in the case of structured observation) the quality of the research instrument and the number of observations undertaken — the greater the number, the more reliable the outcome is likely to be. Measure of inter-rater/coder reliability is important here: different researchers should be able to achieve highly correlated results by use of the same instrument. In the case of informal observation, measures of reliability relate mainly to 'blind' coding of transcribed data, that is, the transcriptions being given to different researchers who need to achieve similar outcomes from the categories determined. Hammersley (1990) refers to the processes as:

> Validity . . . [is] the extent to which an account accurately represents the social phenomena to which it refers. (1990: 57).

> Reliability [is] . . . the degree of consistency with which instances are assigned to the same category by . . . observers. (1992: 67).

Figure 11.3 shows how a combination of semi-structured observations, questionnaire survey and interviewing research methods contributed to the overall findings of one particular project.

> **Moyles, J. and Suschitzky, W. (1997)** *Jills of All Trades? Classroom Assistants in Key Stage One Classes,* London/Leicester: ATL/University of Leicester.
>
> Research was undertaken to examine the working roles and relationships of Key Stage One teachers and classroom assistants working together (Moyles and Suschitzky, 1997). The research was designed in such a way that overall information was achieved through a survey (questionnaire) of a sample from a nationally distributed population. Respondents who expressed interest and willingness were then contacted and observed in the classroom context. Both a structured tracking schedule (see Appendix A) and a frequency schedule (see Appendix B) were designed. The former was intended to track every 20 minutes what the teachers and classroom assistants were doing so that activities could be compared.
>
> From their own experiences of infant classrooms, the observers decided the likely common activities and potential location of the teacher/assistant which it would be helpful to include in the tracking schedule. The schedule recorded where the person was located in or around the classroom, what main role s/he was fulfilling and whether the activity (also recorded) involved a single child or a group of children or another adult. *Findings revealed that teachers did three times more class management tasks than TAs and spent double their time on direct instruction. TAs spent nearly twice as much time as teachers in supporting learning, five times more than teachers on providing resources, and twice as much time as teachers in dealing with the social and physical needs of children.*
>
> The frequency schedule was filled in by the observer for one minute of teaching time four times during a 3-hour class session. This schedule was designed from a review of the relevant literature on child/teacher interactions and the anticipated behaviours in which the two individuals were likely to engage. Again, this allowed post-analysis comparison of interactions with children. *Little difference was evident in the interactions of teachers and TAs with children except that teachers made greater use of praise and were more likely to make suggestions to children in support of learning.*

Figure 11.3 An example of a multi-instrument approach to research methodology

Piloting observations

Piloting of observations, whether systematic or informal, should always be undertaken, in the former case to evaluate the instrument in use and in the latter case to get a feel for the relevancy of different types of field notes. Piloting can also act as a meaningful training for the observer and it should also enable the researcher to see whether it is possible to collect data using another's instrument(s) and achieve inter-observer reliability.

Conclusion

Observation is a useful and interesting tool for all researchers including those working in schools and colleges. Is it the 'best' method? If your purpose is to 'see' what happens and what is enacted then the answer is 'Yes!' Evidence-informed practice is now prominent in research thinking — the establishment of such bodies as the National Educational Research Forum (NERF) in Britain is evidence in itself of government funding with the desired intention of making better use of all research and methods including observation to inform school and classroom practices. Observation is a key means of obtaining both 'hard' and 'soft' evidence about what currently exists in those arenas. Well-conceived structured and informal observational methods can measure what exists and how this changes over time. It cannot, of itself, produce change. Interventionist studies can, however, include the use of video observations to begin the process of change. Observational processes, with all their complexity, can meet a range of intentions and be used for a range of purposes to inform current and future debates in education.

References

Anderson, L. with Arsenault, N. (1998) *Fundamentals of Educational Research*, London: Falmer Press.

Bell, J. (1993) 'Negotiating access and the problems of 'inside' research', in Bell, J. *Doing Your Research Project*, Buckingham: Open University Press.

Burgess, R. (1989) (ed.) *The Ethics of Educational Research*, Lewes: Falmer Press.

Coffey, A. and Atkinson, P. (1996) *Making Sense of Qualitative Data*, London: Sage.

Cohen, L. and Manion, L. (1994) *Research Methods in Education* (4th edn.), London: Routledge.

Cohen, L., Manion, L. and Morrison, K. (2000) *Research Methods in Education* (5th edn.), London: Routledge/Falmer Press.

Coolican, H. (1999) *Research Methods and Statistics*, London: Hodder and Stoughton.

Cortazzi, M. (1993) *Narrative Analysis*, London: Falmer Press.

Croll, P. (1986) *Systematic Classroom Observation*, London: Falmer Press.

Delamont, S. (1992) *Fieldwork in Educational Settings: Methods, Pitfalls and Perspectives*, London: Falmer Press.

Denscombe, M. (1998) *The Good Research Guide for Small-scale Social Research Projects*, Buckingham: Open University Press.

Dey, I. (1993) *Qualitative Data Analysis: A User-Friendly Guide for Social Scientists*, London: Routledge.

DfEE (1998) *The National Literacy Strategy: A Framework for Teaching*, London: DfEE.

Flanders, N. (1970) *Analysing Teaching Behaviour*, Reading, MA: Addison-Wesley.

Fletcher, S. and Whitehead, J. (2000) 'The "look" of the teacher: using digital video to improve the professional practice of teaching'. Paper presented to BERA annual conference, 7–9th September, University of Cardiff.

Foster, P. (1996) 'Ethical issues in observational research', in Foster, P. *Observing Schools: A Methodological Guide*, London: Paul Chapman.

Galton, M., Simon, B. and Croll, P. (1980) *Inside the Primary Classroom*, London: Routledge Kegan Paul.

Galton, M., Hargreaves, L., Comber, C., Wall, D. and Pell, A. (1999) *Inside the Primary Classroom: 20 years On*, London: Routledge.

Guba, G. and Lincoln, Y. (1987) 'Naturalistic enquiry', in Dunkin, M. (ed.) *The*

International Encyclopaedia of Teaching and Teacher Education, New York: Pergamon.

Hammersley, M. (1990) *Reading Ethnographic Research: A Critical Guide*, London: Longmans.

Hammersley, M. (1992) *What's Wrong with Ethnography? Methodological Explorations*, London: Routledge.

Hitchcock, G. and Hughes, D. (1997) *Research and the Teacher: A Qualitative Introduction to School-based Research* (2nd edn.), London: Routledge.

Huberman, A. and Miles, M. (1994) 'Data management and analysis methods', in N. Denzin and Y. Lincoln (eds.) *Handbook of Qualitative Research*, Thousand Oaks, CA: Sage.

King, R. (1978) *All things bright and beautiful?: a sociological study of infants' classrooms*, Chichester: Wiley.

LeCompte, M. and Preissle, J. (eds.) (1993) *Ethnography and Qualitative Design in Educational Research*, London: Academic Press.

Maykut, P. and Morehouse, R. (1994) *Beginning Qualitative Research: A Philosophical and Practical Guide*, London: Falmer Press.

McNamara, O., Jones, L. and Van-Es, C. (2000) 'Evidence-based practice through practice-based evidence: the global and the local'. Paper presented to BERA annual conference, 7–9th September, University of Cardiff.

Moyles, J., Hargreaves, L., Merry, R., Paterson, A. and Esarte-Sarries, V. (eds.) (2002) *Digging Deeper Into Meanings: Interactive Teaching in the Primary School*, Buckingham: Open University Press.

Moyles, J., Adams, S. and Musgrove, A. (2000–2001) *SPEEL: Study of Pedagogical Effectiveness in Early Learning*, DfES funded project.

Moyles, J., Adams, S. and Musgrove, A. (2001) *Study of Pedagogical Effectiveness in Early Learning*, Unpublished report to the DfES on the Effective Pedagogy Project. Chelmsford: APU/London: DfES.

Moyles, J., Adams, S. and Musgrove, A. (2001) 'The study of pedagogical effectiveness in early learning: challenges in defining terminology and engaging with conceptual dissonance', paper presented at the annual BERA Conference, Leeds, September 2001.

Moyles, J., Suschitzky, W. and Chapman, L. (1998) *Teaching Fledglings to Fly? Mentoring in Teacher Education*, London: Association of Teachers and Lecturers/University of Leicester.

Moyles, J. and Suschitzky, W. (1997) *Jills of All Trades? Teachers and Classroom Assistants Working Together in Key Stage 1*, London: Association of Teachers and Lecturers/University of Leicester.

Moyles, J. and Suschitzky, W. (1997) *Jills of All Trades . . .? Classroom Assistants in Key Stage 1 Classes*. London: ATL/University of Leicester.

Moyles, J., Hargreaves, L. and Merry, R. (1999–2001) 'SPRINT: a study of primary interactive teaching. ESRC funded project (R000238200).

Neill, S. and Caswell, C. (1993) *Body Language for Competent Teachers*, London: Routledge.

Paterson, A. and Moyles, J. (2001) 'The reflective dialogue process', paper presented at the APU annual Research Conference, Colchester, June 2001.

Prosser, J. (1998) *Image Based Research: A Sourcebook for Qualitative Researchers*, London: Falmer Press.

Robson, C. (1993) *Real World Research*, Oxford: Basil Blackwell.

Silverman, D. (2000) *Doing Qualitative Research*, London: Sage.

Simpson, M. and Tuson, J. (1995) *Using Observations in Small-scale Research*, Edinburgh: Scottish Council for Research in Education.

Walliman, N. (2001) *Your Research Project: A Step-by-step Guide for the First-time Researcher*, London: Sage.

Whyte, W. F. (1981) *Street Corner Society* (3rd edn.), Chicago: University of Chicago Press.

Willliams, G. L. (1994) 'Observing and recording meetings' in Bennett, N., Glatter, R. and Levačić, R. (eds.) *Improving Educational Management through Research and Consultancy*, London: Paul Chapman.

Woods, P. (1996) *Researching the Art of Teaching*, London: Routledge.

Wragg, E. (1994) *An Introduction to Classroom Observation*, London: Routledge.

Wragg, E. (1999) *An Introduction to Classroom Observation* (2nd edn.), London: Routledge.

Other useful references

Cavendish, S., Galton, M., Hargreaves, L. and Harlen, W. (1990) *Observing Activities*, London: Paul Chapman.

Denzin, N. and Lincoln, Y. (2000) *Handbook of Qualitative Research*, Thousand Oaks, CA: Sage.

National Primary Centre (1991) *Language Observed: Approaches to Classroom Assessment 3–13*, Birmingham.

Shostak, J. (2000) *Understanding, Designing and Conducting Qualitative Research in Education*, Buckingham: Open University Press.

Web sites

Nud*Ist http://www.qsr.com.au
Atlas http://www.atlasti.de
Scolari http://www.sagepub.co.uk/scolari

Observation schedule — tracking
(teacher/assistant)

SCHOOL:

DATE:

YEAR GROUP:

	[Child interaction]			[Adult interaction]				
Time	T. Position	Ch. no:	Ch. Position	Ch. activity	T. role	Ad. Who?	Ad. Position	Ad. activity	Interpretational Notes
8.55									
9.15									
9.35									
9.55									
10.15									
10.35									
10.55									
11.15									
11.35									
11.55									

Positions coded as: cl st = classroom standing; cl sit = classroom sitting; cl fl = classroom floor; cor = corridor; pl = playground; h = hall; o = other

Adult role: man = management, mon = monitoring, dir = direct instruction, sup = supporting learning, soc = social/physical needs, ass = assessing, rec = recording, res = resources, cont = control, h = help

N.B. TA tracking differed by one minute in the time column, being effected one minute later than the T's tracking.

Observation schedule — frequency of predetermined types of adult/child interaction (teaching assistant and/or teacher)

| Date | Time | School | Round | 1 | 2 | 3 | 4 |

Context/Activity	Main resources	Size of group
		same/different

Category[1]	Type	Tally	Code	Other or comment
SOCIAL	Attention		1	
	Name		2	
	Social		3	
	Joking/comment		4	
BEHAVIOUR	Encourage		5	
	Praise		6	
	Reprimand		7	
	Negotiate		8	
QUESTION	For information		9	
	Elicit understanding		10	
	Prompting		11	
TEACHING MODE	Suggest		12	
	Explain		13	
	Instruct – content		14	
	Direct – admin		15	
	Describe		16	
	Remind		17	
	Inform		18	
LISTENING	Silence		19	
	Response		20	
	Reflect back		21	
	Ignore		22	

[1] These categories were either too broad to identify small differences or teachers and teaching assistants (as we concluded) operate very similarly in the classroom, probably because TAs model their behaviour on the teacher.

Schedule for post observation video coding

The following schedule from Moyles *et al.* (1998) was devised for post-observation analysis of video-taped interactions between student teachers/newly qualified teachers and their school-based mentors. Categories were devised from the main literature on mentoring which were the categorised into Role Dimensions and Strategies. The video itself then provided Action categories and examples which, in turn, supported analysis of the video and inter-observer reliability measures.

Role Dimensions	Strategies	Code[1]	Actions	Code	Examples
PROFESSIONAL					
Supporter	To support	A	Praising (general)	1	'Good'
	To accept	B	Praising (specific)	2	'That was good'
	To reassure	C	Listening positively	3	Nodding, 'Yes', 'U-huh'
	To encourage	D	Listening negatively	4	Still, closed body posture
	To protect	E	Offering practical support	5	'I'll take a group'
	To confirm	D	Offering professional support	6	With parents, backing up
			Prompting	7	
			Waiting	8	Anticipatory silence
			Telling/stating	9	'You should . . .' 'Do this . . .'
			Neutral comment	10	'Oh well . . . laugh . . . repetitions
			Sharing professional perception	11	. . . of children, school . . .
			Sharing professional knowledge	12	'I've done . . .' 'I think . . .'
			Empathising	13	'I understand/remember'
			Allaying doubts	14	'Don't worry'
Trainer (procedural)	To coach	G	Suggesting	15	'You could . . .'
	To review	H	Reminding	16	'Do you remember when . . . ?'
	Identify needs	I	Explaining (procedural)	17	'This is because . . .'
	Clarify needs	J	Explaining (rationale)	18	Reasoning behind actions
			Criticising constructively	19	'This didn't work . . . that did'
			Criticising negatively	20	'It didn't work'
			Modelling (suggestion)	21	'You could do it like this'
			Modelling (expectation)	22	'Do it like this . . .'
			Modelling (arrangement)	23	'I'll do it on Monday'
			Questioning (open)	24	'How do you feel it went?'
			Questioning (closed)	25	Yes/no answer.

			Questioning (prompt)	26	'What about that group?'
			Questioning (open but limiting)	27	'Could you do this . . . or this . . . ?
			Questioning (rhetorical)	28	'Shall we . . . ?
			Giving background info	29	About children/school
Educator	To perceive needs	K	Generalising	30	About context
	Analyse needs	L	Extending (suggestion)	31	'That would be good to do in assembly'
	Encourage reflection	M	Extending (expectation)	32	'You can do the assembly'
	To challenge	N	Setting targets (suggestion)	33	'You should concentrate on . . .'
	To action plan	O	Setting targets (expectation)	34	'So you will concentrate on . . .'
	To evaluate	P	Setting targets (NE)	35	'Decide what you will concentrate on'
Assessor	To assess	Q	Formalising	36	Written outcomes/ assessment (summative)
PERSONAL	To counsel	R	Chatting	37	Small talk; jokes etc.
	To befriend	S	Informing	38	About school procedures
			Arranging	39	. . . to speak to someone, to introduce, etc.
STRUCTURAL	To induct	T			
	To accept	U			
	To facilitate	V			
	To negotiate	W			
	To promote	X			

[1]Both alphabetic and numerical coding were done to facilitate analysis, e.g. M24 = educator role, analysing needs through open-ended questioning.

12
Analysing narratives and documents
Martin Cortazzi

Introduction: narratives and documents as texts

Narrative analysis and documentary analysis offer fresh ways to explore the meanings and social functions of texts in educational research. These approaches complement other approaches and can readily be used alongside them. At the same time, insights from these approaches can extend and challenge some aspects of research that might otherwise be overlooked.

There are some interesting harmonies and counterpoints between narrative analysis and the analysis of documents. Both clearly involve verbal data: while documents are by definition written texts, narrative accounts can be oral (say in the form of stories of personal experiences of teachers and managers in education); or written (as parts of histories, case studies, journals and diaries, accounts of teachers' life stories and professional careers). Yet narratives as oral accounts can be recorded and transcribed to be largely treated as text, while some documents, such as committee minutes, also have a clear oral provenance in group talk which is selectively summarised to become text. Here, both narratives and documents will be treated as texts; this means that both are semiotic, or cultural units of meanings constructed through words.

Documentary analysis has a long tradition in research. It often has an aura of respectability, perhaps due to the high regard in administrative circles and educational systems in which written text is held. In education, as elsewhere, text is evidence in a way in which speech is not. Text is held to be evidence of past and current realities or future plans, for example in written examinations and assignments, in the documentation made available for school inspections and other quality assurance procedures, or in mission statements and policy or strategy documents. Narrative analysis is a much more recent approach to research; and to some extent proponents of it still face the feeling that narratives are only anecdotal evidence, slight and transitory tellings of experience which are at best illustrations of something else. Yet many educational researchers, like those in many social science and humanities disciplines, have turned to narrative research methods to explore participants' perspectives on events and to see what their experience means. Both documents and narratives can be treated quantitatively, for example by analysing frequency counts of the mentions of key words or concepts or through other forms of content analysis. More usually, both are seen in qualitative terms, where what matters is how meanings are generated through a certain textual form, with particular textual functions, in certain contexts and with particular effects. Documents and narratives, then, can be treated as texts where the focus is on what is said, how it is said, and what that means.

This chapter will present some ways of analysing narratives and documents as texts, treating them in terms of discourse and culture. In this discourse view, narratives and documents do not simply reflect reality, they also construct it and contribute to subsequent views of it. The chapter will show why these research approaches are considered valuable and it will illustrate with examples some ways in which such analyses might proceed. The analyses will be set broadly within an ethnographic framework, asking about the social meanings and interpretations from the perspectives of insiders within a cultural group or community. The chapter will also look at the nature of this kind of research in terms of being reflexive, raising questions about the nature of the process of such research, in this case by asking about the culture of research. In this way, the chapter should be useful not only as information and exemplification about research methods but as a methodological window through which to raise some general research issues.

Some features of discourse

In treating narratives and documents as texts, it is useful to have in mind some features of discourse. This discourse perspective is important because it encourages researchers to think of narrative accounts and educational documents as rather more than simply stories or pieces of paper that constitute evidence. That is, the perspective helps new researchers to go beyond the obvious and to look at the language and social dimensions of the evidence, to see it in broader contexts, and to question previous assumptions about it. Some major features of discourse will be briefly outlined and illustrated using the example of documents involved in a staff appointment to an educational institution.

Texts are sequences of words or units of language and one could analyse them only from this linguistic angle of looking at what the text says. However, texts are never isolated — whether we can identify them or not, they all have writers and readers, sometimes unintended readers, and even unknown other writers, such as ghostwriters, unacknowledged sources, editors or annotators. So although texts need to be seen as instances of language, they are inherently social because they are socially produced and used, often in social networks.

Texts as units of meanings will have some kind of overall structure. This can be seen in the ways in which particular words relate to other words in the text and how sentences hang together in sequence (this is called *cohe-*

sion) and also in the ways in which the ideas in the text follow in from one another and how these are likely to be understood (this is called *coherence*). Texts may well be expressed in a certain socially expected style (or *register*), using particular kinds of vocabulary or typical phrases, for example as 'legal English' or 'academic English'. Texts in education also generally conform to various other social expectations (*genres*) that relate to the social context in which they are used; these expectations may determine to varying extents the format, style, and organisation of meaning.

Thus educational managers have certain expectations of how texts related to educational employment, for example, should be written and organised and how they are to be read and interpreted. In dealing with staff appointments, there are a series of documents, each of which has its own textual organisation, or genre. This chain of documents may include the job advertisement, documents with details of the institution and requirements of the post, such as the job and person specification, the letters of application with accompanying curricula vitae, copies of qualifications, letters of recommendation from referees, the notes of the interview panel, and letters of rejection or the letter offering an appointment with an accompanying contract and salary scales. Each of these documents might be analysed in slightly different ways because they have different structures and conventions, especially in different cultures. In this example, all the documents might relate to each other and some might refer to or quote other documents (showing relations of *intertextuality*). Each type of document will express the different intentions of the writer through various communicative devices and each may be read or interpreted differently by educational managers or members of an appointments board, or researchers, according to their knowledge of the writer, the context, expected and unexpected readers, and their own purposes. Each text, in other words, is surrounded by a context of expectations and patterns of knowledge and meaning held by those who use the text and who inevitably — and quite normally — bring these to their own interpretation and use of the text.

Text users, of course, may have expectations which differ from each other and so the range of ways of reading the text may depend on how prior knowledge of the context varies: headteachers, parent governors, and applicants for a job will frequently see the chain of documents involved in the full appointment process in quite different ways. The documentary chain is actually different for different participants because some of the documents are public (e.g. the job advertisement) while others are restricted or private and will be seen by selected readers only (e.g. letters of recommendation, which may be confidential). The job applicant often has less access to information, or fewer documents, than the employers (job and person specifications are often only selectively shared with applicants and applicants rarely see each other's papers). Different users in the documentary chain may therefore have access to different sets of links. This differential access to information goes further when one considers others who will be interested in the appointment; although physically peripheral, teachers and learners in the institution, and families or current colleagues of applicants are part of the social network surrounding the application and interview process and they are equally interested in the outcome.

Since the documentary links in this chain interact with each other, and since readers and writers interact with the texts and with each other verbally, the process of producing and using such texts needs to be seen in terms of *interaction*: how the writers and readers interact with the text and with each other's knowledge, expectations and interpretations is highly interactive. Moreover, each text in the chain has some kind of social function or *social action* that it performs: it gives information, displays knowledge and skills, promotes an image of the writer or institution, requests or recommends further action, wards off challenges or anticipated negative reactions, and so on. In fact, such social actions generally work in combinations, as do the social interactions and all the other features of texts mentioned above, so the concepts of texts needed for analysing narratives and documents are quite complex.

Further explanation of discourse concepts can be found in accessible current introductions, most of which contrast narrative and non-narrative discourse. Some are more language oriented (Georgakopoulou and Goutsos, 1997; Hoey, 2001), others feature more socially oriented approaches (Gee, 1999; Wood and Kroger, 2000; Titscher *et al.*, 2000), relating genre and context (Chimombo and Roseberry, 1998), or revealing how discourse can be used for social control (Caldas-Coulthard and Coulthard, 1996; Fairclough, 1995). Collections of articles introducing approaches and examples of analysis are useful (Coulthard, 1994; van Dijk, 1997a; 1997b; Jaworski and Coupland, 1999). It is worth emphasising that the ability to see educational documents and narratives as texts, and to take a discourse-informed view of the language and social features, greatly amplifies the strategies available to a researcher in education to examine such texts, and to explore their meanings and functions in ways that go beyond simply looking at what the words say.

Narrative analysis in education

The data for narrative analysis can include teachers' biographies and autobiographical accounts, teachers' life stories, teachers' or learners' personal accounts and experiences of significant educational events or examples of classroom learning. The data can therefore range from a carefully written and revised career history to a spontaneous anecdote of a classroom incident. Many narrative data will be brought into being through interviews with the researcher, although some may be written for non-research purposes in their own right.

Narrative analysis seems important for at least four reasons. First, it focuses on participants' *experience* and the meanings given by them to that experience. As researchers collect and examine accounts of educational events and how teachers or learners interpret those events, they are concerned with the *interpretations* of participants and how these relate to knowing, explaining, or evaluating what goes on in classrooms or institutions. Since narratives are generally also memories of one sort or another, narrative research can also explore individual or institutional histories and personal or collective perceptions of the past and hence how professional and institutional identities are constructed. For educational managers and those adopting leadership roles, some understanding of such aspects of how institutions work and how people see and remember events is crucial.

Second, narrative analysis is often concerned with *representation* and *voice*. This means that the focus is often on the stories or experiences of minorities or of those whose voices might otherwise go unheard with the aim that others may know education as they know it. The research thus allows for the analysis of changing interests and involvements in education and perhaps may give information about, or publicity to, minority groups that decision makers and the public may need to know in more equitable educational contexts. Thus, some researchers analyse the narratives of ethnic minority teachers, (Osler, 1997) particular groups of teachers, (Armour and Jones, 1998) or women professionals (see Adler *et al.*, 1993) who are perhaps a minority in positions of responsibility.

Third, a collection of narratives of personal experiences in education often has a characteristic that many researchers fail to emphasise. This characteristic is the emphasis given to such personal/professional qualities as dedication and devotion, patience and persistence, enthusiasm, struggle and sacrifice, hard work and humour. Narrative research may thus quite naturally find itself tackling the all-important but often research-neglected humanity of teaching and learning and of its leadership (Ribbins and Marland, 1994).

Fourth, a narrative perspective allows the exploration of *research activity itself as a story*. That is, much research writing (not only narrative research) is reported and presented as a story, with a kind of constructed plot, which is in effect a rhetorical design aimed at persuading readers of the interest, if not the truth, of the research. Ethnographic studies, for example, are often written up as quests of discovery and interpretation, as a research journey from outsider to insider understanding. The researcher thus makes a story of the research, and constructs a narrative while relaying and interpreting the accounts of informants (van Maanen, 1988; Atkinson, 1990; Golden-Biddle and Locke, 1997; Walcott, 2001).

There are a number of accounts of multidisciplinary approaches to narrative analysis (Polkinghorne, 1988; Riessman, 1993; Cortazzi, 1993) and life story materials (Linde, 1993; Lieblich *et al.*, 1998) that can readily be applied to education. Narrative analysis has been applied to British primary teachers' accounts of teaching (Cortazzi, 1991) and American elementary school teachers' narratives of their work (Nelson, 1993). There are American (Hatch and Wisniewski, 1995), British (Thomas, 1995; Erben, 1998), Swiss (Huberman, 1993), and Finnish (Antikainen *et al.*, 1996) studies of life histories and biographies in education, similar studies from women's perspectives (Munro, 1998; Weiler and Middleton, 1999), and collections of studies of teachers' stories (McLaughlin and Tierney, 1993; Jalongo *et al.*, 1995) which emphasise personal and professional insights, teachers' identity, educational change and particular classrooms, such as those where writing is taught (Trimmer, 1997). Other collections of narrative studies attempt to construct what might be called 'educational narratology' or a theory of narrative in teaching and learning (Witherell and Noddings, 1991; McEwan and Egan, 1995). These book-length collections are worth mentioning because they demonstrate the variety of published material on educational narrative analysis. For novice researchers who wish to see and try narrative analysis there is a wealth of data here, some of which could be submitted to a secondary analysis from the perspectives of educational management to make an original study. This is a useful thought because it is time consuming and sometimes difficult to obtain narrative data first hand.

Documentary analysis in education

The data for documentary analysis (beside those already mentioned) include policy documents, regulations, official statistics, curriculum documents, schemes of work and course handbooks, inspection reports, school prospectuses and newsletters, material on noticeboards and grafitti on walls, textbooks and worksheets, pupils' written work, memoranda, letters to schools and letters to parents, email communications and information found on web sites. These are all printed or written data, which already exist independently of the researcher, and most can be used for research as they are found. Many documents can be unobtrusively obtained at low cost; they are easily stored and can readily be re-analysed. For example, it may be a great deal easier for a researcher to study the minutes of a meeting than to observe the meeting or interview the participants. By extension, some researchers include more visual formats as documents, such as maps and plans, photos, films and videos. Such a range of documents implies that there is a great variety of social and administrative functions in educational documents.

In handling documents, researchers consider a range of questions:

- What are the range, location, and feasibility of access for target documents?
- How representative are the documents in hand and how do they link with other documents in a chain or complementary set?
- Is there a need to sample a range of documents such as minutes?
- What is the source, who is the author and what are the channels of transmission or dissemination for the documents?
- What is the status, accuracy, credibility, personal or institutional voice and normal context or setting of use for the document?
- What is the intended purpose, how would different participants interpret this and what are the intended or unintended effects of its use?
- What orientations, values, and ideologies does the document represent?
- What is the nature and social functions of the document as text?

In attempting to answer such questions, the researcher would be aware that the research purpose may be different from the purposes behind the original document: documents can be read for embedded meanings as unwitting evidence for such aspects of educational institutions as the exercise of power and control, the presentation of real or contrived images, the leaking of attitudes, values and social expectations which the authors might have thought hidden.

A crucial issue behind these questions is the relation of the document to its social context. Like narratives and other texts, documents do not simply arise from a context and reflect the reality of that context. That is only part of the story. More interestingly, once a document is in use it is itself part of that context and therefore contributes to the construction of later contexts of use. This is easily understood in relation to committee minutes or records of a staff meeting: they often refer to previous minutes; parts of them tend to inform or be the focus of later talk as matters arising; and as a record of decisions or planned actions they may be referred to as reminders or checks of who should do what and whether this has been done. Such minutes do not, therefore, simply reflect what happened at the meeting but critically contribute to action. Such minutes also tend to construct their own reality: once an item is recorded in them, the record is taken as true and agreed, despite disagreements or counterarguments which may have been expressed, but not necessarily recorded or accorded due weight, yet alone those other views which may not have been expressed. To chair such a discussion or control the minutes is thus to have a strong hand in creating a documentary reality.

Documentary analysis can focus on the analysis and classification of themes, keywords, and meanings. Generally this is done through selecting particular units of analysis, such as mention of important themes, and counting frequencies or occurrence of categories. This is part of a long research tradition of *content analysis* (Berelson, 1952; Holsti, 1969; Krippendorf, 1980; Scott, 1990; Weber, 1990, Robson, 1993). However, as indicated earlier, documentary analysis can employ many techniques and methods from discourse analysis, which essentially means seeing the document as a text in its social context. If the documents are held on a computer, or can be scanned in, the analysis can also use techniques of corpus linguistics, including *concordancing*, in which target words can be rapidly called up on screen in their sentence contexts to see their meanings and whether they are being used in different ways (Stubbs, 1996; Kennedy, 1998). Further approaches can be seen in on-line research and virtual ethnography based on Internet documents (Hine, 2000; Mann and Stewart, 2000), which can be particularly useful for researching current educational events and for getting international or cross-cultural perspectives.

Examples of narrative analysis

One of the best known models for analysing narratives is the socio-linguistically oriented model of Labov (Labov, 1972; Cortazzi, 1993; Linde, 1993). The model shows a narrative to have a structure with up to six elements:

- an *abstract* to summarise the point or state a general proposition which the narrative will exemplify;
- an *orientation* to give details of time, place, persons and situation;
- a *complication* to give the main event sequence and show a crisis, problem or turning point;
- an *evaluation* to highlight the social point of telling the story, marking this part out from the rest;
- a *result* to show a resolution to the complication; and
- a *coda* to finish the story.

These elements occur in various sequences and combinations. The evaluation can occur anywhere and it can overlap with the other parts, since it is a rhetorical underlining of the narrative's meaning.

The following brief example is a spontaneous anecdote told by a British primary teacher who was asked about the children in his classroom (Cortazzi, 1991).

> I've got quite a nice bunch at the moment. They've got a very nice sense of humour, **(A)**

> but one . . . I think it was one day last term I put a row of fossils out, animal fossils, **(O)**

> and I put '120 million years old'. **(C)**

And as one of the kids walked by he started, 'Happy birthday to you.' **(R)**

That's the sort of sense of humour they've got. It just sort of kills me, it kills me. **(E)**

The abstract (A) gives advance notice of the main point which the narrative will illustrate. The orientation (O) shows the time and circumstance: a display of fossils in the classroom with what is later seen as a complication (C), the teacher's written notice showing the age of the fossils. The result (R) or resolution recounts a child's spontaneous reaction to the notice by singing the 'Happy birthday' song, as if the notice had been a birthday greetings card. The evaluation (E) reiterates the main point, that this shows the children's sense of humour and that this incident characterises the class as a whole. Yet the story is not only about the children's humour; it emphasises the teacher's reaction to their humour which the teacher obviously enjoys as part of the teacher-class relationship, as shown by the colloquial, 'It kills me', which is evaluated by being repeated. The teacher, through the narrative, shows an appreciation of the children's humour and his enjoyment of it, but he does not simply report the child as singing — he actually sings as the child did. This re-enactment dramatises, but it does more: by imitating the child through narrative performance the teacher gives him credit and at the same time gets some himself, as a performer.

A second example comes from a study of racism and corporate discourse (van Dijk 1993: 152–153; the analysis is my own). A manager (M) of a Dutch supermarket recounted to an interviewer (I) how his board had agreed to allow Muslim cashiers to wear headscarves at work. He had previously denied that there was any discrimination among company personnel.

> M: I know one of our stores, where someone like that was offered by the employment agency, like, 'we have someone who could work for you, it is a fundamentalist Muslim who wears one of those scarves.' And then the store manager he got his personnel together, his own personnel in the canteen, and they had a discussion about that, shall we do it or won't we? Personnel said, 'Yes, what are we fussing about, it is so difficult to get people, and we can't bypass someone like that. That would be very stupid.' And he said, 'Let her come.' And she also worked at the cash register, and . . . the customers stayed away. They did not queue up at her cash, but at the others.

> I: Even after a while, when they got used to it?

M: Yes, and then, well, then they said ... and there was rather a big perceptible difference it was, a marked difference, for the other customers. Then the manager, who panicked, again got his employees together, and again had discussions about, come and have a look at what's happening. And again the employees said, 'We should not be put off, we go on with this, and then those women should stay away. We don't care', and then they persisted and after some time she got other, so there were other customers, I don't know, or the same customers, who went to her, and it was quite a bright girl, it was really a very good girl.

The manager concludes this story of his organisation's affirmative action and discrimination by explaining that the employee was extraordinarily friendly with the customers yet some customers threw the money on the floor instead of handing it to the cashier. Also she was still being taken to work by her father ('That was really quite a different culture'). He continues with a second episode about the store manager's effort to promote the cashier.

M: He wanted that she would go to work as a supervisor, because she was simply a very good girl. But then he really had to, because in that case she would have to be transferred to another store, but that man went to great lengths, also in these meetings with his personnel, with his supervisors to get this settled, that she would be transferred. Yes, and then she nearly had to be sanctified, and he got away with that, but what happens, as usual, she is taking a vacation in Turkey, stays away for 4 weeks, and she doesn't come back.

I: That is not exactly inspiring.

M: Yes, but you have to place yourself in the position of that manager, how he feels. Damn it! Then you think, then he thinks, he thinks, this is once, but never more. Why did I go through all this trouble? . . . That shows how it is a very difficult matter, and that it is also very difficult to have people accept using different values and norms, that it is a very slow process, that you have to do that very carefully, but at the same time not evade it.

Tellers evaluate, in their own terms, the principal people or institutions featuring in their narratives. Here, the company is portrayed as an equal opportunities employer which employs members of ethnic minority groups despite the actions of some racist customers. This is not simply stated but is demonstrated and dramatised through narrative. The store manager is presented positively as someone who faces predicaments of outsider discrimination against his staff and goes to some lengths to get good people from minorities promoted, yet finds it difficult to accept personnel from other cultures. The cashier's co-workers support the policy even when the manager panics. An extended analysis would relate this to other narratives of racism.

There are different voices in the story: we hear the corporate voice of the personnel manager and his staff, and the voice of the store manager who probably recounted events to personnel. The voice of the cashier is notably absent, and so are those of other employees and the customers. Ideally, we would collect their narrative versions of events to obtain more inside voices.

As to human feelings, the manager's panic, persistence, and frustration are shown, as are the supposed difficulties of putting policies into practice. Yet the story gives some, presumably unintended, insight into a lack of under-standing of religious customs (the cashier is 'a fundamentalist' who 'wears one of those scarves') and incomprehension (at the employee's failure to reap-pear). There is no indication of any understanding of the cashier's feelings. Apparently, the teller is reporting events in order to present a positive image of his company. The narrative is given as evidence in an argument to show social responsibility and openness to change, to show positive evaluations about company recruitment and promotion practices; any problems with this are imputed to outsiders (racist customers or people of a different culture). The account seems designed to give credibility and might enter manage-ment circles as an exemplar of trying to put policy into practice as a part of institutional identity. The story telling may somehow bolster the pro-fessional self of the teller (as person or as personnel) as may be seen in the slippage into his own and others' relayed attributions and personal inter-pretations ('fundamentalist', 'a very good girl', 'those women', 'as usual . . . she doesn't come back', 'Damn it! Then you think . . . this is once but never more').

This supermarket story could be briefly analysed as having the following gloss or cyclical structure of narrative elements:

A: This is an example of discrimination.
O: Hiring personnel in one of the supermarkets.
C1: One applicant is a Muslim 'fundamentalist' who wears a scarf.
R1: Personnel agreed to hire her; management allowed her to wear the scarf.
C2: Some customers avoided her; one threw money on the floor.
R2: Personnel decided to keep her and ignored discriminatory acts.
E1: She was a very good a friendly employee.
O2: The manager did his best to get her promoted.
C3: She went to Turkey and did not come back.
E2: The manager was very frustrated.
E3: It is very difficult to have personnel from another culture.

Further analysis might depend on more familiarity with the original context or on having access to other versions of the same incidents or on obtaining further stories of discrimination to detect other patterns of meaning.

The nature of narrative research

Such examples do not fully reveal the interactive nature of narratives, which in this respect differ from documentary data. Narratives are nearly always told to *someone*, and oral stories are nearly always *performed* to that person. Some narratives are indeed *jointly negotiated* with other speakers or hearers, even with interviewers. Thus interviewees often wonder what an interview is really for, and after answering will add, 'Is this the kind of thing you want?' or 'Is that any use?' Such checking reveals that interviewees often pay close attention to the interviewer's responses to glean clues about their own further replies. Since the interviewer's responses are rarely in the interview schedule, but are spontaneous reactions to narratives, comments and answers, many interviewers are not aware of their contribution to what is actually a jointly negotiated interactive text, even when they hear their own voices on a tape. Narratives are shaped by the on-going discourse and the teller's perception of what the audience knows or is interested in, and this shaping is often constructed during the telling itself. This suggests a need for reflexiveness, for the researcher to engage in self-critical reflection on one's own biases, preferences and presuppositions, and to critically inspect the whole research process.

This and the foregoing suggests a series of ten questions to ask about narratives in research (there are parallel questions about documents):

- What kinds of narrative are there?
- Why is the teller sharing a narrative?
- How do we compare narratives?
- How much context is needed to interpret a narrative, or does it contain its own context?
- What are the relations between the teller, the told, the audience and the researcher?
- How do we account for performance features in narratives?
- What model of narrative analysis is appropriate (there are at least forty)?
- How does the researcher know when interpretations of narratives and their evaluations are appropriate to what the teller means; and how does one check with the teller?
- How does the analysis represent meaning, voice and human qualities?
- What are the standards or criteria to judge narrative analyses?

Answers to the final question include: coherence, trustworthiness, plausibility, persuasiveness, generalisabilty, verisimilitude, reflexiveness, harmonisation with results from other data sources, and member validation (i.e., checking with the respondents).

Examples of documentary analysis

Documentary analysis can be used as a subsidiary form of research; for example to provide triangulation within a case study. Alternatively, it can be the major method. In one example of documentary analysis, Goodman (1997) examines annual committee reports of British schools of the early nineteenth century to show the ways in which women managed schools prior to the rise of technocratic or rational management and the consequences for those women when such practices were introduced. In another example, Placier (1998) analyses historical research to inform a contemporary study of American junior high schools but finds that some studies provide a limited or biased point of view in the documentary construction of history. In a third example, Hextall and Mahony (2000) examine the genesis of official documentation through processes and procedures of consultation with teachers in 1997, processes which were used to develop the British standards for qualified teacher status for newly trained teachers. They show that successive versions and drafts of the documents show signs of severe editing by officials and the suppression of some points of view as positive elements of teachers' responses were over-reported and criticisms were down-toned.

Smith (1999a) in studying the history of Maori women's education in nineteenth-century New Zealand, comments on the uses of old photographs, official records, and 'as told to' biographies. She observes that the historical documentary material requires oral narrative accounts from the indigenous participants to be understood; even the biographies distort these participants' perceptions and experiences, because the written versions (recorded by white outsiders as scribes) are edited into chronological sequences which were quite different from the original order of telling, obscuring the culture of expression of background and details in the tellers' presentations of their own lives and ignoring any reasons for the original order.

Researching culture and cultures of research

This last example raises issues relating to the culture of research. As did Smith (1999a), Brumble (1990) found that white researchers and editors imposed their own values on Native Americans telling their own life stories to make them conform to their own ideas of what an autobiography should be and how it should be told. Brumble cites an editor as concluding:

> Indian narrative style involves a repetition and a dwelling on unimportant details which confuse the white reader and make it hard to follow the story. Motives are never explained — emotional states are

summed up in such colourless phrases as 'I liked it'. For one not immersed in the culture, the real significance escapes. (1990: 80)

Clearly, this is collecting stories and generating data without taking the participants' views into account; it ignores the local culture. These respondents had their own views, however, on the researchers' motives:

they come here and they say they want to be my friend, then they go away and put down what I say in books and make a lot of money. (1990: 90)

Smith (1999b) argues that indigenous peoples may have their own research agendas and that to avoid cultural imperialism and preserve their identities they must research their own environments themselves, employing their own culturally appropriate research methods. In much documentary and narrative research, there is this larger framework of culture and ideology, of both the researched and the researchers, and this needs to be taken into account.

This, however, requires a double vision: that of the insider, with the participants' perceptions of educational meanings; and that of the outsider, with the academic community's conventions and the ability to interpret the research to audiences of readers in other cultural communities. A solution, adopted by Cortazzi and Jin (Cortazzi and Jin, 1996, 2001; Jin and Cortazzi, 1998), in their uses of narrative and visual ethnography to study classrooms in China, is for two researchers from different backgrounds (in this case British and Chinese) to work together to draw on the strength of their identities and cultures of research to work toward a research synergy.

For some learners of research the opposite can happen. Students from one culture often learn about research from those of other cultural traditions, and there are times when the two groups do not enter each other frameworks of research easily. This uneasy juxtapositioning of perceptions is shown in a narrative observation (author's data) of a new postgraduate student from the Middle East who had just heard a professor's lecture about various alternatives in research methodology. From the perspective of his academic culture, the student believed one method must be the right one, but that for some reason the professor was keeping the knowledge of this to himself. The following dialogue ensued, with the student (S) asking the professor (P) a series of questions. The professor was quite happy to be challenged but was puzzled by the inability of the student to understand his answers. Researchers would, of course, choose documentary or narrative analysis because these approaches match their research purposes: the classic question is what questions are you asking, why are they worth asking, and then (only) what approaches or method will help you to find the answers?

S: Which research method is the best?

P: Well, as I say, there are many different methods. Each method has advantages and each has disadvantages. You are asking the wrong question. You ought to be asking about which method is appropriate to a particular research situation or problem.

S: Well, which method is used in this department?

P: We use a lot of different methods. Different people use different methods for different purposes.

S: Well, which method do you use?

P: Lots of different methods. It depends on the research questions. There are different methods which are appropriate for different research questions.

S: But which method is the right one?

P: As I say, there isn't a right one. It depends on the research questions. What kind of research question do you have in mind? Your question is relatively absolute but my answer is absolutely relative.

In this exchange, the participants hear and understand each other's words but do not enter the framework of interpretation within which the words are uttered. In a discourse perspective and an ethnographic framework, we see documents and narratives as texts in their context of use, and we seek to understand them from the perspectives of the users and tellers, no matter what our own perspective might be. We seek to acquire a double vision: an inside view and an outside view.

References

Adler, S., Laney, J. and Packer, M. (1993) *Managing Women: Feminism and Power in Educational Management*, Buckingham: Open University Press.

Antikainen, A., Houtsonen, J., Huotelin, H. and Kauppila, J. (1996) *Living in a Learning Society: Life-histories, Identities and Education*, London: Falmer Press.

Armour, K. and Jones, R. (1998) *PE Teachers' Lives and Careers*, London: Falmer Press.

Atkinson, P. (1990) *The Ethnographic Imagination, textual constructions of reality*, London: Routledge.

Berelson, B. (1952) *Content Analysis in Communications Research*, New York: Free Press.

Brumble, H. D. (1990) *American Indian Autobiography*, Berkeley: University of California Press.

Caldas-Coulthard, C. and Coulthard, M. (eds.) (1996) *Texts and Practices: Readings in Critical Discourse Analysis*, London: Routledge.

Chimombo, M. P. F. and Roseberry, R. L. (1998) *The Power of Discourse: An Introduction to Discourse Analysis*, Mahwah, NJ: Lawrence Erlbaum Associates.

Cortazzi, M. (1991) *Primary Teaching: How it Is — a Narrative Account*, London: David Fulton.

Cortazzi, M. (1993) *Narrative Analysis*, London: Falmer Press.

Cortazzi, M. and Jin, L. (1996) 'Cultures of learning: language classrooms in China', in Coleman H. (ed.) *Society and the Language Classroom*, Cambridge: Cambridge University Press.

Cortazzi, M. and Jin. L. (2001) 'Large classes in China: "good" teachers and inter-action', in Watkins, D. A. and Biggs J. B. (eds.) *Teaching the Chinese Learner: Psychological and Pedagogical Perspectives*, Hong Kong: CERC/ACER.

Coulthard, M. (ed.) (1994) *Advances in Written Text Analysis*, London: Routledge.

Erben, M. (ed.) (1998) *Biography and Education: A Reader*, London: Falmer Press.

Fairclough, N. (1995) *Critical Discourse Analysis: The Critical Study of Language*, London: Longman.

Gee, J. P. (1999) *An Introduction to Discourse Analysis, Theory and Method*, London: Routledge.

Georgakopoulou, A. and Goutsos, D. (1997) *Discourse Analysis: An Introduction*, Edinburgh: Edinburgh University Press.

Golden-Biddle, K. and Locke, K. D. (1997) *Composing Qualitative Research*, Thousand Oaks, CA: Sage.

Goodman, J. (1997) 'A question of management style: women school governors, 1800–1862', *Gender and Education*, 9(2): 149–160.

Hatch, J. A. and Wisniewski, R. (eds.) (1995) *Life History and Narrative*, London: Falmer Press.

Hextall, I. and Mahony, P. (2000) 'Consultation and the management of consent: standards for qualified teacher status', *British Educational Research Journal*, 26(3): 323–342.

Hine, C. (2000) *Virtual Ethnography*, London: Sage.

Hoey, M. (2001) *Textual Interaction: An Introduction to Written Discourse Analysis*, London: Routledge.

Holsti, O. R. (1969) *Content Analysis for Social Science and Humanities*, Reading, MA: Addison-Wesley.

Huberman, M. (1993) *The Lives of Teachers*, London: Cassell.

Jalongo, M. R., Isenberg, J. P. and Gerbracht, G. (1995) *Teachers' Stories: From Personal Narrative to Professional Insight*, San Francisco: Jossey-Bass.

Jaworski, A. and Coupland, N. (eds.) (1999) *The Discourse Reader*, London: Routledge.

Jin, L. and Cortazzi, M. (1998) 'Dimensions of dialogue: large classes in China', *International Journal of Educational Research*, 29: 739–761.

Kennedy, G. (1998) *An Introduction to Corpus Linguistics*, London: Longman.

Krippendorf, K. (1980) *Content Analysis: An Introduction to its Methodology*, London: Sage.

Labov, W. (1972) 'The transformation of experience in narrative syntax', in Labov, W. *Language in the Inner City*, Philadelphia, PA: University of Pennsylvania Press.

Lieblich, A., Tuval-Mashiach, R. and Zilber, T. (1998) *Narrative Research: Reading, Analysis, and Interpretation*, Thousand Oaks, CA: Sage.

Linde, C. (1993) *Life Stories: The Creation of Coherence*, New York: Oxford University Press.

Mann, C. and Stewart, F. (2000) *Internet Communication and Qualitative Research: A Handbook for Researching Online*, London: Sage.

McEwan, H. and Egan, K. (eds.) (1995) *Narrative in Teaching, Learning, and Research*, New York: Teachers College Press.

McLaughlin, D. and Tierney, W. G. (eds.) (1993) *Naming Silenced Lives, Personal*

Narratives and Processes of Educational Change, New York: Routledge.

Munro, P. (1998) *Subject to Fiction: Women Teachers' Life History Narratives and the Cultural Politics of Resistance*, Buckingham: Open University Press.

Nelson, M. H. (1993) *Teacher Stories: Teaching Archetypes Revealed by Analysis*, Ann Arbor, MI: Prakken Publications.

Osler, A. (1997) *The Education and Careers of Black Teachers*, Buckingham: Open University Press.

Placier, M. (1998) 'Uses of history in present-day qualitative studies of schools: the case of the junior high school', *Qualitative Studies in Education*, 11(2): 303–322.

Polkinghorne, D. E. (1988) *Narrative Knowing and the Human Sciences*, New York: State University of New York Press.

Ribbins, P. and Marland, M. (1994) *Headship Matters*, Harlow: Longman.

Riessman, C. K. (1993) *Narrative Analysis*, Newbury Park, CA: Sage.

Robson, C. (1993) *Real World Research: a Resource for Social Scientists and Practioner-researchers*, Oxford: Blackwell.

Scott, J. (1990) *A Matter of Record*, Cambridge: Polity Press.

Smith, L. T. (1999a) 'Connecting pieces: finding the indigenous presence in the history of women's education', in Weiler, K. and Middleton, S. (eds.) *Telling Women's Lives: Narrative Enquiries in the History of Women's Education*, Buckingham: Open University Press.

Smith, L. T. (1999b) *Decolonising Methodologies: Research and Indigenous Peoples*, London: Zed Books.

Stubbs, M. (1996) *Text and Corpus Analysis: Computer-assisted Studies of Language and Culture*, Oxford: Blackwell.

Thomas, D. (1995) *Teacher's Stories*, Buckingham: Open University Press.

Titscher, S., Meyer, M., Wodak, R. and Vetter, E. (2000) *Methods of Text and Discourse Analysis*, London: Sage.

Trimmer, J. F. (ed.) (1997) *Narration as Knowledge: Tales of the Teaching Life*, Portsmouth, NH: Boynton/Cook.

van Dijk, T. A. (1993) *Elite Discourse and Racism*, Newbury Park, CA: Sage.

van Dijk, T. A. (ed.) (1997a) *Discourse as Structure and Process: Discourse Studies — A Multidisciplinary Introduction*, vol. 1, London: Sage.

van Dijk, T. A. (ed.) (1997b) *Discourse as Social Interaction: Discourse Studies — A Multidisciplinary Introduction*, vol. 2, London: Sage.

van Maanen, J. (1988) *Tales of the Field: On Writing Ethnography*, Chicago: University of Chicago Press.

Walcott, H.F. (2001) *Writing Up Qualitative Research* (2nd edn.), Thousand Oaks, CA: Sage.

Weber, R.P. (1990) *Basic Content Analysis* (2nd edn.), London: Sage.

Weiler, K. and Middleton, S. (eds.) (1999) *Telling Women's Lives: Narrative Enquiries in the History of Women's Education*, Buckingham: Open University Press.

Witherell, C. and Noddings, N. (eds.) (1991) *Stories Lives Tell: Narrative and Dialogue in Education*, New York: Teachers College Press.

Wood, L. and Kroger, R.O. (2000) *Doing Discourse Analysis: Methods for Studying Action in Talk and Text*, Thousand Oaks, CA: Sage.

13
Using diaries in research

Marlene Morrison[*]

Introduction

Diaries are among a wide and often complex array of documentary materials that may be of interest to researchers in the field of educational management and leadership (see Figure 13.1). While personal chronicling and self-narratives have long and distinguished histories, their use in research is more recent. This chapter focuses upon diary-focused research as a distinctive genre that straddles both quantitative and qualitative approaches. Diary-keepers are either researchers or research participants or both. For the purposes of this chapter, diary keeping is seen, in process and outcomes, as essentially social, even though historic or romantic associations with the term might be to view diaries as intimate or personal (Morrison and Galloway, 1996). Much of the attention in this chapter is given to diary use by research participants, and to diaries that are solicited rather than unsolicited accounts (for the latter, Scott (1990) provides a useful framework).

However, initial attention is also given to the importance of diaries for researchers, especially qualitative researchers, for whom diaries are more than procedural tools for managing and documenting research stages (important though this is for all research) but are also integral to the production of the analytic record 'that underpins the conceptual development and density' (Strauss, 1987: 5) featured in qualitative accounts of educational experience. The discussions that follow are not exhaustive. Researchers in educational management and leadership, for example, will always need to recognise that the potential contributions of diaries, and roles for diarists, may disguise important differences in meaning and use depending upon cultural contexts, discussed elsewhere in this volume (see Chapters 2 and 12).

[*]I would like to record my thanks to Dr. Sheila Galloway, Senior Research Fellow at the Centre for Educational Development Appraisal and Research, University of Warwick, a long time colleague and friend with whom I have shared valuable and formative insights about the intentions and purposes of diaries in educational settings.

Q. How might primary school managers improve the effectiveness of temporary (supply) teacher use in school?

Time	Main activities	Other activities
13.00	Children in. Did register. Didn't tally. Incorrect from morning! Took ages to sort out; some children's names difficult to pronounce. Register not very clear. Need to be accurate for swimming.	A mum came with me. — an older lady — very nice but not very effective. Very noisy in changing areas. I was dotting from one to to the other.
13.20	Eventually set off. Took a while to get as kept starting and stopping. Worn out when I arrived!	
14.00	Eventually we got there down to the pool instructor. He took the more able group — leaving me alone with 20 children in a small pool. We worked hard but they didn't tire. Changing took ages. Walked back after a great lecture from me. Got back 14.40. Too late for play.	I have never felt so worn out after swimming. Only I had to get out of the water for a a short while. Miracles never cease.
15.00	I kept them out for 10 min. play while I had a drink. An ESN teacher took a group for reading. I let rest finish off any Work then get an activity while I heard Readers. Behaviour improving.	Didn't think they'd settle to a story and they hadn't read all week.
15.30	Dismiss children. Write note for teacher.	Dep. wished I was going back as I'd controlled class.

Q. What was the most demanding task or situation you had to deal with today? Any additional comment on today's activities?

A. Swimming — very dangerous situation — particularly at the baths. 1:20. Ridiculous.

(Morrison and Galloway, 1996: 50)

Figure 13.1 A diary extract: a supply teacher's afternoon

Researchers' diaries

Until recently, published references to diaries referred mainly to their importance for researchers (Burgess 1981; 1984). Diaries kept by researchers are examples of documentary evidence that can be used for a range of purposes. In earlier accounts, distinctions are made between logs, diaries and journals. Holly (1984; 1989) differentiates between a log — a truncated record of information that relates to specific situations, rather like an aide-mémoire —

and a diary, which is seen to contain more 'personal' information, and includes interpretation as well as description 'on multiple dimensions' (1984: p.5). According to Holly, journals, a third form of research record, are carefully structured to combine both objective notes and free-flowing accounts. As Burgess (1994) suggests, these distinctions are probably more useful analytically than in practice, since the umbrella term — 'diary' — can frequently comprise substantive, methodological and analytic elements, as in the case of Griffiths (1985) who recorded distinctive elements of his work as 'Diary 1'and 'Diary 2'.

A diary or log serves a range of elementary yet critical purposes for the researcher. It provides a tool for charting both progress and critical research moments. These can be plotted against the planning checklist agreed among the research team, or with the research supervisor. It might, for example, include contact dates with the supervisor or research team, and chart agreement and progress on the tasks and targets for the research.

For the qualitative researcher, the diary performs a range of functions. Burgess (1981; 1984) focused on the principles that are associated with it, raising questions about the recording and categorising of data, and the issue of inclusion or otherwise of diary data in the final account.

Of course, not every researcher has the time, resources, or the epistemological 'will' to record in the depth and detail deployed by Okely (1994), for example. The brief extract below gives some sense of a daily journal that often consumed a whole notebook per day. Her approach is in the traditional anthropological tradition:

> With minimal success, I had combed the anthropological . . . literature for guidance and reassurance in the face of increasing scepticism among my employers about non-questionnaire research. Then a chance meeting with the African anthropologist Malcolm Mcleod afforded me the best and only detailed methodological advice I was to find at the outset of fieldwork. From his experience, he suggested 'write down everything you hear, smell, and see; even the colour of the carpets. . . . Ideally you should fill an exercise book each day.' So I jettisoned my earlier, increasingly unsatisfactory attempts at writing notes under prescribed headings. I had been deciding what was relevant and in the process omitting other details, possibly for ever. My notes took the form of a chronological diary . . . Events were written up as soon as possible . . . Ideas, tentative interpretations and dominant themes were also written in the text, as the field experience developed . . . As both fieldworker and future author, I was free to allow the ideas to germinate in their own time, and through my thinking, not by proxy. Subsequent participant observation and extended contemplation would sort the wheat from the chaff. (1994: 23–24)

This extract raises at least two questions: How structured should the researcher's diary be? And what role will the diary 'jottings' play in the analysis of data and in the final report/dissertation/thesis?

Okely's account appears to be at one end of a diary continuum that extends from a mainly free-flowing account to a highly structured summary of timed events using specific headings. From my earliest experiences as a researcher, I have kept a diary for every project in which I have been involved; a diary whose format and style straddle the middle of the continuum introduced above. Basically, they comprise three columns. Column 1 is a daily record of all events, frequently substantive, sometimes methodological, and usually completed at the end the day; column 2 is used for analytic memos, records emerging themes and ideas, and poses questions; while column 3 is used for retrospection and introspection (what I call the R and I column). This provides an opportunity to note and refine ideas and thoughts after time has elapsed from the original diary entry. The diary with its columns was kept in an exercise book but it is now stored as a computer file. Most recently, software packages for qualitative data analysis provide further opportunities for the enthusiastic diarist. None of the above is meant to imply that the diary is ever a complete record, or a neutral medium of production, or that it will remain unaffected by other writing and reading that is part of the qualitative research process (see also Atkinson, 1992).

Miles and Huberman (1994: Chapter 4) sound a note of caution for researchers new to qualitative studies, and argue strongly against allowing any data, including diary data, to accumulate over weeks and months without engaging in early analysis of that data:

> Some qualitative researchers put primary energy into data collection for weeks, months, even years and then retire from the field 'to sort out their notes'. We believe this is a mistake. It rules out the possibility of collecting new data to fill in the gaps, or to test new hypotheses that emerge during analysis. It discourages the formulation of 'rival hypotheses' that question a field-worker's routine assumptions and biases. And it makes analysis into a giant, sometimes overwhelming, task that demotivates the researcher and reduces the quality of the work produced. (1994: 50)

Researchers' diaries have been utilised as important elements of action research, where the diary may be seen as an important tool for reflection and as a vehicle for the provocation of personal and professional change, as for example in Walker (1988), a study of general practitioner trainees. In combination with other forms of data such as interviews, photographs, and video records, etc., diary data can also make an important contribution to ethnographic accounts of educational experience.

For example, Burgess and Morrison (1998) conducted a project between 1993 and 1994 that investigated the ways in which adults, children, and young people in English primary and secondary schools experienced food and eating. It formed part of a larger ESRC programme entitled *The Nation's Diet: the Social Science of Food Choice* (Burgess and Morrison, 1998). Recommendations were for educationists (policy makers and practitioners), nutritionists, and sociologists, and the methodological approach was ethnographic. As the principle researcher, Morrison (1995) spent a term in each of four schools, observing the institutional dynamics of food and eating in a range of formal and informal settings for teaching and learning: classrooms, dining halls, playgrounds, school corridors, journeys to and from school, neighbouring ice-cream vans and chip shops. Events were recorded daily in diary form and some diary extracts were published, both in the final report and subsequently. In the following example, the data from the diary is used illustratively to inform readers about lunch-time eating experiences in a school:

Monday
Today 365 £1 purchases have been recorded by the canteen supervisor. Am told by several members of staff during first break that it's like a zoo in there [the dining hall]. First day's observation supports that impression. Children are literally herded to the hatch in groups. When queuing gets unmanageable students are sent outside and return when it appears to be quieter. Dinner ladies' role appears to be one of gatekeeping: keeping out, letting in in batches. Food eaten is a nutritionist's nightmare. Most children eat cake and chips. The most popular combination is cake, chips, and a packet of tomato ketchup.

Thursday
Those in receipt of FSM [free school meals] are not checked to see what they purchase, so chips in combination with three or four cakes is not uncommon. There is a shortage of knives and forks, and no water. Cheap coloured drinks are very popular. Latest habit appears to be to ignore the straw supplied with drinks, turn the carton upside down, suck plastic carton, tear into with teeth, and suck contents from the resultant tear. Interesting noises! Some pupils leave the dining hall with half eaten purchases. Two observed with bags of chips in coat pockets. (1995: 246)

In such ways, ethnographic accounts using diaries illustrated ways in which schools are important arenas for assessing the ambiguities and contradictions of food consumption which are features of adult populations, and which, for a variety of reasons, Morrison found replicated in learning environments.

Having introduced aspects of the usefulness of diaries for researchers, the chapter now turns to diary keeping by research informants as tools for data collection and analysis.

Research informants' diaries

As do all personal accounts, diaries exhibit the strengths and weaknesses of information that is solicited from research informants: 'they are partial, and reflect the interests and perspectives of their authors' (Hammersley and Atkinson, 1995: 165). In educational research, where there may have been a tendency to privilege both the 'oral' and the 'observed' — what people say they do and what they are observed doing — over the literate, diaries provide an interesting counterpoint, since diarists are invited to write what they do and/or think. Whether or not this is because we tend to assume that 'the spoken account is more "authentic" or "spontaneous" than the written account'(1995: 165), diaries have specific uses in 'picking up' the minutiae of vicarious educational experience in ways which the other major form of solicited written information, questionnaires, do not. However, even this brief introduction suggests a view of diaries as rather traditional, paper-bound instruments. Diary research now links to recent literary styles of development, and advances in recording diary information such as audio-visual, or through developments in the use of electronic diaries (Saris, 1989) and schema for coding sensitive information (Coxon *et al.*, 1992). Further technological developments include qualitative software packages that have allowed diary data to be considered alongside other forms of data analysis. Diaries are used in a wide variety of contexts, formats and styles; they can also be both large-scale and highly structured (Gershuny *et al.*, 1986).

Whatever forms diaries take, a number of fundamental assumptions about diary keeping need to be considered.

- Diaries rest on the view that research informants are in especially advantageous positions to record aspects of their lives and work. Such a perspective does more than extol the virtue of self-report. Implicit in this statement are interpretive ideas discussed in the first chapter of this book, namely, that participants in education are social actors who, through personal logs and reports, make available 'inside' information that might not otherwise be available or visible to the researcher.
- Diaries allow researchers access to evidence that may not be otherwise available to the researchers, whether on *logistical* (researchers cannot be everywhere) or *ethical* (researchers should not be everywhere) or *pragmatic* (researchers need to be elsewhere) grounds. The extent to which diary data constitutes 'substitute observation' (Morrison and Galloway, 1996) might be seen as a challenge for diary design and use (see below).
- Combined with other forms of data collection and analysis, diaries are

based on a premise, shared by both qualitative and quantitative research, that the researcher can collect, aggregate, collate, and analyse diary records, in order to produce a wider and/or deeper picture of what educational experience means to groups, as well as to individuals.

• Diary accounts have the potential to produce large amounts of data. Researchers need, therefore, to convince themselves, as well as potential diarists, that the activity is worthwhile and for specific educational purposes, and to reach agreement with diarists about which aspects of individuals' lives that will be open to public scrutiny, and in what forms. Simultaneously, researchers need to be very clear about *why* they are inviting diary participation; from the planning stage, this extends to knowledge about how the data is going to be analysed and includes how, and when, analytic categories and codes are to be assigned.

Diary designs

Diaries can be used qualitatively and quantitatively to illuminate a range of educational issues. For interpretive as well as 'action' researchers, who may be encouraged to complete diaries as personal accounts, reflections, or confessionals about daily experience, the notion of designing diaries might seem 'a contradiction in terms' (see also Galloway and Morrison, forthcoming). This means that researchers need to design diaries that maximise their usefulness in relation to the research topic and the main questions to be addressed:

> Diary booklets or proforma need to suit the contexts and the ways in which diary data are expected to articulate with data from other sources. Written and oral instructions for use will probably need reinforcement by personal contact during the data collection period ... Ostensibly a relatively low cost method of collecting data, obtaining agreement, briefing diary-writers (sometimes individually), and making progress calls are tasks requiring research time to be adequately costed. (Galloway and Morrison, forthcoming)

Some published guidance on the use of diaries appears to narrow the focus to specific, limited uses. For example, Bell (1999) asserts that diaries:

> are not records of engagements or personal journals of thoughts and activities, [Why not?] but rather logs of professional activities ... Do you really want to know that someone had a cup of tea, paid the milkman, or had a bath, [You might need to ... it depends on the research problem] or are you only interested in professionally related activities [perhaps]? (1999: 148–149; the insertions are mine)

Surely the key issue is the need for clarity about the research problem addressed, and its relation to diary use? If the core intention, for example, is to examine the ways in which school departmental and faculty heads manage time for professional activities (Earley and Fletcher-Campbell, 1989), then the use of a timed weekly log of professional activities seems apt. But if the purpose of the research is to investigate the ways in which managers, teachers, and/or students make connections between the public and private spheres of their lives, then the times afforded to personal hygiene, refreshments, and shopping might take on a specific significance, and should therefore be included.

Part of the rationale for using diaries proposed (Galloway and Morrison, 1993 discussed in Morrison and Galloway 1996: 35) in a project entitled 'Supply teaching: An Investigation of Policy, Processes and People', was 'to make connections between private and public aspects of supply teachers' lives which showed infinite variation' (Morrison and Galloway, 1996: 35). Earlier, Morrison had used diaries as a way of exploring how mature women students, who entered a college of education after a lengthy period of non-participation in education, managed to 'juggle' study with paid and unpaid work such as child-rearing, and with leisure activities (Morrison, 1996; see below).

Design challenges

Diarists are usually invited to complete diaries over specified time periods. Because diaries are time-consuming, instructions to accompany diaries, and the layout and appearance of the diary 'booklet' may take on a specific significance. Ultimately, diaries have the potential to become onerous; tendencies to non-completion are, therefore, only partially overcome by meticulous attention to cosmetic appearance and clear instructions.

Large-scale time budget studies have used diaries in leisure research, and the investigation of household work strategies and the sexual division of labour. Diary surveys feature in studies of food purchase and consumption choices and in investigation of income and financial matters among individuals and households. The period covered is usually either one or seven consecutive days; but two-to-four non-consecutive day diaries and part-day diaries are also possible. For both qualitative and quantitative purposes 'time slots' in the diary can be open or fixed and activity categories precoded or open. Gershuny *et al.* (1986) describe the 'Szalai' system devised in the 1960s (with 190 activity codes) as a *de facto* standard for time budget surveys (Szalai, 1972).

The choice of format is rarely straightforward. A large-scale, one-day survey of the distribution of activities in a population might be very useful descriptively, but less useful interpretively than diary surveys over a longer period. Researchers have used seven-day time frames, aware that 'time budget researchers who wish to improve the quality of their estimates have an alternative to increasing their sample size; they can increase the period covered by the research instrument' (Gershuny *et al.*, 1986: 18).

Large-scale designs of this kind are clearly not an option for the single-handed researcher. But some of the challenges remain similar. Objections to diaries of longer duration are that agreements to participate become more difficult to secure, and the quality and rate of response may vary and/or decline. The propensity to respond may vary at different times in the day/night, and the gap between the event and its record and interpretation by the diarist may widen. All this suggests that research design for small- or large-scale use of diaries must accommodate practical constraints. Earley and Fletcher-Campbell (1989) used weekly diaries to investigate educational management but, recognising how these encroached on time, excluded diary-writers from other elements of their research.

Illustrative examples

Studying time

Researchers have used diaries as an instrument for investigating time, to locate individuals 'in time', and to pursue experience and the passage of time, specifically during *transitions* in the life, work, or study cycles of educators and students. Bradley and Eggleston (1976) used diaries in their study of probationer teachers who were asked to keep weekly diaries on three separate occasions during the term. Such an approach might be adapted for studies about the professional activities of newly appointed heads or those aspiring to headship, for example, or in studies of transitions from careers in educational leadership to retirement.

As introduced earlier, Morrison (1996) used informant diaries to study the gendered experience of mature women returning to study in a college of further education after a long period of absence. The resultant analysis formed the basis for recommendations to college managers about how qualitative improvements in the experience of study time at college, that was, for students, part of an ongoing negotiation between study, work, family, and leisure time, might improve both student retention and examination success rates. Diaries were based on a similar format to that shown as Figure 13.1 at the beginning of this chapter. The three columns in the format used denoted 'Time', 'Main activities' and 'Other activities' respectively. The time column addressed the 'When?' question; this included the timing of daily activities (from 7 am to 10 pm for up to 10 days) and the sequencing in which activities occurred. Responses in the two remaining columns addressed, in part, the 'What?' question; in other words, the diarists' descriptions of the activities in which they were engaged. As importantly, these two columns were also designed to address a thematic issue that was emerging from the preliminary data, namely women students' repeated references to the need to 'juggle' time. Thus respondents were asked to describe what they considered to be the main activity of the time period, and to give a description in 'their own terms' about what activities, if any, they considered to be 'other' or supplementary during that period. Findings revealed that 'studying' activities occurred simultaneously with activities like cooking, ironing, loading the washing machine, and listening to children read. It was possible to plot the times when study was considered to be the main or only activity (usually on college premises), when it was combined with other activities, and the priority given to study (or not) at specific times of the day, or on specific days. Instructions to answer the question 'What?' were not infrequently extended by the diarists to address the question 'Why?'; this supports earlier comments about the mixing of description and interpretation (Holly, 1984) that the act of diary writing often evokes. This provided added insights about how mature women students defined 'wasting', 'worrying', and 'waiting' time(s). Unexpectedly, the diary also revealed a range of understandings about what the word 'study' meant; for some students, 'reading' was relegated as a study activity which lacked status because it did not entail the act of 'doing'; open-ended suggestions from tutors 'to read', for example, could be construed as 'wasting' time when there were 'more important' things to do, like writing an essay, cooking dinner, or collecting children from school.

A 'substitute' for observation

Researching supply teaching, diary accounts were used by Galloway and Morrison to investigate supply work in schools, a phenomenon that is both ordinary (occurring frequently, if irregularly), and extraordinary, in that it sometimes brings into schools teachers who are total strangers to the pupils for whom they are fleetingly responsible (Galloway, 1993). Explaining the mechanics of diary use, they comment:

> Seventeen supply teachers completed diaries, enabling experience to be tracked in detail. The selection did not purport to be a representative sample; rather they exemplified a range of different situations pertaining to individuals doing supply work *that went beyond what researchers could observe given the practical constraints affecting the field work*. In total, diaries provided data on eighty days to support that being obtained elsewhere. However, unlike interviewing (where self-report sometimes occurs over a lengthy time span), daily accounts would add an immediate and alternative dimension to verbal accounts of experience. (Morrison and Galloway, 1996: 37; my emphasis).

Previous writers have used diaries as a 'observational log, maintained by sub-

jects which can then be used as the basis for intensive interviewing'
(Zimmerman and Wieder, 1977: 481). Not only do Morrison and Galloway
(1996) give detailed attention to the extent to which 'writing about experience adds an element of artificiality and superficiality to already complex
features of data recording in "natural settings" ' (1996: 41) they also caution against simplistic assumptions about diary data as a substitute for observation by the researcher. On occasion, diary accounts *were* at variance with
observations recorded by researchers. (In other circumstances, Oppenheim
(1966) has noted the tendency either for diarists to record what they think
researchers will wish to read, or amend 'usual' behaviour during the recording period.) In this sense, diaries share the strengths and weaknesses of all
forms of self-report. In the supply teaching example, in place of statistically
representative information, the semi-structured diary method provided the
research informant with opportunities to represent varied experience, and,
for the research team, afforded 'glimpses of the infinite variety of life as the
stop-gap teacher' (1996: 45).

Pupils' diaries

So far, all examples of diary use have considered diary accounts solicited
from adults. In studying food and eating in schools, Burgess and Morrison
(1995; Burgess 1994) designed diaries to be used by primary school pupils.
It was important for Morrison, the principal researcher, to talk with pupils
about what needed to be done and to design a booklet that was both appropriate and attractive to children. Diary keeping was restricted to one week,
including a weekend, and a cover letter inside the diary, signed by the
researcher, was addressed personally to each child (Figure 13.2).

As Bell (1999: 150) comments: 'diarists must be at a certain educational
level to understand the instructions, let alone complete the diary'. The
method poses questions about the capacity of a mixed ability group to articulate a written record at similar levels of detail. Yet, the main challenge of
the approach pertained to the wide variety of responses evoked. In Figure
13.3 two extracts (also noted in Burgess, 1994) illustrate how two pupils
(among 60 respondents) interpret the instructions for diary use differently.

Qualitatively, 60 diaries produced a rich source of data about children's
lives, but as the extracts suggest, they also presented challenges. The first
diary entry is a kind of free-flowing account; the second treats each of the
questions raised in the introductory letter from the researcher as topics to
be answered, albeit briefly, and maintains this style throughout the week. In
particular, the extracts illustrate challenges in comparing data across diaries,
an important issue if the research intentions are to trace the use of time for
eating, for example; or the extent to which children exercised 'choice' in the
selection of foods they record as having eaten. Readers might also wish to

---

Dear [name of pupil]

A FOOD AND DRINK DIARY

I hope you will help me. I am a researcher who would like to know more about what children eat and drink. If you write in this diary, it will help me to know more.

So, next MONDAY, TUESDAY, WEDNESDAY, THURSDAY, FRIDAY, SATURDAY, AND SUNDAY, please write in your diary. It may help you to write if you think about answering these questions:

WHAT DID YOU EAT AND DRINK TODAY?

WHEN DID YOU EAT AND DRINK TODAY?

WHERE DID YOU EAT AND DRINK TODAY? (at SCHOOL,HOME, SOMEWHERE ELSE?)

DID YOU GO ON A VISIT and EAT THERE?

DID YOU ENJOY A CELEBRATION? (like BIRTHDAY or ANNIVERSARY)

DID YOU LIKE WHAT YOU ATE AND DRANK?

PLEASE WRITE ABOUT HOW YOU FELT.

Thank you very much for your help. Please return the diary to school after seven days.

Yours sincerely

Marlene Morrison
Research Fellow

(Burgess and Morrison, 1995: Appendix)

Figure 13.2 Diary instructions: sample letter

consider the extent to which diaries pose ethical issues in terms of the level of intrusion into the lives of the diarists and their families; in this case, as for all diary keeping, intentions and purposes for use needed to be clear. Ethical issues for research are also featured in Chapter 5.

Critical incidents, problem portfolios, and new possibilities: the 'shared' diary

Of key interest to researchers of educational management and leadership, is the need to understand effective ways of managing. Understanding needs to extend beyond the use of time for professional activities on a daily or weekly basis, and to include interest in how managers decide what it is more (or less) important that they give their attention (or time) to. Bell (1999: 151–153) records a range of approaches that have been applied in the area of educational management.

An investigation by Oxtoby (1979) focused on the ways in which heads

---

Diary extract 1 21/6/93
Today at dinner time I ate sandwiches, a chocolate, crisps and drank some coke. In the morning I drank some tea. When I came back from school I ate rice pudding, chappati, and curry. Then later some fruit. I ate in the morning and in the afternoon and at night. I ate at Birmingham museum and at home. At dinner time I ate with my friends, and in the morning and at night I ate with my family. I went on a visit and ate there. No, I did not enjoy a celebration. Yes I did like what I ate and drank today. I felt very hungry today.

Diary extract 2 Monday 21st June 1993
1)   Today I ate 2 turkey batches, crisps and a bottle of pop.
2)   I ate and drank at dinner time.
3)   I ate and drank somewhere else.
4)   I ate with my friends.
5)   Yes.
6)   Yes.
7)   I liked what I ate and drank.
8)   I enjoyed eating and drinking.

(see also Burgess,1994)

Figure 13.3 Children's diaries: sample entry

of department sifted the more significant aspects of their jobs from the more trivial ones. He writes:

> The critical incident approach is an attempt to identify the more 'noteworthy' aspects of job behaviour and is based on the assumption that jobs are composed of critical and non-critical tasks ... The idea is to collect reports as to what people do that is particularly effective in contributing to good performance and then to scale the incidents in order of difficulty, frequency, and importance to the job as a whole. The technique scores over the use of diaries in that it is centred on specific happenings, and what is judged to be effective behaviour. (1979: 240)

Marples' (1967) use of 'problem portfolios' that record 'information about how each [management] problem arose, methods used to solve it and so on', is further recommended by Oxtoby (1979) because, he argues, it maximises the usefulness of self-report whilst minimising the 'weaknesses' of the diary method — its 'time-consuming' and 'trivial aspects'. His strong positivist leanings are also apparent; concern about the absence of 'objective quantification' in diaries and 'critical incidents' (Oxtoby, 1979) is partly overcome by the potential for the statistical analysis of problem solving that 'problem portfolios' provide.

More recently, 'shared' or group diaries have been suggested for research into educational management issues. Burgess (1994) suggests that 'diary groups' at school senior management level offer the potential to share day-to-day practice. For a different purpose, Galloway *et al.* (1995) employed a hybrid diary/log to investigate the use of interactive video in educational and training institutions. Diary booklets attached to workstations invited users to record date, time and place used, start and finish times, software used, and whether the equipment was used by a group, on a course, or individually. Given space for more qualitative comment on their experience, numerous contributors made entries: some minimal, others more extended reflections. 'The assumption is that a diary has one author and represents one perspective, but a hybrid version like this can effectively serve several research purposes' (Galloway and Morrison, forthcoming).

Diary data analysis

Theoretical emphases affect how diaries are analysed. Diarists are creators of written texts that are open to descriptive or perspective analysis (Purvis, 1984). In the case of descriptive analysis, diary keepers are 'witnesses' to the educational phenomena of interest to the researcher. But diary data can also be used as representative indicators of the perspectives of the group to which the writer belongs. In descriptive analysis, the diary's accuracy is centrally important; in perspective analysis, its contribution lies less in its 'truthfulness' and more in the representativeness of the category to which the diarist is assigned. Analytically distinct, the two types of analysis are potentially complementary.

Like any document, diaries can be considered in terms of 'authenticity, representativeness, credibility, and meaning' (May, 1993: 144). As with data collection, data analysis can take qualitative or quantitative forms; the balance of concerns may differ between approaches, but the essential components remain the text, the audience and the diarist.

Content analysis may be quantitative or qualitative with computer analysis of diary records becoming more commonplace, examining, for example, the frequency with which certain phrases and words appear in the diary text. Quantitative analysts derive categories from the data in order to compare and count them. In the context of diaries, research priority goes to what is written rather than the decisions and situations that inform the writing. Qualitative data analysis views diary writing as a process or construct in which diary-writers address potential and actual readers. 'Reading' of the text accompanies consideration of data from secondary sources, interviews, and observation. Some research accounts of diaries focus increasingly on complementary use of both quantitative and qualitative approaches (for example, Marsh and Gershuny, 1991) on work history data in a publication that attempts to bridge the quantitative-qualitative divide (Dex, 1991).

Diary design must consider how diaries will feature in the final report.

Platt's (1981) advice on the presentation of findings from documents is instructive, especially her suggestion for a clear enunciation of the role of diaries from the outset, and the use of diary extracts as illustrative data for general themes emerging from the research overall. For large numbers, sampling and coding procedures need explanation. In ethnographic and case study research, the sources and reasons for selecting diaries and diarists need to be clearly articulated (Morrison and Galloway, 1996).

Combining diaries and diary interviews

While diary use has been advocated as a means of obtaining information that might not be readily available from an initial face-to-face interview or by means of observation, readers will be also have become aware that diaries are rarely used alone. Rather, diaries are frequently used in combination with interviews. At first sight, this appears to be a rather uneasy combination of a form of 'mute evidence' which 'endures physically and thus can be separated across space and time from its author, producer or user' (Hodder, 1994: 393); and the interview, which might be seen as a more 'spontaneous' form of verbal interaction.

Researchers choose these strategies to gain data that will help understand and explain educational phenomena. Interviews prior to diary-writing explain the purpose of the exercise, reinforcing the agreement to participate. The commitment required of diary writers *demands* an initial face-to-face approach. Indeed, mid-diary progress interviews may also be necessary in order to maintain momentum and commitment on the part of diarists. Post-diary interviews use diary data to explore issues in greater depth.

Both pre- and post-diary interviews were essential elements in the qualitative study of substitute teaching (Morrison and Galloway, 1996) referred to elsewhere in this chapter. Planned and unplanned meetings in the field probably encouraged diary-writers; scheduled diary-interviews and telephone contact undoubtedly sustained commitment.

Post-diary interviews allow matters recorded briefly, as they happen, to be retrospectively discussed in detail (Burgess, 1984). Fuller, more reflective styles of recording offer a rich seam to be mined in interview (Galloway and Morrison, forthcoming). The extent to which the diary method risks becoming intrusive and/or unduly time-consuming has already been noted: post-diary interviews exacerbate this and important ethical questions also arise. Research compromises balance, breadth, and depth of information against the degree of intrusion into private as well as public areas.

Diary accounts stimulate additional explanation and data. Studying counter-culture life-styles, Zimmerman and Wieder (1977) used seven-day diaries as a basis for individuals to talk about: 'less directly observable features of the events recorded, of their meanings, their propriety, typicality, connection with other events' (1977: 484). The diary method gives some access to events that researchers cannot personally record, whilst post-diary interviews produce even richer data. Combining the two gives informants some control over the information that is given and how it is imparted.

Post-diary interviews allow reinterpretation in an interactive process: the diary-writer can review the original data, even construct a 'new' version of events. They complement the original diary exercise, and one practical research decision is whether or not to share sight of the original text with its author during the interview. Specific details mean that the researcher can address themes that emerge as being important in the diary-writing evidence, or in the research generally; familiarity with diary entries is a preliminary to identifying key issues. 'Questions in mind' helped Zimmerman and Wieder (1977) to find answers but also to sense omissions and to 'probe our inform-ants about the reasons they had not done something' (1977: 492). Post-diary interviews sometimes help verify facts, contribute to 'triangulation' proce-dures or serve as a channel for interim feedback.

Above all, the diary interview sets side by side the written word and the oral evidence of one person. Interviews may confirm diary accounts but they may not. Finding differences between data, for example, may relate to the nature of each method. Ball (1981) used a combination of diaries and ques-tionnaires (rather than interviews) in his ethnography of Beachside Comprehensive School. Commenting on the pupil data, he notes that:

> The sociometric questionnaires failed to pick up the casual friendships that existed between pupils outside school, and made it appear that they had no such contact. In addition, they failed to pick up cross-sex friendships that were established at this time . . . The entries in the diaries that several of the pupils wrote for me did, however, refer to these contacts. (Ball, 1981: 100)

If such dissonances between methods appear, this may provide new direc-tions for analysis. As a research tool, the strengths of diary interviews linked to diary accounts are many. However, some limitations inherent in the diary method extend to diary-interviews, since the quality of original diary data partly shapes the success or otherwise of subsequent interviews. Overall, post-diary interviews make additional demands on informants but enrich data col-lection; it is the combination of oral and written data that makes them exciting.

Not for everyone?

Researchers have tended to request diary information from certain groups, and culture, power, status and education can play a part. Diary-writers have been predominantly people with adequate writing skills, at ease with reflecting on paper; people with sufficient resources who are stable and/or secure enough to produce coherent accounts; and those whose culture values written rather than spoken accounts.

At first sight, educational managers and leaders seem particularly well-suited as diary writers. However, the method has been seen as less appropriate for very 'busy' people with 'limited time'. This depends on whose interpretation of busy-ness is accepted, of course. It is possible to argue that managers are no 'busier' than other educational research participants from whom diary assistance has been sought and frequently obtained; moreover, at senior levels, the principles and practices of diary keeping are central to daily work schedules, overseen and monitored by secretarial guardians of 'the diary'. One recent example of the use of diaries with secondary heads monitored the impact of their values on their daily work (McEwen *et al.*, 2000).

Meanwhile, diaries continue to be used mainly with women, children and young people. Could it be the case, ask Galloway and Morrison (forthcoming):

> that the method is so intrusive and revealing that people [such as senior educational managers] who have more power and higher status have resisted it, whilst those who are less well placed may see it as an empowering process? Future studies may put this to the test as researchers develop further the flexibility and effectiveness of diary writing as a research tool. (Galloway and Morrison, forthcoming)

Summary

In an introductory research methods course for postgraduate Masters degree students at the School of Education, University of Leicester, Rob Watling and I emphasise six key points about the use of diaries in educational research:

- *Point 1: Clarity* It must be clear to participants what sort of views and/or activities need to be recorded in the diary and (if appropriate) what period of time needs to be sampled and recorded in it.
- *Point 2: Ease of completion* It is quite likely that the completion of a diary or a log is going to be an added burden for the participant. If they are already busy (perhaps because of the nature of the experience you are asking them to record) it may be particularly important that the diary should not take too much time to complete.
- *Point 3: Flexibility* It is one of the great advantages of diaries that they are able to be used not just to record what happened, or what people did, but also some of the vital contextual information that relates to these events and peoples' reactions to them.
- *Point 4: Purpose* While the researcher's ambitions must be clear, they are

not enough in themselves to convince someone to participate in the project. Ask yourself what the participants are likely to get out of the process for themselves and attempt to enlist their support on that basis.

- *Point 5: Format* The most common formats for diary research are paper-based. But what are the advantages in collecting the information on tape recorders or by video? What are the disadvantages of such methods?

- *Point 6: Analysis* Consideration must be given from the outset to how the material generated by research diaries will to be analysed. How much pre-coding is appropriate in the diary in question? How open and responsive can the analytic categories afford to be before they become random stories collected from vague areas of people's experiences?

Diaries can be used qualitatively and quantitatively to illuminate a range of educational issues. This is an essentially interactive genre: writing, reading and interpreting are complex processes involving several parties. New directions in diary research attend equally to the interpretation of diary accounts and to methodological concerns. Some limitations have been noted of diary-writing as a research tool. But as diaries are increasingly used to gain insights into current patterns of educational life, the need for clarity among researchers about their design and fitness for purpose with a wider range of participants becomes increasingly important.

References

Atkinson, P. (1992) *Understanding Ethnographic Texts*, Qualitative Research Methods Series 25, London: Sage.

Ball, S. J. (1981) *Beachside Comprehensive*, Cambridge: Cambridge University Press.

Bell, J. (1999) *Doing your Research Project: A Guide for First-time Researchers in Education and Social Science* (3rd edn.), Buckingham: Open University Press.

Bradley, H.W. and Eggleston, J. F. (1976) 'An induction year experiment', Report of an experiment carried out by Derbyshire, Lincolnshire and Nottinghamshire LEAs and the University of Nottingham School of Education.

Burgess, R. G. (1981) 'Keeping a research diary', *Cambridge Journal of Education*, 11(1): 75–81.

Burgess, R. G. (1984) 'Methods of field research 3: using personal documents', in *In the Field: an Introduction to Field Research*. London: George Allen and Unwin.

Burgess, R. G. (1994) 'On diaries and diary keeping', in Bennett, N., Glatter R. and Levačić, R. (eds.), *Improving Educational Management*, London: Paul Chapman.

Burgess, R. G. and Morrison, M. (1995) 'Teaching and learning about food and nutrition in school', in *The Nation's Diet Programme: The Social Science of Food Choice*, Report to the ESRC.

Burgess, R. G. and Morrison, M. (1998) 'Ethnographies of eating in an urban primary school', in Murcott, A. (ed.) *The Nation's Diet. The Social Science of Food Choice*, Harlow: Addison, Wesley, Longman.

Coxon, A., Davies, P., Hunt, A., Weatherburn, P., McManus T. and Rees, C. (1992) 'The structure of sexual behaviour', *Journal of Sex Research*, 29(1): 61–83.

Dex, S. (ed.) (1991) *Life and Work History Analysis: Qualitative and Quantitative Developments*, London: Routledge.

Earley, P. and Fletcher-Campbell, F. (1989) *The Time To Manage? Department and Faculty Heads at Work*, Windsor: NFER-Nelson.

Galloway, S. (1993) 'Out of sight, out of mind': a response to the literature on supply teaching, *Educational Research*, 35(2): 159–169.

Galloway, S., Budgen, A., Burgess, R. G., Hurworth, R., Pole, C. and Sealey, A. (1995) *School Management Training with Interactive Technology*, Coventry: National Council for Educational Technology.

Galloway, S. and Morrison, M. (1993) '*Supply Teaching in Schools: An Investigation of Policy, processes and people*', a report to the Leverhulme.

Galloway, S. and Morrison, M. (forthcoming) 'Diaries, diary interviews and designing diaries', in Pole, C. and Burgess, R.G. (eds.) *Encyclopaedia of Social Research Methods*, London: Macmillan.

Gershuny, J., Miles, I., Jones, S., Mullings, C., Thomas, G. and Wyatt, S. (1986) 'Time budget: preliminary analyses of a national survey', *Journal of Social Affairs*, 2(1): 13–39.

Griffiths, G. (1985) 'Doubts, dilemmas, and diary keeping', in Burgess, R. G. (ed.), *Issues in Educational Research: Qualitative Methods*, Lewes: Falmer Press.

Hammersley, M. and Atkinson, P. (1995) *Ethnography. Principles in Practice* (2nd edn.), London: Routledge.

Hodder, I. (1994) 'The interpretation of documents and material culture', in Denzin, N. and Lincoln, Y. (eds.), *Handbook of Qualitative Research*, Thousand Oaks, CA: Sage.

Holly, M. L. (1984) *Keeping a Personal Professional Journal*, Australia: Deakin University press.

Holly, M. L. (1989) *Writing to Grow*, Portsmouth, NH: Heinemann.

Marples, D. L. (1967) 'Studies of managers: a fresh start', *Journal of Management Studies*, 4: 282–299

Marsh, C. and Gershuny, J. (1991) 'Handling work history data in standard statistical packages', in Dex, S. (ed.), *Life and Work History Analysis: Qualitative and Quantitative Developments*, London: Routledge.

May, T. (1993) *Social Research: Issues, Methods, and Process*, UK St. Edmundsbury Press for the Open University.

McEwen, A., McClune, B. and Knipe, D. (2000) 'Management and values: the changing role of the secondary headteacher', *Teacher Development*, University of Leicester, No. 2, 222–240.

Miles, M. and Huberman, A. M. (1994) *Qualitative Data Analysis. A Source Book* (2nd edn.), London: Sage.

Morrison, M. (1995) 'Researching food consumers in school: recipes for concern', *Educational Studies*, 21(2): 239–263.

Morrison, M. (1996) 'Part-time: whose time? Women's lives and adult learning', in Edwards, R., Hanson, A. and Raggatt, P. (eds.), *Boundaries of Adult Learning*, London: Routledge for the Open University.

Morrison, M. and Galloway, S. (1996) 'Using diaries to explore supply teachers' lives', in Busfield, J. and Lyons, E. S. (eds.), *Methodological Imaginations*, London: Macmillan in Association with the British Sociological Association.

Okely, J. (1994) 'Thinking through fieldwork', in Bryman, A. and Burgess, R. G.

(eds.), *Analysing Qualitative Data*, London: Routledge.

Oppenheim, A. N. (1966) *Introduction to Qualitative Research Method*, London: Wiley.

Oxtoby, R. (1979) 'Problems facing heads of departments', *Journal of Further and Higher Education*, 31: 46–59.

Platt, J. (1981) 'Evidence and proof in documentary research: 2. Some shared problems of documentary research', *Sociological Review* 29(1): 53–66.

Purvis, J. (1984) *Understanding Texts*, Open University Course E205, Unit 15, Milton Keynes: Open University Press.

Saris, W. (1989) 'A technological revolution in data collection', *Quality and Quantity*, 23(3–4): 333–349.

Scott, J. (1990) *A Matter of Record. Documentary Sources in Social Research*, Cambridge: Polity Press.

Strauss, A. (1987) *Qualitative Analysis for Social Scientists*, Cambridge: Cambridge University Press.

Szalai, A. (ed.) (1972) *The Use of Time*, The Hague: Mouton.

Walker, M. (1988) 'Training the trainers: socialisation and change in general practice', *Sociology of Health and Illness*, 10(3): 282–302.

Zimmerman, D. H. and Wieder, D. L. (1977) 'The diary: diary-interview method', *Urban Life*, 5(4): 479–98.

Part D
Analysing and Presenting Data

14

Analysing quantitative data

Anthony Pell and Ken Fogelman

Introduction

This chapter is intended to serve as an introduction to some of the basic techniques and concepts in analysing quantitative data generated by our research. Its main focus is on inferential statistics — the various tests which we might use to help to assess the confidence which we can have in our findings — but equally important is the descriptive and exploratory stage of analysis. This is usually the first stage of analysis, when we might produce the first results in terms of simple distributions and/or summary statistics such as averages and measures of dispersion.

However, it is important to emphasise that this exploratory stage also serves other important purposes such as checking for possible errors in the data or your sample and that your instruments have worked as you would have hoped. Perhaps most important of all is that this early stage should be used to get to know and understand your data, to appreciate both its potential and its limitations. The power of modern computers and software can make it very tempting to proceed straight to the more complex stages of analysis, but most experienced researchers would acknowledge the importance of the exploratory stage — and preferably of some of this analysis being done by hand and calculator.

We can then move on to the stage where we are using statistics to inform the inferences which we may draw from our data: to begin to answer our research questions. These may be quite complex but they are virtually always some version of questions about differences between groups or about relationships between variables. The nature of the question which we want to ask of our data is part of what determines exactly which technique or test we might use, but the other issue that we need to take into account is the nature of the data with which we are working. It is this issue that is discussed below.

Types of data

Data collected for educational, and indeed for all research investigations, can be: nominal, ordinal, interval or ratio data.

Nominal data simply distinguishes between categories, for example 'Yes',

'No' or 'Don't know' in answer to some question. A further example would be the use of code numbers, such as 1 or 2, to distinguish between boys and girls. Because these numbers are essentially 'markers', it would make no sense to add or multiply them, for example, but there are special statistics called *non-parametric*, which you can use to study the numbers in each of the categories.

With *ordinal* data, the size of the numbers is meaningful. A pupil rated 3 on achievement does better than one rated 2; and a pupil rated 2 does better than a pupil rated 1. Here the numbers indicate an *order*, whereas nominal data only indicates *difference*. Again, non-parametric statistics allow you to analyse the implications of this ordered data.

When the differences between adjacent numbers on an ordinal scale are the same (as they would be on a pupil language test marked as percentage scores, for instance), then the data becomes *interval*, and can now be subjected to the usual arithmetical processes of addition, multiplication, etc. More powerful statistics of the *parametric* type (see later) then become available.

However, be warned: the interval scale of the pupils' language test is *not made up of equal intervals*, because the human abilities and behaviours we try to measure in educational research cannot be recorded with the precision that is possible in recording natural science data, for example.

The natural sciences generate *ratio* data scales, where *the apparent similar differences of the interval scale can be shown to be identical*. Thus, on a ruler, 10 millimetres measured from 30 mm to 40 mm is the same as 10 millimetres measured from 70 mm to 80 mm.

On, for example, a language test, because language ability cannot be measured in fixed 10 percent units, the difference between pupils scoring 30 per cent and 40 percent is unlikely to be the same as the difference between pupils scoring 70 percent and 80 percent.

Uncertainties in the measurement of human behaviour limit social and educational research analyses to interval data, at best. Further, it is this uncertainty that limits the interpretation of social statistics. While people generally attribute precision to all quoted figures, which by implication are seen as 'scientific' from ratio-type data, the probable errors brought about by the educational research treatment of mostly interval data has been shown in the past to lead to gross misunderstandings (Shipman, 1972).

Handling distribution-free data

Parametric and non-parametric analyses

Parametric tests and analyses are those performed on *ratio* and *interval* data, assumed to be drawn from a wide, *normal population* that has certain special, technical characteristics, which are explained later. Non-parametric analyses can be performed on simple *nominal* and *ordinal* data, having no particular pattern or distribution, hence the occasional use of the term 'distribution free' to describe non-parametric statistics.

Non-parametric tests usually treat data, such as continuous test scores, as ranks or orders, whereas the parametric tests operate directly on the raw scores. One advantage of using a non-parametric test is that your conclusion is not qualified by uncertainty about the kind of data you used, and whether it was part of a 'normal' population and so really best suited to the parametric statistic you used. Another important point to bear in mind is that non-parametric tests can work on much smaller data sets, perhaps made up of fewer than ten pupils.

This chapter only covers a small selection of the wide range of non-parametric statistics. Consult Siegel (1956), still in print after forty years, for a more comprehensive treatment.

The Chi-square test

The one variable, two category test

The one-variable chi-square (χ^2) test is a non-parametric statistical procedure which can be used with 'counts' of pupils falling into two or more categories.

For example, researchers observed 36 low achieving and 36 high achieving pupils working in the classroom. Forty-eight pupils were seen to be reading, including 34 of the high achievers but only 14 of the low achievers. Do these figures mean that high achievers read more, or were these observations just chance events? The chi-square test gives an answer.

This is what you do.

1. Draw up a contingency table (Table 14.1), entering the number of pupils actually seen reading (this is called the *observed frequency*, f_o).
2. As the pupils observed comprised equal numbers of low and high achievers, it would be expected (by chance) that equal numbers of each would be seen to be reading. Because 48 pupils were actually seen reading, it is expected that there would be 24 low and 24 high achievers (these are *expected frequencies*, f_e).
3. Calculate the difference between f_o and f_e, ignoring whether it is positive or negative.
4. For this simple example, with only *two* columns of low and high achievers, we have to make a correction by subtracting 0.5 (Yates's correction) from the difference $|f_o - f_e|$, and then we square the result. (You do *not* have to use Yates's correction and subtract 0.5 if you have *more than two columns or rows* of data.)
5. Divide the square you get by f_e, the number expected.

Table 14.1 Observed and expected readers

Number	Low achievers	High achievers	All
Observed f_o	16	32	48
Expected f_e	24	24	48
Difference $|f_o-f_e|$	8	8	
$(|f_o-f_e|-0.5)^2$	56.25	56.25	
$(|f_o-f_e|-0.5)^2/24$	2.34	2.34	
$\Sigma(|f_o-f_e|-0.5)^2/24$	4.68		Chi-square

6. Finally, add your answers for the low and high achievers to get 4.68, which is the chi-square statistic for the observed numbers of readers.
7. Look at Table 14.2, which shows critical values of chi-square. If your calculated statistic ever reaches or passes these values, you could have a meaningful, non-chance effect. Your chi-square value is then said to be 'significant' (this is discussed more fully below).

You can see that the calculated value of 4.68 reaches and passes the lower of the two highlighted, critical significance levels, so the researchers can conclude that 'high achieving pupils do more reading in class than low achievers'; the observed number frequencies are unlikely to be due to chance.

The explanation of the 'degrees of freedom' column of Table 14.2 is best postponed until after the next chi-square example, but when observed numbers fall into two categories only, in this instance readers and non-readers, there can only be one degree of freedom. This is because although the number of readers, say, can have any value from 0 to 48 (it is 'free'), the number of non-readers is immediately fixed (at 48 less the number of readers), once the number of readers is known: only *one* of the two categories is free to have a value.

Table 14.2 Critical values for the chi-square statistic

Degrees of freedom	Critical chi-square value	
	For 5% significance	For 1% significance
1	3.84	6.63
2	5.99	9.21
3	7.81	11.34
4	9.49	13.28

Note on statistical significance

This term, used frequently by educational researchers, always accompanies statistical tests of research results. Consider this everyday life example:

Imagine a coin is tossed ten times. You might expect to get five 'heads' and five 'tails'. If you found you had six heads and four tails, would this mean that there is something wrong with the coin, or is it due to chance? Your experience tells you that this is just 'chance'. But what if you got *eight heads and two tails*, or even ten heads? Is something wrong? Is the coin biased?

If a second coin, which you knew was fair, was taken and tossed ten times . . . and then again for another ten . . . and again, and so on for a hundred times, recording the number of heads in each set of ten tosses, you could get experimental evidence for the number of chance appearances of *eight heads and two tails*. If you have a few hours to spare you could try this for yourself; if not, you will have to take on trust the results. Only in 5 out of 100 sets of ten tosses, would you find *eight heads and two tails*: it is not impossible, just not a very likely chance occurrence.

Go back to the first coin. There is a 5 in 100 chance (said to be 5 percent) of getting *eight heads and two tails* just by the natural course of events. This outcome of *eight heads and two tails* is said to have *statistical significance at the 5 percent level*.

So in educational research, for measurements of human behaviour with their built-in natural variations, by convention an arbitrary critical value is set; this value is the 5 percent we have just met. As long as the research results have less chance than 5 percent of being natural variations, the results are said to be *statistically significant*.

The two variables, multi-category test

Here, frequencies of occurrence are cross-tabulated for two variables, and then an extended method used to calculate the chi-square statistic.

Primary pupils were asked to rate themselves on a three-point 'self-image' scale. Researchers also had three-point achievement ratings for each pupil so a contingency table comprising the two variables of achievement and self-image could be built up. The data appear in Table 14.3 as the highlighted numbers for f_o.

To calculate the value of the chi-square statistic:

1. For each of the nine cells in Table 14.3, calculate the expected number of pupils by using simple proportion in terms of the 'all' numbers. For cell A:

$$\frac{79}{417} \times 101 = 19.1$$

In general, should the expected frequency, f_e, fall to 5 or below, the chi-square test should not be used.

2. For each cell, calculate

$$\frac{(f_o - f_e)^2}{f_e}$$

Table 14.3 Achievement and self-image

Achievement		Self-image			
		Low	Average	High	All
Low	f_o	42	28	31	101
	f_e	A (19.1)	B (28.6)	C (53.3)	
$\frac{(f_o-f_e)^2}{f_e}$		27.4	0	9.3	
Average	f_o	34	79	94	207
	f_e	D (39.2)	E (58.6)	F (109.2)	
$\frac{(f_o-f_e)^2}{f_e}$		0.7	7.1	2.1	
High	f_o	3	11	95	109
	f_e	G (20.6)	H (30.8)	I (57.5)	
$\frac{(f_o-f_e)^2}{f_e}$		15.0	12.6	24.5	
All		79	118	220	417

To calculate the value of the chi-square statistic:

3. As a formula,

$$\chi^2 = \frac{\sum (f_o-f_e)^2}{f_e} \quad\cdots\cdots\cdots\cdots\cdots\cdots\cdots\cdots\cdots\cdots\cdots\cdots \quad 1$$

Now add all the values of $\frac{(f_o-f_e)^2}{f_e}$ to find chi-square (χ^2). This gives a value of 98.7.

4. Find the degrees of freedom for chi-square by studying the cells in Table 14.3. If you work along the first row, where the total number of pupils is 101, you are free to fill the first two cells as you choose, but the third is then determined for you by the row total of 101. Similarly, when moving down the first column, after the first two cells are filled, then the third is fixed by the column total of 79. This means that, overall, you are free to fill just four of the cells before their composition becomes predetermined: you have *four degrees of freedom*.

> In general, the number of degrees of freedom can be found by multiplying the number of rows, less one, by the number of columns, less one.

5. Use the value of chi-square, 98.7, and the number of degrees of freedom to check the critical, significant figures from Table 14.2. You can see that the highest significant figure of 13.28 is easily exceeded, so the researchers can conclude that 'high achieving pupils have the highest self-image'.

Correlation and the contingency coefficient

In the earlier example, the chi-square test showed that pupils with the best self-image are those with the highest achievement. In statistical terms, it is said that 'self-image and achievement are positively *correlated*'.

Some researchers eagerly seek correlations as evidence for relationships otherwise hidden away under the surface of their data. If you have found that high achievement and a strong self-image go together, you have a reason for allowing your pupils to occasionally tackle relatively easy tasks so that the satisfaction of achievement can boost their feelings and self-image. This is a practical example of using *correlation as a measure of association*. Beware of reading too much into correlation, though. It does not mean, for instance that high self-image *causes* pupils to do well, simply that high self-image often (but not always) accompanies high achievement.

Figure 14.1 displays the self-image scores and attainment scores (in maths

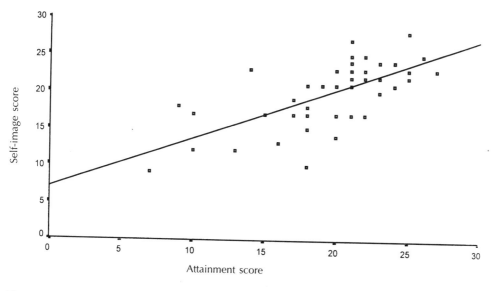

Figure 14.1 Scatterplot of scores showing positive correlation

and English, combined) for 48 primary pupils. See how this *scatterplot* shows the positive correlation by allowing us to draw a line sloping upwards, an idea which is further developed later. The degree of correlation is given by a *correlation coefficient*, which can have positive or negative values from zero.

One of two correlation coefficients you might meet up with in non-parametric statistics is called the *contingency coefficient*, C. It can be calculated directly from chi-square χ^2:

$$C = \frac{\sqrt{\chi^2}}{\sqrt{N + \chi^2}} \dots\dots\dots\dots\dots\dots\dots\dots\dots\dots\dots\dots 2$$

where N is the number of pupils.

In the earlier example, $\chi^2 = 98.7$ and $N = 417$, so C is calculated as 0.44, which is a significant correlation for the simple reason that chi-square is itself significant.

If there had been no correlation between achievement and self-image, C would have been zero. Had there been perfect positive correlation so that high achievement always accompanied high self-image, C *would not* have been an expected +1.00, which is what you find with other correlation coefficients such as the Spearman rank order and Pearson correlation coefficients. The maximum value of C depends upon the size of the contingency table: the value for the 3 × 3 table is 0.82.

The advantage of using the contingency coefficient is that it can be used for any type of data, including *nominal data*, which otherwise would lack a statistical correlation treatment.

The Spearman rank-order correlation coefficient

From its name, you can deduce that this correlation coefficient operates with ordinal data, but it can be used with the higher level interval data if the Pearson coefficient is felt to be unsuitable. The coefficient, which takes values from − 1.00 (perfect negative correlation), through 0.00 (no correlation at all) to + 1.00 (perfect positive correlation), measures the degee of association between, for example, two sets of scores for a sample of pupils.

Researchers were investigating how primary pupils improved their scores in 'tables' over a year's maths lessons. The pupils were tested at the beginning and at the end of the year. Table 14.4 shows the pre-test and post-test scores for ten such pupils.

To calculate the rank order correlation coefficient, this is what you do.

1. Work out the rank on each test. If there are any ties, find the average of the two rank places which otherwise would have been used, for example a tie on the pre-test with score 26 at rank 1 (and 2) becomes 1.5.

Table 14.4 Pre-test and post-test scores

Pupil	Pre-test score	Post-test score
A	26	52
B	10	68
C	16	4
D	24	40
E	4	56
F	6	32
G	22	64
H	6	40
I	26	24
J	12	60

Table 14.5 shows the rank orders.

2. For each pupil, calculate the difference in the pre-test and post-test rank orders (D).

Table 14.5 Calculating the rank order coefficient

Pupil	Rank order		Difference in rank order, D	D²
	Pre-test	Post-test		
A	1.5	5	−3.5	12.25
B	7	1	6.0	36.00
C	5	10	−5.0	25.00
D	3	6.5	−3.5	12.25
E	10	4	6.0	36.00
F	8.5	8	0.5	0.25
G	4	2	2.0	4.00
H	8.5	6.5	2.0	4.00
I	1.5	9	−7.5	56.25
J	6	3	3.0	9.00

3. Calculate the values of D² and add them all up. This gives 195.00.
4. Use the Spearman rank order formula for the correlation coefficient, R for N sets of data

$$R = 1 - \frac{6\Sigma D^2}{N^3 - N} \quad \dots\dots\dots\dots\dots\dots\dots\dots\dots\dots\dots\dots\dots\dots\dots \; 3$$

$$= -0.18$$

We have negative correlation between the pre- and post-test scores which, if meaningful, tells us that there is a trend for post-test scores to be below pre-test scores. But what if the calculated figure of 0.18 is due to chance? We need to use a table of statistical significance to find out the critical value that R must reach before our rank order correlation can be thought of as other than a chance association.

In fact, our coefficient of (–) 0.18 falls well short of the required value, so the researchers can conclude, only, that 'tables' mastery at the end of the year *is not related* to that at the beginning.

Statistical significance

In a recent research study of the primary classroom, one hundred high achieving and one hundred low achieving pupils were observed in several schools. The pupils were either working by themselves with the teacher alongside, or working in a group with the teacher, or being taught together as a class. In Table 14.6, you can see the work pattern observed by the researchers.

Table 14.6 Significant differences

Pupil working with teacher	Observed for this number of time units		Chi-square	Significance
	Low achievers	High achievers		
Individually	90	60	5.60	5% level
In group	50	120	28.0	1% level
As part of the class	460	500	1.58	Not significant
Total number of observation 'units'	2,000	2,000		

The question a researcher now has to answer is: 'Do the different figures for each of the three categories of teacher interaction mean that the teacher *does* spend more time working individually with low achievers, or is the 90:60 ratio *due to chance* (so if the research were to be carried out again, it would be just as likely to give a 60:90 ratio)?'

From what was said about the chi-square test, you can see how we can calculate expected 'individual' category numbers for low and high achievers, which should be an even split because 2,000 observations were made on each group. When the chi-square statistic is calculated from Table 14.6, its value is 5.60, which is said to be significant at *the 5 percent level*. This means that *the chance of the 90:60 ratio being a random occurrence is less than 5 percent*.

The table is completed by the statistical calculations for the group and class categories. The chance of the 50:120 ratio for 'group' interaction being a random occurrence is less than 1 percent, which means it is even more likely than the individual interaction to describe a real, meaningful event.

However, the 'class' teaching difference in observations is not significant in the statistical sense, which means that *the chance of it being a random occurrence is **more** than 5 percent.*

The 'cut-off' figures of 1 percent and 5 percent are usually applied, conventionally, for all statistical analysis work, and can appear as decimals of 0.01 and 0.05.

You will appreciate that in social research, we can never be absolutely certain that differences are real: there is always a slight possibility that chance is at work, but you will discover that if you can obtain differences at the 5 percent or 1 percent level, your findings will be received seriously.

Now, after testing the scores of Table 14.6 'for significance', the researchers could conclude that 'low achievers are more likely to receive individual help from the teacher: high achievers interact more often with the teacher when working in groups, but in general class teaching neither group is particularly favoured by the teacher'.

You can see that statistical significance has a key role in educational research when interpreting the results.

Distribution dependent data

Introducing the normal distribution and standard deviation

As discussed previously, a large amount of data, probably of the *interval* type, can make up what is called a *normal population* and a precise *parametric statistic* can be brought into play to investigate it.

Here is an example of a normal distribution set of data. Several hundred primary pupils were tested on mathematics achievement using a 36-item test, where the maximum mark was exactly 36. Table 14.7 shows how the scores were spread out: the scores have been grouped to keep the table a convenient size.

The scores are shown graphically in Figure 14.2, where the average score of each pair, called the *interval mid-mark*, has been used on the horizontal axis. The *frequency* is the name used for the number of pupils who obtained the scores in each box of the *histogram* chart.

The *mean* of the maths scores is 18.33. This is the sum of all the scores divided by the number of pupils.

The *standard deviation* of the scores is 5.06, which measures how much the scores are spread out either side of the mean. How to calculate the standard deviation is shown in the next section. In this practical example, about 75 percent of all the pupils' scores are within one standard deviation of the mean: about 97 percent are within two standard deviations of the mean.

All the scores follow a near *normal distribution*, which is shown by the

Table 14.7 Distribution of maths scores

Score	Score at mid-interval	Number of pupils (N)
Below 5	0	0
5/6	5.5	3
7/8	7.5	11
9/10	9.5	29
11/12	11.5	38
13/14	13.5	58
15/16	15.5	85
17/18	17.5	100
19/20	19.5	92
21/22	21.5	78
23/24	23.5	55
25/26	25.5	42
27/28	27.5	19
29/30	28.5	11
31/32	29.5	0
33/34	31.5	2
35/36	33.5	1

smooth, symmetrical curve of Figure 14.2. If the scores were to have a smaller standard deviation than 5.06, then the curve would be narrower with a sharper peak, but the mean would stay at 18.3 (Figure 14.3).

A true normal distribution of data always has 68.3 percent of its values, such as pupils' maths scores, within one standard deviation of the mean: it always has 95.4 percent within two standard deviations.

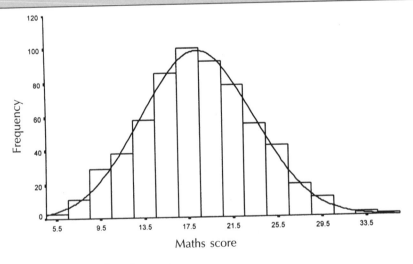

Figure 14.2   Histogram of maths scores

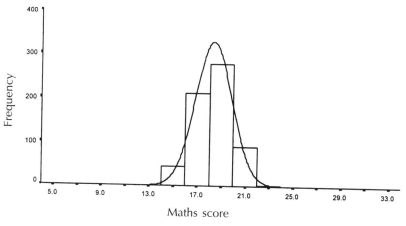

Figure 14.3 Histogram of another set of scores (small standard deviation)

Calculating standard deviations

From Table 14.7, you would probably agree that if you tested your pupils on the same maths test with your class being just a small *sample* of a much larger *population*, the mean score for your pupils would almost certainly differ from the value of 18.33 already found. Further, if your colleague were also to test her pupils, then her sample of pupils would probably differ on mean score from yours as well as from the greater population. This is typical of *sampling* in educational research: the samples selected are likely to have different means, at least, although their standard deviations could be similar. Nevertheless, you can see that means and standard deviations are going to be important in working out *differences* with parametric statistics to see if one teaching method is really better than another or whether pupils have improved over the year.

Table 14.8 shows how to calculate the standard deviation from basic principles, using just a few pupils' scores from Table 14.7 as an example.

1. Calculate the mean μ of the marks for the N pupils from

$$\mu = \frac{\Sigma X}{N} \quad\text{.................................}\quad 4$$

$$\therefore \mu = 19.0$$

2. Calculate the *variance* σ^2, and hence the *standard deviation* σ from

$$\sigma^2 = \frac{\Sigma (X - \mu)^2}{N} \quad\text{...................}\quad 5$$

$$\therefore \sigma = 6.66$$

Table 14.8 Calculating a standard deviation

Pupil	Test mark X	Deviation from mean $(X - \mu)$	Squared deviation $(X - \mu)^2$
A	16	−3	9
B	23	+4	16
C	10	−9	81
D	31	+12	144
E	19	0	0
F	15	−4	16
	114		266

The square of the standard deviation, the variance, is often used in more advanced parametric statistics instead of the standard deviation.

You will see that the mean and standard deviation of the sample of just six maths scores differ from the values for the population. What will happen if we take several different samples? Of course, if we chose a *biased sample* from, say, just the pupils who scored between 28 and 34 marks, we would expect a very high mean and a small standard deviation, but what if we chose a *random sample*, which is a selection made from the general population where every member has an equal chance of being chosen, would the mean and standard deviation always be the same?

Table 14.9 shows what happens when forty random samples of six scores are drawn from the original population of maths scores.

The mean for these forty samples of six is 18.75 with a standard deviation of 1.79. You can see that the means of the random samples are certainly not the same; neither are their standard deviations.

At 18.75, the mean of all the sample means differs a little from the general population mean of 18.33, but there is a considerable difference between the *standard deviation of the sample means*, at 1.79, and the standard deviation of the population of scores at 5.06. The spread of sample means shows a very *rough approximation to a normal curve*, but if the size of the samples is increased to fifty random maths scores each, and if the number of samples drawn becomes eighty, there is likely to be a closer approximation.

Because sample means are less spread than the individual scores that make up the whole population, the *sample means standard deviation*, which is named *the standard error of the mean* (s.e.m.), is expected to be quite different to the standard deviation of the population.

In general statistical terms, drawing samples of size N from a large population of scores of standard deviation σ results in a standard error of the mean equal to the standard deviation divided by the square root of N.

Table 14.9 The means and standard deviations of samples of six maths scores

Mean maths score	Standard deviation	Mean maths score	Standard deviation
17.16	4.72	15.85	1.86
20.04	7.37	21.03	4.33
17.93	2.38	18.29	4.91
19.08	4.84	17.76	6.93
22.56	6.94	15.19	4.89
22.10	4.74	21.57	4.45
19.05	3.02	16.07	3.55
19.33	5.97	18.78	2.96
20.49	4.03	18.25	4.22
18.21	4.33	17.01	6.46
17.77	4.03	17.02	4.87
19.41	2.99	15.50	4.51
19.83	3.22	18.81	6.31
21.39	6.63	20.41	4.43
18.15	6.89	19.31	5.94
18.09	1.97	19.54	6.10
19.46	3.73	19.90	4.53
21.09	3.81	16.97	5.82
19.39	4.33	18.34	5.43
17.29	3.65	16.72	4.50

The population of maths scores has $\sigma = 5.06$, so for samples of size 50,

$$\text{s.e.m.} = \frac{5.06}{\sqrt{50}}$$

$$= 0.72$$

It is by using the s.e.m. that you can test whether your pupils' test scores are above or below the standards of the population as a whole. Say your class of 32 pupils scored a mean of 17.45. For your sample,

$$\text{s.e.m.} = \frac{5.06}{\sqrt{32}}$$

$$= 0.89$$

With a population mean of 18.33, about 95 percent of all sample means would be expected to fall by chance within the range of 18.33 + twice 0.89 and 18.33 − twice 0.89 (in other words, between 20.11 and 16.55). Your class mean is within this chance band so it is unlikely to be any different to the average performance. Yet, other colleagues and administrators, unskilled in statistics and education and research, might well judge that you and your pupils were 'failing'.

Z-scores and other standardised scores

With the mean score and the standard deviation having such an importance, it is worth introducing a modification to test scores, such as the mathematics set, so that they include this information. This is done by calculating a z-score (z) from each raw score (X) by subtracting the mean score (μ), and then dividing by the standard deviation (σ), as shown in Equation 6.

$$z = \frac{X - \mu}{\sigma} \quad \dotfill \quad 6$$

Z-scores will have a mean of 0.00 and a standard deviation of 1.00. As an example of the calculation, a maths test score of 26 in the population of scores where the standard deviation is 5.06 has a z-score given by

$$z = \frac{26 - 18.33}{5.06}$$
$$\therefore z = +1.52$$

The z-score is positive because it is above the mean: a score of 15, which is below the mean, has a negative z-score.

$$z = \frac{15 - 18.33}{5.06}$$
$$\therefore z = -1.52$$

Table 14.10 shows the percentage of scores in a normal population lying between certain critical z-score values.

The critical values are needed to judge whether results are statistically significant or not. It has already been used indirectly with the maths scores to see if a class mean score of 17.45 was significantly different to a population of *means* centred on a score of 18.33 and s.e.m. of 0.89. In this case,

$$z = \frac{17.45 - 18.33}{0.89}$$
$$\therefore z = -1.26$$

which does not reach the critical value of 1.96 needed for significance at the 5 percent level.

Table 14.10 Some critical values of z-score

| Z-score range | | % of normal |
Lower	Higher	population
−1.96	+1.96	95.0
−2.58	+2.58	99.0
−∞	+1.65	95.0
−∞	+2.33	99.0

Differences between means: large samples

Researchers are often interested in the difference in the mean scores obtained by two groups or samples that might have been exposed to, say, different teaching methods. Alternatively, you might want to compare the performance of your students with that of others in another school. In either case, the analysis requires a study of *sample mean differences*. Working from tables such as Table 14.9, you find that you get a normal distribution of sample mean differences centred on 0.00, which is shown in Figure 14.4. Critical statistical tails are shown: if the difference of two sample means falls into these areas, then 'significance' is achieved in this '*two-tail*' test.

Taking an international comparison, say a sample (n_1) of 220 ten year-olds in the USA had a mean score on the maths test (m_1) of 16.91 with a standard deviation (s_1) of 4.34. A sample of (n_2) 163 ten year-olds in Hungary had a mean score (m_2) of 18.28 with a standard deviation (s_2) of 4.91.

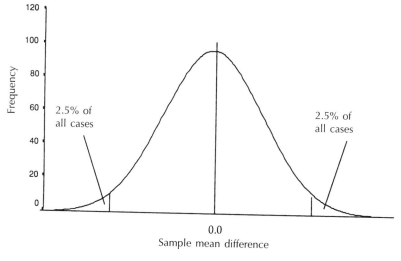

Figure 14.4 Normal distribution of sample mean differences

Hypothesis testing

We now meet up with *hypothesis testing*.

> In general terms, a hypothesis is an educated guess about the meaning of information, which is then to be subsequently investigated with a view to either supporting or rejecting the guess.

The international data can provide us with at least two hypotheses:

1. 'that there is no difference between the USA and Hungarian means', that is called a neutral or *null hypothesis* (H$_o$), and presumes that the USA sample is drawn from a population that has the same mean as the population from which the Hungarian sample is drawn (so we write H$_o$: $\mu_1 = \mu_2$); and

2. 'that the Hungarian mean is more than the USA mean', an *alternative hypothesis* (H$_A$), that presumes that the Hungarian sample is drawn from a different population to the USA one with a greater mean (so we write H$_A$: $\mu_2 > \mu_1$).

The difference between the the national sample means is 18.28 – 16.91, or 1.37. If the standard deviation of the distribution of sample mean differences ($\sigma_{m_1-m_2}$) were known, then the z-score for the difference of 1.37 could be calculated.

To find the standard deviation,

$$(\sigma_{m_1-m_2})^2 = \frac{(s_1)^2}{n_1} + \frac{(s_2)^2}{n_2} \quad \dots\dots\dots\dots\dots\dots\dots\dots\dots 7$$

This gives:

$$\sigma_{m_1-m_2} = 0.483$$

The z-score for the difference of the means is thus:

$$z = \frac{1.37}{0.483}$$

$$\therefore z = 2.84$$

Such a high z-score is beyond the 99 percent critical value of 2.58, which means that such a difference has less than a 1 percent probability of being a chance occurrence. The *null hypothesis* that the USA and Hungarian pupils have the same mean scores on the maths test is *rejected* at the 1 percent level.

Note that when testing a null hypothesis, it does not matter which of the two means is the larger: only the suspicion that they are not the same is under test. This requires a *two-tail test of significance* with 2.5 percent of 'probability' in each tail at either end of the normal distribution curve. The situation is different when testing the alternative hypothesis that the Hungarian pupils actually score better. In this case, a *one tail test of significance* has the normal curve with its 5 percent of critical probability all in one tail, so any z-score outside the range of minus infinity to + 1.65 will be statistically significant at the 5 percent level. As the z-score is 2.84, it can be concluded that the *alternative hypothesis is supported* at the 1 percent level of significance, and the Hungarians score higher than the USA.

Differences between means: small samples

If sample sizes fall below 40, the z-score method of statistical analysis is usually replaced by the *t-test*, a more reliable test for small samples in this range. The t-test has a specific requirement that the two populations from which the samples are drawn have *the same standard deviation*. If this condition is obeyed then the common population standard deviation for both samples and the standard deviation of the sample mean differences are calculated from the equations below.

The t-test calculation is made clear by taking the general science scores for the two African village schools of Jim Rhangane and Vukuzenzele. The population comprised some 13,000 pupils taking the end-of-year regional examination. The two samples were the entire year group entries of the two schools (Table 14.11).

Initially, you might think that Jim Rhangane pupils did better than the Vukuzenzele pupils, but then, looking at the standard deviations, perhaps there is no significant difference. These thoughts lead to your two hypotheses:

1. 'that there is no difference between the two sample means', the *null hypothesis*: H_o: $\mu_1 = \mu_2$; and
2. 'that the Jim Rhangane sample mean is greater than the Vukuzenzele mean', the *alternative hypothesis*: H_A: $\mu_1 > \mu_2$.

The variance σ^2 for the common, regional population of 13,000 pupils is

Table 14.11 Small samples for a t-test

School	Number of pupils	Mean score	Standard deviation
Jim Rhangane	$n_1 = 16$	$m_1 = 30.12$	$s_1 = 6.18$
Vukuzenzele	$n_2 = 29$	$m_2 = 27.04$	$s_2 = 6.46$

estimated from Equation 8.

$$\sigma^2 = \frac{n_1 (s_1)^2 + n_2 (s_2)^2}{(n_1 - 1) + (n_2 - 1)} \quad \dots\dots\dots\dots\dots\dots\dots 8$$

This gives

$$\sigma^2 = 42.35$$

The variance of the population of sample mean differences $(\sigma_{m_1-m_2})^2$ is found from:

$$(\sigma_{m_1-m_2})^2 = \frac{\sigma^2}{n_1} + \frac{\sigma^2}{n_2} \quad \dots\dots\dots\dots\dots\dots\dots 9$$

So, substituting $\sigma^2 = 42.35$ gives:

$$(\sigma_{m_1-m_2})^2 = \frac{42.35}{16} + \frac{42.35}{19}$$

$$\therefore \sigma_{m_1-m_2} = 2.208$$

The t-score for the difference in sample means is given by an equivalent form of the z-score calculation of Equation 6, which becomes

$$t = \frac{m_1 - m_2}{\sigma_{m_1 - m_2}} \quad \dots\dots\dots\dots\dots\dots\dots 10$$

The difference in the schools' means thus has a t-score of

$$t = \frac{30.12 - 27.04}{2.208}$$

$$\therefore t = 1.40$$

The t-score values needed for statistical significance actually depend upon the sample sizes. A number called the *degrees of freedom* (df) has to be calculated from

$$df = (n_1 - 1) + (n_2 - 1) \quad \dots\dots\dots\dots\dots\dots 11$$

and then the t-score value is read from a statistical table.

As the combined degrees of freedom for the Jim Rhangane and Vukuzenzele schools has a value of df = (16 − 1) + (29 − 1), or 43, then, the minimum critical score to test the null hypothesis that the two means are the same is 2.02 for a two-tail test at the 5 percent level. The calculated t-score of 1.40 falls well short of this value so the *null hypothesis* is retained: the Jim Rhangane and Vukuzenzele schools do not score significantly different in the general science examination.

The Pearson correlation coefficient

It is now time to meet the widely-used Pearson correlation coefficient, which is widely used with interval data to investigate associations between different variables.

Researchers tested 48 eleven-year-old girls to compare attainment in maths and reading with feelings about going to school, such as 'enjoyment' of school life and being 'miserable'. Figure 14.5 shows the first of three *scatterplots* of the results.

You can see that, generally, the higher the reading score, the higher the maths score. A line-of-best-fit is drawn through the points to 'average out' the variation of the positions. This line slopes upwards, which implies a *positive correlation* between the maths and reading scores. The Pearson correlation coefficient is calculated to be +0.68 (see below).

The scatterplot of Figure 14.6 shows that 'misery' is *negatively correlated* with attainment in reading. The line-of-best-fit slopes downwards. The implication is that *the worst readers are more likely to be miserable at school*, which is itself an interesting research finding. This time, the Pearson correlation coefficient is –0.40.

Sometimes, a scatterplot shows no recognisable trend at all: this is the case

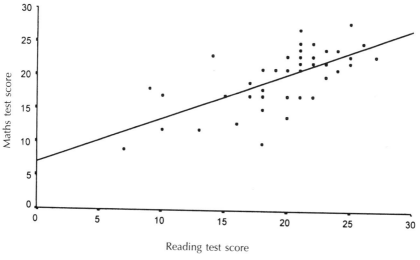

Figure 14.5 Scatterplot of scores showing positive correlation

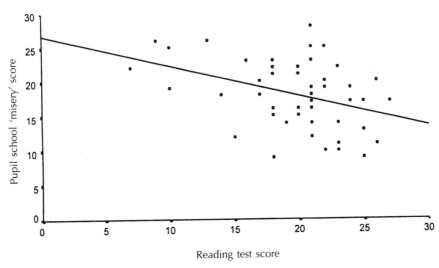

Figure 14.6 Scatterplot of scores showing a negative correlation

with Figure 14.7, where enjoyment of school is compared with attainment in language. The line-of-best-fit appears to be almost horizontal, indicating little correlation. The Pearson correlation calculation gives an insignificant +0.03. The conclusion has to be that there is no association between language attainment and school enjoyment.

We shall now calculate a Pearson correlation coefficient using an example of pre-test and post-test scores.

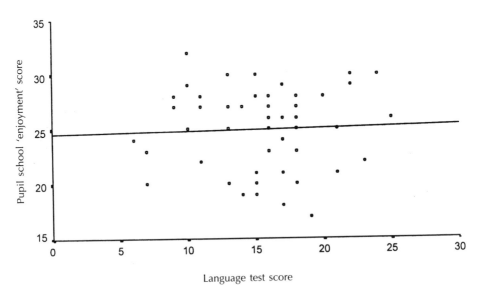

Figure 14.7 Scatterplot of scores showing no correlation

Table 14.12 Calculating the Pearson correlation coefficient

Pupil	Pre-test score X	Post-test score Y	$(X - \mu_x)$	$(Y - \mu_y)$	$(X - \mu_x)(Y - \mu_y)$	$(X - \mu_x)^2$	$(Y - \mu_y)^2$
A	26	52	10.8	8.0	86.4	116.64	64.00
B	10	68	−5.2	24.0	−124.8	27.04	576.00
C	16	4	0.8	−40.0	−32.0	0.64	1,600.00
D	24	40	8.8	−4.0	−35.2	77.44	16.00
E	4	56	−11.2	12.0	−134.4	125.44	144.00
F	6	32	−9.2	−12.0	110.4	84.64	144.00
G	22	64	6.8	20.0	136.0	46.24	400.00
H	6	40	−9.2	−4.0	36.8	84.64	16.00
I	26	24	10.8	−20.0	−216.0	116.64	400.00
J	12	60	−3.2	16.0	−51.2	10.24	256.00
Sum	152	440			−224.0	689.60	3,616.00

1. Find the mean of the X-scores by calculating the sum (152) and dividing by the number of pupils (N = 10):

$$\mu = \frac{\Sigma X}{N}$$

$$\therefore \mu_x = 15.2$$

2. Similarly, find the mean of the Y-scores by calculating the sum (152) and dividing by the number of pupils (N = 10).

$$\mu = \frac{\Sigma Y}{N}$$

$$\therefore \mu_y = 44.0$$

3. Calculate the difference of $(X - \mu_x)$ by subtracting the mean X-score, μ_x, from each value of X.
4. Calculate the difference of $(Y - \mu_y)$ by subtracting the mean Y-score, μ_y, from each value of Y.
5. Multiply $(X - \mu_x)$ by $(Y - \mu_y)$ to get the values in Column 6. Then add up the ten products to get

$$\Sigma (X - \mu_x)(Y - \mu_y) = -224.0.$$

6. In Column 7, square the $(X - \mu_x)$ values from column 4, then add up all ten squares to get

$$\Sigma (X - \mu_x)^2 = 689.60$$

7. To calculate the standard deviation, σ_x, of the X-scores:

$$\sigma_x^2 = \frac{\Sigma\,(X - \mu_x)^2}{N}$$

$$\sigma_x^2 = 68.96$$

$$\therefore\ \sigma_x = 8.30$$

8. In Column 8, square the $(Y - \mu_y)$ values from Column 5, then add up all ten squares to get

$$\Sigma\,(Y - \mu_y)^2 = 3616.00$$

9. To calculate the standard deviation, σ_y, of the Y-scores:

$$\sigma_y^2 = \frac{\Sigma\,(Y - \mu_y)^2}{N}$$

$$\therefore\ \sigma_y = 19.02$$

10. Finally, use the Pearson formula to calculate the correlation coefficient r_{xy} between the pre-test and post-test scores:

$$r_{xy} = \frac{\Sigma\,(X - \mu_x)\,(Y - \mu_y)}{N\,\sigma_x\,\sigma_y} \quad\dots\dots\dots\dots\dots\dots\dots\dots 12$$

So,

$$r_{xy} = \frac{-224.0}{10 \times 8.30 \times 19.02}$$

$$\therefore\ r_{xy} = -0.14$$

For small sets of data, say with up to 30 pupils, the easier calculations of the Spearman coefficient make it a real alternative to the more reliable Pearson index, even if the interval data has to be ranked first. Whichever of the two coefficients you use, when you have your final value the problem of the *significance* of the correlation has to be addressed.

Statistical significance of the correlation coefficient

The research with the 48 eleven-year-old girls reported above produced the set of correlation coefficients shown in Table 14.13: these include the three coefficients already considered from the scatterplot diagrams.

Faced with an array of coefficients, how much weight can you give to the values? If language and reading scores are really correlated because the

Table 14.13 Pearson correlation coefficient for the pairs of tests (48 pupils)

Test scale	Enjoyment	Misery	Maths	Language
Enjoyment				
Misery	0.30			
Maths	0.28	−0.31		
Language	0.03	−0.40	0.59	
Reading	0.12	−0.40	0.68	0.62

Significantly different from zero at the 5 percent level

Significantly different from zero at the 1 percent level

coefficient is high (0.62), then are language and enjoyment scores not cor-related because the coefficient is low? How high must a coefficient be before it ceases to be a chance occurrence and becomes an indicator of a real asso-ciation?

To answer these questions, you should consider the 48 pupils to be just a sample of a broad population of eleven-year-old girls who could equally as well have been tested. Some of the critical correlation coefficients appear in Table 14.14.

It should now be clear that only the enjoyment-language and enjoyment-reading pairs of tests show no significant statistical correlation. All the other

Table 14.14 Critical values for the correlation coefficient

Sample size (N)	Correlation coefficient needed to differ significantly from zero (in a one-tail test)	
	at 5% level	at 1% level
1,000	0.05	0.07
500	0.07	0.10
200	0.12	0.16
100	0.16	0.23
50	0.23	0.32
48	0.24	0.32
40	0.26	0.35
30	0.30	0.40
25	0.33	0.44
20	0.36	0.48
15	0.42	0.54
10	0.50	0.63
5	0.68	0.80

Critical values for the sample of 48 eleven-year-old girls

pairs are worthy of further analysis to establish what are the implications for the classroom teacher. Namely, for eleven-year-old girls in primary school, valid conclusions are:

1. Those with high maths scores are likely to be those that enjoy going to school the most.
2. Feelings of misery and inadequacy are associated with low levels of general attainment.
3. There is a strong association between attainment in maths, language and reading.

It would be wrong to say that *because* the child likes being at school, high maths scores will follow; significant correlation coefficients do not mean that one of the variables causes the other: simply that there is a recognisable trend in the pattern of the two sets of scores.

There is one further point which must be made: make sure that your correlation sample reflects the known groupings of your pupils. For instance, the practial example we have used has been restricted to eleven-year-old girls. This is because the pattern of correlations is not exactly the same for boys of this age. Further, girls at nine years of age do not show the same pattern as the eleven-year-old girls. If you choose a sample that mixes together both girls and boys, as well as different age groups, do not expect a very meaningful pattern: most of the correlation coefficients will be 'not significant', and you may have missed important findings.

Conclusion

This chapter has focused on relatively straightforward statistical analysis technique, concerned with distributions of one variable and with relationships between no more than two variables. For more complex situations, where questions relate to relationships among three or more variables, you will need to know about multi-variate techniques. If you wish to extend your understanding of statistics you will need to consult one or more text books. Choosing the right book is a personal matter — it very much depends on your starting points and the level of mathematical treatment detail that you require. Some suggested titles are given below, but you should dip into them — and some others — before deciding which is the most appropriate for your needs.

References and further reading

Freedman, D., Pisani, R. and Purves, R. (1998) *Statistics*, London: W. W. Norton & Co.

Lewis-Beck, M. S. (ed.) (1994) *Basic Statistics*. International Handbooks of Quantitative Applications in the Social Sciences, Volume 1, London: Sage.

Marsh, C. (1988) *Exploring Data*, Oxford: Polity Press.

Shipman, M. D. (1972) *The Limitations of Social Research*, London: Longmans.

Siegel, S. (1956) *Non-parametric Statistics for the Behavioural Sciences*, Tokyo: McGraw Hill.

15
The analysis of qualitative data
Rob Watling

Introduction

Analysis is the researcher's equivalent of alchemy — the elusive process by which you hope you can turn your raw data into nuggets of pure gold. And, like alchemy, such magic calls for science and art in equal measure. It is understandable, therefore, that the editors of this book chose to place the chapters on data analysis towards the end. It is understandable because the transformation of data into wisdom is often seen as something that can only be done in the later stages of a research project, once the raw material has been safely gathered in. And it is also understandable because the sorts of analysis you do in your project will inevitably depend on the types of research you have been undertaking. You would expect to analyse interview transcripts differently to the notes you make during participant observation, for example. And both of these would be different to the way you would handle the information you find during your literature search. So of course, some key decisions about analysis will *need* to be taken late on in your project.

But locating these chapters at the end of the book is interesting because analysis is not, in practice, something that *can* only be considered at the end. This is for two main reasons. Firstly, the types of analysis that you are in a position to carry out may determine the types of research you are able to do. If, for example, you do not have the time or resources to analyse 100 in-depth, face-to-face interviews; or to process 1,000 questionnaires; or to use diaries with 25 managers, you had better choose another approach. If you feel that qualitative analysis will be too imprecise for your purposes or too vague to act as the basis for generalisation, you may already have chosen to adopt a more quantitative approach which will require different analytic techniques. So the first point to recognise is that some decisions about analysis may actually *precede* important decisions about methods. But the second point is just as important. With qualitative data in particular (but also with quantitative data as we have seen in Chapter 14) it is simply not possible or desirable to treat analysis as a separate activity which is only done at the final stages of a project. The analysis of data takes place throughout the project. It is an iterative and persistent part of the research process.

Imagine that you are going to conduct a series of interviews with managers at a further education college. In selecting the college that you want to visit you will already be considering some of its key features (its size, its general type, its suitability for your project, and so on). You will certainly do some basic background research about its policies and practice (deciding if it seems to be a forward-looking institution or one which is constrained by local conditions). When you arrive at the college to conduct your interviews you will form some important first impressions of the place, such as the neighbourhood in which it is located, the state of the college buildings, the demeanour of the students, whether it is welcoming to visitors, and so on. Before you start the interviews you may have general discussions with the people you have come to meet, and these are likely to give you more information about the place. By now you will understand quite a lot about the college you have chosen for your research. Indeed you will have started to analyse some important qualitative data. Throughout the interview itself, you will be 'reading' the situation — making sense of the interviewees' words and interpreting their body language. You are bound to form judgements, hunches, prejudices, theories, hypotheses and further questions as you go along.

By the end of the day you will have conducted the interviews, responded to the managers' answers in order to get more detail, added a new question to your schedule, formed some key judgements, come to some tentative conclusions about their management style, left the building, reflected on the visit, challenged some of your own assumptions and written up your field notes. You will, in the process, have analysed a huge amount of qualitative data. And that is just in one field visit.

This key recognition — that analysis pervades each and every aspect of qualitative inquiry — may even lead, in extreme cases, to the termination of an entire research project (Gummesson, 2000):

> During an interview, I found that a company had engaged an advertising agency to set up a campaign designed to improve the company's image. The media cost of the campaign was expected to be around $300,000. In my judgement the campaign was meaningless; the company lacked business mission, goals, and strategies and hence had no corporate image to communicate. After a brief examination of the project, I got in touch with the chief executive and proposed that the campaign ought to be stopped. It turned out to be possible to cancel the contract with the media. The chief executive was satisfied because he wanted to cut costs.

This example illustrates that information gathering, analysis, con-clusions, recommendations, and implementation can take place more or less simultaneously. This contrasts with the stage-by-stage approach (albeit partly iterative) recommended in scientific research. Care has to be taken here, however. There is a considerable risk that without an understanding of the institutional conditions, consultants and researchers may put forward naïve, standard solutions. (2000: 127–8)

Whether he/she realises it or not, any qualitative researcher will have to analyse parts of the data while they are designing the project; when they are conducting their desk-based research; when they are doing their fieldwork; while they are storing, retrieving and handling their records; when they are building and testing theories; and when they are writing up their report. This chapter will consider some of the main ways in which this analysis can take place at any or all of these stages and will encourage you to realise that data analysis is rarely a separate or distinct activity in its own right.

Methods and methodology

As has been pointed out repeatedly throughout this book, researchers are constantly faced with a series of choices and options about research methods. What they are doing when they make these choices is less about making the 'right' choice, than about making the 'best' choice in the partic-ular circumstances in which they find themselves — the optimum choice. It is not necessarily 'right' to take a positivist or interpretivist position, to use a standardised measure of literacy or to organise a focus group. The deci-sion needs to be made and justified in the particular context of the research you are undertaking.

The same is true of the approach that you take to analysing your data, whether these data are qualitative, quantitative or — as is far more likely — a mixture of both. The important thing is that you, the researcher, make the decisions thoughtfully, systematically, critically and in ways which can be accounted for. In this way, when you come to defend your work, you will be able to justify your choice of methods (the tools, techniques, instruments and approaches you have adopted) through a clear methodology (a study and an account of the arguments and the philosophical underpinnings of your work).

In the analysis of qualitative research (which is what interests us here) that means making a series of deliberate, critical choices about the meanings and values of the data you have gathered, and making sure that your decisions can be justified in terms of the research, the context in which it was carried out, and the people who were involved in it. Nothing less will do.

Denzin and Lincoln (1998) describe this collection of processes as bricolage — 'a pieced-together, close-knit set of practices that provide solutions to a problem in a concrete situation' (1998: 3) and go on to look at some of the key skills of the bricoleur — the flexible, creative, intuitive qualitative researcher who seeks to produce an in-depth understanding of complex social phenomena:

> The bricoleur is adept at performing a large number of diverse tasks, ranging from interviewing to observing, to interpreting personal and historical documents, to intensive self-reflection and introspection. The bricoleur reads widely and is knowledgeable about the many . . . competing and overlapping perspectives and paradigms.
>
> The bricoleur understands that research is an interactive process shaped by his or her personal history, biography, gender, social class, race, and ethnicity, and those of the people in the setting. The bricoleur knows that science is power, for all research findings have political implications. There is no value-free science. The bricoleur also knows that researchers all tell stories about the worlds they have studied . . .
>
> The product of the bricoleur's labour is a bricolage, a complex, dense, reflexive collage-like creation that represents the researcher's images, understandings, and interpretations of the world or phenomenon under analysis. (1998: 4)

Six elements of qualitative data analysis

I have already said that data analysis inevitably takes place throughout the entire research process. I have also implied that each piece of research will follow a different route, and that the types of analysis you are engaged in will always depend very heavily on the nature of the project, the people involved and the focus of the investigation. How then can we provide any guidelines for the newcomer to research? Are they always on their own, making the best they can of a difficult problem and fearing the examiner who is lying in wait, ready to criticise (and mark down) their choices? It is not that fearful a prospect. There are precedents, both in the general traditions of research and in specific examples of researchers who have looked at similar topics before and identified some of the best ways of operating in different circumstances. The task for the new researcher is to take what he/she can from these past experiences, to adopt the ones that fit their circumstances best, to adapt those that are nearly suitable, and to reject those that are irrelevant or uncomfortable. All these decisions need to be taken critically, and with adequate reflection.

And it is wise to realise that there is nothing so unique about the research of educational management and leadership that it will not be raised in the literature relating to educational research in general or in many other aspects of the social sciences. You will find as much support for your research activity in the writings of teachers, curriculum theorists, policy analysts and other educationalists, and you will find as much relevance in the writings of nurses, lawyers, engineers and social workers who have also decided to adopt a more qualitative approach to their work. Read widely for your research, and develop the fruitful links which are the hallmarks of the sophisticated and mature practitioner. For in many ways, qualitative research is similar to the sorts of process by which we make judgements and arrive at understandings throughout our everyday working lives. But when we call it 'research' we need to be more reflective, more systematic, more critical and more accountable in the ways we proceed.

When we look at other people's research, and at our own, we can identify a series of different stages where analytic processes can be found. For the purpose of this chapter, I have chosen six (though some research projects will have more or fewer than this) and I would like to go through them in turn, suggesting the types of analysis that might occur under any of them (Figure 15.1). I will illustrate my points by referring to recent writings on educational and social scientific research. What I do not want to imply, however, is that this diagram represents a blueprint for action. This is not designed as a system for moving simply through the research process: you would miss out a number of key stages if you did. Rather, it is a guide to some of the ways in which analysis might be located throughout a qualita-

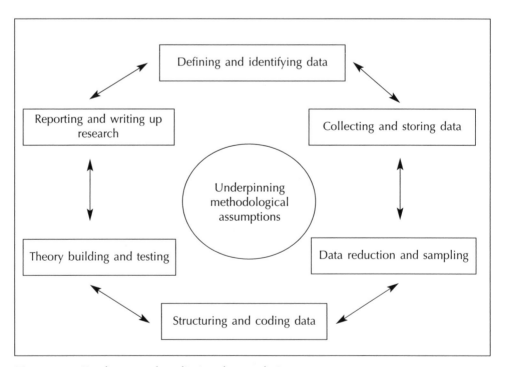

Figure 15.1 Six elements of qualitative data analysis

tive research project, instead of being left till the end of the process where it would loom over you as a final reckoning.

Defining and identifying data

What do we mean by 'data' — especially in a qualitative study? It is a term with distinctly positivist origins, coming from the Latin and meaning 'things that are given'. It implies a scientific, objective approach to reality in which there is a fixed (a given) world of known and knowable facts for us to discover. As we have seen elsewhere in this book, such a view is not always accepted, especially by those who argue that reality is socially constructed and that truths are negotiated by actors in specific contexts:

> Fundamentally, we think that social phenomena exist not only in the mind, but in the objective world as well, and that there are some lawful, reasonably stable relationships to be found among them. The lawfulness comes from the sequences and the regularities that link phenomena together; it is from these that we derive the constructs that account for individual and social life. (Huberman and Miles, 1998: 182)

The qualitative researcher, especially one working within such an epistemological framework, is likely to be searching for understanding, rather than knowledge; for interpretations rather than measurements; for values rather than facts. And the scientific notion of 'data' sometimes sits uncomfortably in such discussions. Some researchers are not happy with the word at all, preferring to write about evidence, information, or material rather than data. For the purposes of this chapter, however, I have retained the term even though it sounds too precise to me.

But whatever you decide to call those things that the quantitative researcher readily refers to as 'data', it is important to acknowledge what you are including in the term. Once you move away from the analysis of given, measurable, and objectively verifiable facts, to the analysis of thoughts, feelings, expressions and opinions which are open to debate, there is a clear requirement for the researcher to make justifiable choices about what to include and what to leave out of your account. In doing so you are already involved in a process of analysis — weighing up the value and worth of specific things and deciding whether or not they are likely to 'count' in the research. How much of an interview, for example, will you count as evidence? Is it only the spoken words? Is it also the gestures and body language of the interviewee (Keats, 2000)? Is it also the things they omit to say which you will regard as important?

Even at the design stage we can see that the researchers are weighing up alternatives and making choices about the appropriateness of the people they will be working with and the quality of the data that they are likely to pro-

vide. In describing the methods used in their study of the HEADLAMP training programme for newly appointed headteachers, for example, Blandford
and Squire (2000) make a series of points about their sample, all of which
we are entitled to presume are relevant to their ultimate analysis:

> All 20 respondents selected by the researchers participated: these were
> a representative sample of 16 newly appointed headteachers employed
> in a range of schools, and four LEA inspectors/advisers. As in phase
> one (of the project) the geographical range was wide; the schools were
> situated in five different LEAs across England and drawn for the full
> spectrum of county, unitary, metropolitan and city authorities. One
> school was grant-maintained. Respondents' schools varied in size from
> a nursery school to a community secondary school (with adult educa-
> tion provision) of 1,800 school age pupils. The range of schools
> included nursery (1), infant (1), primary (5), junior (1), secondary co-
> ed (5), secondary single-sex (1), special educational needs, residential
> (1) and day (1). There were eight male and eight female headteachers
> in the sample; only one of the female heads was appointed to a sec-
> ondary school. The respondents had between 9 and 27 years' teaching
> experience in mainstream schools and had been in post from two to
> seven terms. The number of pupils on roll in the respondents' schools
> ranged between fewer than 100 and over 1,000. (2000: 25)

This kind of sampling is inextricably linked to analysis, but it is not only
done at the beginning of the project. Finch and Mason (1990) point out, for
example, that one of the main differences between qualitative fieldwork and
social surveys is the stage at which sampling of people and situations can
take place:

> In surveys such decisions are made once-and-for-all at the beginning of
> the project, and follow formalized statistical procedures for sampling.
> In fieldwork, such decisions are taken at various stages during the
> course of the project on the basis of contextual information. To out-
> siders who are not privy to the changing contextual basis of this pro-
> ject, research decisions can look rather ad hoc. (1990: 25)

It is important to recognise that these preparatory processes of selection
involve analysing as well as defining the phenomenon. Drawing on the work
of Doyle and Carter (1984), for example, Simco (1995) discusses the difference between academic 'tasks' and 'activities'. This is an important pre-
cursor to their study in the classroom — it helps the researcher decide what
to observe and how to analyse it:

Essentially 'academic tasks are devised by the answers students are required to produce and the routes that can be used to obtain these answers' (Doyle, 1983: 161). They have a number of elements in their definition . . . (and) it is within the precision of the definition of 'task' that the crucial differences between task and activity emerge. Activity is to do with classroom occurrences within specified periods of time. Tasks are part of activity because they are embedded in it. In essence it is possible to have several tasks and also classroom occurrences which are not tasks but which are part of activity. (1995: 53)

And many other researchers, such as Eslea and Mukhtar (2000), identify what needs to be researched partly by analysing what others have left out of their work:

The study reported here is an attempt to address some of the problems identified in the bullying and racism research to date. Clumsy definitions, inappropriate questionnaires, white researchers and the unnecessary lumping together of non-white ethnic groups mean that little can be concluded about the real experiences of ethnic minority children in British schools. Any hypothesis must therefore be tentative: experiences of racism and bullying may vary according to country of origin, language, religion, clothing, food, rituals, and so on. On the one hand, one might expect the political tensions between India and Pakistan to be reflected in hostility between children of these nationalities, and on the other hand, that tension between Hindu and Muslim children might be found regardless of nation. Another possibility is that bullying may reflect the relative proportions of different ethnic groups in the local population. This study attempts to begin the process of untangling these possibilities, in order to provide a richer understanding of bullying among Asian schoolchildren in Britain. (2000: 210)

Collecting and storing data

During the collection of qualitative data most researchers will start to form opinions and judgements about it. Let us look briefly at some of my own field notes written after a semi-structured interview with a group of teachers piloting a new curriculum project. I was exploring the extent to which the project was trying to be informative (trying to introduce new areas of knowledge into the curriculum) or transformative (trying to support social change):

The discussion then moved on to consider some aspects of the distinction between two aspects of the project identified in the interim report as its informative and transformative goals . . . During the first few minutes of this part of the discussion, I detected a reluctance on the part of the team to acknowledge a transformative ambition. I was not sure whether to put this down to humility, reservation or disagreement with my basic question.

The team began by suggesting that the pilot was interested first in transforming the teachers and the assumptions of teaching and learning that are inherent in some other subjects. There has also been a transformative element of the work as it is carried out in schools, and this needs to be linked (hopefully) to a wider view of what schools are, how they operate, and what they are 'for'. This, in turn, is linked to the wider aspirations of the current review of the curriculum. (Watling: personal fieldnotes)

We can see that it is *during* the interview itself that theories start to form in the researcher's mind. These theories may be tentative, provisional or unfinished. They may be dispensed with later on or may prove to be key elements of the final analysis. But once again it is important to recognise that they are not left till the end of the research, and that their 'value' needs to be judged by the researcher within the context of the data collection. It is also advisable at times like this, to check your analysis by sharing these observations with the people you are working with — whether that is your research and work colleagues, or the participants in your research.

Finally in this section, I would like to encourage you to consider the ways in which you store your data and make them accessible for analysis. Whether your data are on paper, in notebooks, on proformas, on audio or videotape, on computer or anywhere else, you have the opportunity early on to organise them in ways that will be helpful to you later. Some people use card indexes, colour codings, filing systems, photocopies — use whatever works for you and supports the sort of data-retrieval and analysis you need to make. One of the simplest things to do is to print interview transcripts with line numbers (an easy option to select on most word processors) which will make them look like the example of a project transcript below. It will help enormously in identifying specific excerpts from long transcripts (see example below).

Denscombe (1998) offers the following, additional advice:

- As far as possible, get all materials in similar formats (for example, all on A4 size pages or all on record cards of the same size). This helps with storage and when sifting through materials.
- Where possible, the raw data should be collated in a way that allows researchers' notes and comments to be added alongside. So, for example, when taped interviews are transcribed, there should be a

623 We did some Child Protection stuff recently, and it was very simple, in

624 order to get the message over. We brought out pen portraits of three kids

625 I'd selected to be very, very dire and the pictures on the staff faces told it

626 all. Then I said 'What are you going to do when you have a problem with

627 this kid? Are you going to go eye to eye, nose to nose scream and shout at

628 him? You can't do that with this kid. This kid has seen worse than

629 anything you can inflict on him. None of them will work — he'll just go

630 and tell you where to go and walk off on you because you can't do

631 anything.' And it had an effect on a number of people, staff have come

632 and seen me since.

wide margin to the right-hand side of the page left blank, so that the researcher can add notes . . .

- Each piece of 'raw data' material should be identified with a unique serial number or code for reference purposes . . . (This helps with retrieval, checking, audit trails and preserving anonymity.)
- Make a back up copy of all original materials and use the back up copies for any analysis . . . It is time-consuming and can be expensive. But any loss or damage to the material is catastrophic for the research. To save effort it is best to duplicate the raw data as soon as they have been reference coded . . . The original should be stored safely — preferably in a location quite separate from the back-up copies, which now become the 'working copies' that the researcher uses for analysis. (1998: 209–210)

Data reduction and sampling

It is highly unlikely that any researcher will use all the data gathered during their project — especially if they are using the sort of qualitative approaches discussed elsewhere in this book which are likely to produce large amounts of rich, deep data.

In reducing the amounts to a manageable size it is possible to use any of the standard sampling techniques. This can be done before any of the data are analysed (in the strict sense of the word). It would be possible, for example, to use a random sampling technique and to analyse only every third paragraph of an interview, or to look in depth at only 50 percent of the questionnaire returns. But it will usually make much more sense to reduce the data by more purposeful methods — working perhaps on the basis of what you already know to be important or relevant. This may not sound scientific or objective, but the researcher is entitled to make sense of the data they are handling — they merely have to account for what they are doing and justify their choices. Your analysis will thus inform the type of data reduction that you carry out. This means, again, that analysis is not something that can always be done at the end of the project. You need to weigh the value of evidence to your project as you go along, to take informed judgements on its value to your work, to interpret it and to use it as the basis for your understandings and your explanations.

Structuring and coding data

Almost everything that we have considered so far is what we might call *formative analysis*. It reflects the epistemological and ontological aspects of qualitative research projects which seek to provide understandings and explanations, and actively shape the types of data collection that will go on. These perspectives *allow* and *require* the researcher to analyse aspects of their subject iteratively and reflexively. The more-easily recognisable processes of analysis might be thought to begin once the data is safely back in the study (whether this is done during or after the fieldwork). As we listen to our tape-recordings, as we read our transcripts or other documents, as we revisit our research journals, we have to start to make some sense of it all. The ways of proceeding here are varied and largely technical, and include indexing, coding, content analysis, discourse analysis, and others. There are tried and tested methods for coding interviews, for example, and the choice of codes may have been pre-determined, or have emerged from the types of data gathered during the research. If we wish, we can use the results of preliminary coding for some simple quantitative analyses — counting responses in a sub-set of the interviews and using the results as the basis for further analysis.

In Arksey and Knight (1999), 178 teachers were asked whether they saw teaching as a profession and if so, why. A sample of responses was selected for coding. Each distinct idea was written down with similar ideas being written alongside each other, and identical responses being tallied. For example, teaching was said to be a profession where teachers:

272

Wear a suit/neat clothes IIIIII	(g)
Higher education needed III	(e)
Clean shaven	(g)
Mark work regularly III	(f)
Tidy hair I	(g)
Decide how to teach a topic IIII	(d)

The *full set* of ideas (over a hundred were noted) in the sample of transcripts could be collapsed to form eight main categories, which were:

The public standing of teaching	(a)
Teachers' inter-personal skills	(b)
Teachers' possession of standards and values	(c)
Teachers' autonomy and non-routine decision-making	(d)
The possession of specialist knowledge	(e)
Conscientiousness	(f)
Appearance and self-presentation	(g)
Others	(h)

It can be seen that 4 of the ideas in the sample above fell into category (d); 3 into (e); 3 into (f) and 8 into (g).

The categories were discussed by all five researchers, who agreed that they were usable and covered all of the data. Definitions of each category were then written to make public their meanings and to enable any member of the team to apply them consistently.

The categories were then used to index the complete set of interviews. (1999: 165)

Accounts of such techniques are easy to find in any of the quality research methods handbooks. In the courses we teach at the University of Leicester, Marlene Morrison and I steer students towards guides such as: Bell (1999), Blaxter *et al.* (1996), Cohen and Manion (1994) Denscombe (1998), Hopkins (1993), Robson (1993) and Silverman (2000). But we stress that the techniques you choose to manage your data are intricately related to the methodological choices you make elsewhere in your work. It is important to use them critically and not just instrumentally.

These techniques include inductive and deductive processes of analysis for which Tesch (1990) has devised a complex typology of 26 different kinds of approach arranged into four main groups based on the characteristics of language; on the discovery of regularities; on the comprehension of the meaning of text or action; and on reflection. Miles and Huberman (1994), on the other hand, have described a set of 13 'tactics' for generating meaning from qualitative data which they later summarised as follows:

> Numbered 1 to 13, they are roughly arranged from the descriptive to the explanatory, and from the concrete to the more abstract: *Noting patterns and themes* (1), *seeing plausibility* — making initial, intuitive sense (2) — and *clustering* by conceptual grouping (3) help one to see connections (between the various pieces of data). *Making metaphors*, a kind of figurative grouping of data (4), is also a tactic for achieving more integration among diverse pieces of data. *Counting* (5) is a familiar way to see 'what's there' — and to keep oneself honest.
>
> *Making contrasts and comparisons* (6) is a classic tactic meant to sharpen understanding by clustering and distinguishing observations. Differentiation is also needed, as in *partitioning variables*, unbundling variables that have been prematurely grouped, or simply taking a less monolithic look (7).
>
> More abstract tactics include *subsuming particulars into the general, shuttling back and forth between first-level data and more general categories* (8); *factoring* (9) and analogue of a familiar quantitative technique, allowing the analyst to move from a large number of measured variables to a smaller set of unobserved, usually hypothetical, variables; *noting relations between variables* (10); and *finding intervening variables* (11). Finally, assembling a coherent understanding of a data set is helped through *building a logical chain of evidence* (12) and *making conceptual/theoretical coherence*, typically through comparison with the referent constructs in the literature (13). (Huberman and Miles 1998: 187)

Theory building and theory testing

In the accounts from Arksey and Knight (1999) and from Huberman and Miles (1998) above, we can identify an iterative process whereby theories about the data are generated, tested and applied at various stages. Some may need to be rejected, or adapted if they are going to be retained. If there is space in your research report you can describe these changes in your theory base — discussing the alternative viewpoints you have considered and explaining why some of them were not thought suitable. To build and test your theories in this way, as you progress through the research, is one way of showing your critically analytical approach to your work. If you look back through this chapter and at high quality accounts of other people's research, you should be able to identify opportunities for theory building and testing at each and every stage of the research process.

Reporting and writing up research

Some of the 'findings' of qualitative research (again this term has a positivist heritage that not every one is comfortable with) only really start to emerge when you begin drafting the final report. As you construct an argument based on what you have done, the things you have seen and heard, the people you have worked with, and the data you have handled, some more analysis is not just permissible, it is almost inevitable. The final threading together of the piece, the weight you give to each part of the argument, the elaboration of a line of thought — all these constitute a final round of analysis. Richardson (1998) considers our approach to writing as the final frontier in our efforts to make research come alive to a wider audience:

> I write because I want to find something out. I write in order to learn something that I didn't know before I wrote it. I was taught, however, as perhaps you were, too, not to write until I knew what I wanted to say, until my points were organized and outlined. No surprise, this static writing model coheres with mechanistic scientism and quantitative research. But, I will argue, the model is itself a socio-historical invention that reifies the static social world imagined by our nineteenth-century fore parents. The model has serious problems: It ignores the role of writing as a dynamic, creative process; it undermines the confidence of beginning qualitative researchers because their experience of research is inconsistent with the writing model; and it contributes to the flotilla of qualitative writing that is simply not interesting to read because adherence to the model requires writers to silence their own voices and to view themselves as contaminants.

> Qualitative researchers commonly speak of the importance of the individual researcher's skills and aptitudes. The researcher — rather than the survey, the questionnaire, or the census tape — is the 'instrument' … Yet they are trained to conceptualize writing as 'writing up' the research, rather than as a method of discovery. (1998: 347)

Richardson goes on to propose a whole range of creative writing practices that can support analysis in these stages of research, and gives guidance on where to find real examples of the use of 'narratives of the self', fiction, drama, poetry, 'performance science', 'polyvocal texts', 'responsive readings', 'aphorisms', comedy and satire, visual representations and others. She also suggests a series of writing exercises which might encourage you to be more versatile and to adopt new processes for analysis. My only caveat would be to remind students that their work is likely to be assessed by people who are firmly rooted in the writing traditions she is trying to challenge. It may be a strategy which delivers risk as much as it offers liberation.

Systems and software

Some people are free-thinking, free-floating individuals who can live with the organic mess produced by most qualitative research, and come out at the end with a seamless and well-rounded research report. But most people fall back on systems of one sort or another, whether it be field notes, diagrams, card indexes, computer packages or fully-fledged ways of turning interviews into numbers ready for crunching. The important thing is to use a system which you understand, which is reliable, safe and which you can justify.

You can now buy some efficient and highly flexible software packages that support qualitative researchers in the analysis of their data. There is no room in this chapter to consider them in depth and there will, inevitably, be different versions and packages available by the time you read this. But they fall into a number of different groups as described below.

Firstly, there are simple software packages which can easily be called upon to support the qualitative researcher. Even the simple word processor is capable of helping you to store, retrieve, and analyse your data creatively. It can count, tabulate, format, summarise, copy, cut and paste, remove, highlight and annotate. Other, linked, packages such as databases, spreadsheets, and presentation software are now much easier to use than they were a few years ago, and it is certainly easier to transfer data between one package and another. Spending time with the software you already know, and exploring it with the help of the many quality manuals now available can reap benefits.

Also available are packages for specific aspects of data handling, particularly the high quality bibliographic software packages such as EndNote, Pro-Cite, and Reference Manager. At its most basic level, this software provides an electronic version of a card index system, allowing users to store and retrieve details of the documentary materials they have used. At its most extensive, it provides a comprehensive system allowing you to import, store, share, manipulate, retrieve and export this data in a wide variety of ways. One of its greatest strengths is its ability to produce detailed bibliographies for academic publications, and to do so in any of the hundreds of styles required by different publishers. This software is available for individual use, but is also being networked by many higher education institutions (Mulvaney, 2000).

Finally, there is a range of software packages tailor-made for handling qualitative research data and supporting the generation and testing of theories. The current market leaders (in alphabetical order) are ATLAS, EnVive Ethnograph, HyperRESEARCH and NUD*IST; all are based on the principals of storing, coding, searching, retrieving and sorting your data according to the categories and labels that you apply to it. They also, in various ways, support you as you build and test your theories. Details of some of the different approaches which these packages provide can be found in Richards and Richards (1998) but your final choice will frequently depend on cost, availability, and your confidence with computers. The balance on this final point is between the steep learning curve that some of these packages present you with, and the fact that it is often much easier to learn the basics on a small-scale project than on a major piece of research where mistakes and delays can cause serious problems. In a smaller piece of work it is much easier to cut your losses and revert to more traditional (or more radical) systems if you feel out of your depth or constrained by the inevitable limitations of the software. For whichever system you use (and almost every qualitative researcher will use one of these software packages) the important thing is to ensure that the software supports your research, and that it does not dictate your way of working.

Conclusion

I have argued that analysis is an integral part of the whole research process — especially when you are dealing with qualitative data. It informs and responds to the types of research you are able to conduct, it shapes and is shaped by the subject of your work, and it pervades each and every aspect of the research process from project design to the writing of the report. Most important, the processes of analysis are inextricably linked to the other methodological choices you make throughout your work. As such they need to be accounted for, justified, critically evaluated and (we hope) celebrated.

References

Arksey, H. and Knight, P. (1999) *Interviewing for Social Scientists*, London: Sage.

Bell, J. (1999) *Doing Your Research Project* (3rd edn.), Milton Keynes: Open University.

Blandford, S. and Squire, L. (2000) 'An evaluation of the Teacher Training Agency Headteacher Leadership and Management Programme (HEADLAMP)', *Educational Managemant and Administration* 28(1): 21–32.

Blaxter, L., Hughes, C. and Tight, M. (1996). *How to Research*, Buckingham: Open University.

Cohen, L. and Manion, L. (1994) *Research Methods in Education*, New Hampshire: Croom Helm.

Denscombe, M. (1998) *The Good Research Guide*, Buckingham: Open University.

Denzin, N. K. and Lincoln, Y. S. (1998) *Collecting and Interpreting Qualitative Materials*. London: Sage.

Doyle, W. (1983) 'Academic work', *Review of Educational Research* 53: 159–199.

Eslea, M. and Mukhtar, K. (2000) 'Bullying and racism among Asian schoolchildren in Britain', *Educational Research* 42(2): 207–217.

Finch, J. and Mason, J. (1990) 'Decision taking in the fieldwork process: theoretical sampling and collaborative working', *Studies in Qualitative Methodology* 2: 25–50.

Gummesson, E. (2000) *Qualitative Methods in Management Research*, London, Sage.

Hopkins, D. (1993) *A Teacher's Guide to Classroom Research*, Buckingham: Open University.

Huberman, A. M. and Miles, M. B. (1998) 'Data management and analysis methods'. in Denzin, N. K. and Lincoln, Y. S. (eds) *Collecting and Interpreting Qualitative Materials*, London: Sage.

Keats, D. M. (2000) *Interviewing: A Practical Guide for Students and Professionals*, Buckingham: Open University Press.

Miles, M. B. and Huberman, A. M. (1994) *Qualitative Data Analysis: an Expanded Sourcebook*. London: Sage.

Mulvaney, T. (ed.) (2000) *A Quick Guide to Personal Bibliographic Software*, London: UKOLUG.

Richards, T. J. and Richards, L. (1998) 'Using computers in qualitative research', in Denzin, N. K. and Lincoln, Y. S. (eds.) *Collecting and Interpreting Qualitative Materials*. London: Sage.

Richardson, L. (1998) 'Writing: a Method of Enquiry', in Denzin, N. K. and Lincoln, Y. S. (eds.) *Collecting and Interpreting Qualitative Material*. London: Sage.

Robson, C. (1993) *Real World Research*, Oxford: Blackwell.

Silverman, D. (2000) *Doing Qualitative Research*, London: Sage.

Simco, N. P. (1995) 'Activity analysis in primary classrooms', *British Educational Research Journal* 21(1): 49–60.

Tesch, R. (1990) *Qualitative Research: Analysis Types and Software Tools*, London: Falmer Press.

16

Academic writing: process and presentation

Ann R. J. Briggs

Introduction

> Research in isolation serves no purpose. Effective communication, both to other research workers and to teachers and other educationists, is the essence of good educational research. (Nisbet and Entwistle, 1984: 256)

This chapter is intended as general guidance for those who are new to academic writing, and addresses such questions as:

- Who am I writing for — and how does that affect what I write?
- How do I organise and structure my writing?
- What sort of language should I use?
- How authoritative can I be about my findings?
- How do I present my analysed results?
- How should I further disseminate my research?

You will already have gained insight into the presentation of your research from the other chapters in this book, particularly Chapters 14 and 15. You may find it helpful to use this chapter in conjunction with those which deal with the particular methodology you have chosen.

Audience

One important question to ask before writing up your research is, 'Who am I writing for?' The answer might be among the following:

- masters degree, or doctoral, examiners;
- the editor and readers of an academic journal;
- conference delegates; or
- senior staff at my place of work.

The answer is rarely, simply: 'Myself'.

Each of the 'audiences' listed above will have its own expectations, some easy to assess, others less so. All will expect to be presented with something new and engaging: new insight into known situations, new concepts or areas of knowledge. The expectations of examiners and academic journal editors can partly be gauged by reading dissertations, theses and journal articles which have received their approval; look again at material of this type that you consulted for your literature review, to seek out and develop an approach to your audience that is appropriate, both for you and the context in which you are writing.

Other audiences may expect a different focus, and sometimes a selective approach to your material is appropriate. Conference delegates will want to be stimulated to think and debate within relatively tight time constraints; focusing on just one aspect of your research may be right in this context. Choose a research subject that you find particularly intriguing, or that ties in most closely with the theme of the conference, and give a clear presentation of it, rather than trying to present the whole of your research. Indicate to your audience how it can learn about the rest of your findings — if they do not exist in published form, tell people how to contact you. A different approach to selecting your material will be needed for senior staff at your place of work. They will probably need a concise and accessible report — written or oral — which summarises all your findings, together with clear recommendations for action. This may mean that months of investigation, analysis and writing must be distilled into 1,000–2,000 words for easy access by a range of staff. If the intended outcome of your research, school or college improvement for example, is to be guided by what you have learned, then a format that motivates the maximum number of people to read (or listen) and respond will have to be chosen.

The findings of a major research project may be presented many times: perhaps in formats appropriate for all the different audiences listed above, as well as in published books or educational newspapers. The heart of the research — its aims, the investigation itself, the analysis of findings and conclusions — must be there in each case, but the balance of what you present to each audience will differ, as will the level of detail which you include.

So how do you decide what to include? One approach is to assess how much your audience knows already. In the first three cases given above, the audience will be familiar with the broad concepts underlying your research, and the research traditions into which it fits; they will, however, be assessing your ability to present and engage in those concepts and traditions. They may know nothing of the local context of the research, and may not be specialists in the aspect of education that is the subject of your research. Your senior managers, however, though they may well be 'expert' on the local context and phase of education, may be less familiar with the broad concepts that underpin your research and drive your argument.

In all cases there will be areas of information with which you feel your audience will already be familiar, and concepts that you feel that they will already understand but which are germane to the account you are presenting, and which therefore must be included in your presentation. Even if your audience is familiar with the relevant concepts, it will need to know how those concepts fit in with the investigation and analysis that you have undertaken. Whatever your audience's familiarity with the subject, it will expect you to be able to explain it, to take it through your train of thought. Remember, your audience has not 'lived through' your research as you have. What you put in or leave out will depend upon the required length of the piece, but your writing should be internally coherent — that is, it must not depend upon data or concepts which have not been presented or discussed. This means, of course, that conclusions should be based on what has been presented, not on knowledge which is assumed or 'given'.

Above all, your audience wants to feel that you have the authority to speak or write on your chosen subject. 'The essential feature of any research report is to make a claim to knowledge' (Bassey, 1999: 89). Readers need assurance that the research has been properly carried out; that it recognises and builds upon what has been previously researched and understood; that the data collected have been analysed thoroughly and thoughtfully; and that conclusions bear in mind not only the research findings, but also previous knowledge and the constraints imposed by the scale of the research. This kind of authority can be conveyed irrespective of the length of the written piece: from a thesis of many thousand words to a research abstract of a few hundred words.

Structure

Whatever the length of your written piece, it will need a clear structure; this becomes increasingly important both for you and for your reader in longer pieces of writing. For theses and dissertations, and to a certain extent for articles in academic journals, there are conventions to be followed. If you have been given guidelines for the various sections of your thesis, you would be well advised to follow them, or to make it clear in your writing, after discussion with your tutor, why you are deviating from usual practice.

Where no format is given for the writing as a whole, think through what your audience will need to know, and the order in which it will need to be presented, if it is to make sense. You may arrive, predictably, at a presentation sequence such as this:

- the aims of the research and its context;
- a review of related research and knowledge;

- a description and justification of the chosen research methodology;
- a summary of findings;
- an analysis of what the findings show; and
- conclusions and recommendations.

Some contexts allow deviation from this format. In a newspaper article or an internal report, for example, it might be appropriate to catch the reader's attention by presenting the conclusions first: the reader then chooses whether to read on for further detail. The review of related research and knowledge — essential to an academic audience — might be omitted or greatly reduced in journalism or report writing. Writing about your research in a chapter of a book might focus primarily upon the outcomes, with the reader being informed through bibliographical referencing of the existence of fuller accounts of the research.

Developing a good structure for your writing depends also upon your ability to stand outside — or above — your subject, and consider it as a whole. What are the patterns that shape it? Are they your research questions? Are they key issues derived from your literature search? Are they a framework for analysis which you have taken or adapted from other writers, or devised for yourself? Where is the study going, and by what broad routes? Consider this advice from Blaxter *et al.* (1996: 215) about the themes of your research:

> The *themes* of your report or thesis are the key issues, concepts or questions you identify as being of relevance and interest. These will both inform the research you undertake, so will be evident in your contextual discussion, and help to structure your analysis and findings. They are the aspects of your field or discipline to which your research is contributing.

Within the larger sections of your writing, a consistent internal structure can be achieved by using these themes as a framework of sub-sections. If themes are repeated in successive sections of your writing, the reader will be encouraged to follow routes with which he/she will become increasingly familiar. The structure can be both externally visible — as sub-headings replicated in different sections — and embedded, where the concepts are dealt with in the same order in each section. You may be concerned that this approach will make your writing seem repetitive and unexciting. My response would be that if the structure of your argument is clear, the reader will be 'freed up' to become interested in your findings; if there is no clear 'map' of the pattern of ideas you are presenting, the reader may struggle to follow your train of thought and may not engage with the key points you are trying to make.

Within each sub-section, a finer degree of structuring is also essential. Ask yourself questions such as 'What do the readers need to know next?' and,

'What do they need to know already in order to understand what I am writing here?' to help you to order and organise your writing. Use link paragraphs to act as bridges between sub-sections, and offer summaries to give a chance for the reader — and the writer — to 'take stock' of what has just been presented. Using link words and phrases such as 'but', 'however', 'therefore', 'on the other hand' or 'in addition' helps you to build a cumulative argument, rather than simply presenting a succession of statements, and will help to move your document towards the destination you have in mind.

The flow of your argument can also be either enabled or impeded by the way in which tables and figures are placed. These are a valuable — often essential — part of your presentation, making points which it would be difficult to convey in continuous prose. However, they need clear labelling (with figure number and caption) and thoughtful handling if they are to convey their full impact. Remember that your reader is following the text, and is dependent upon you to 'signpost' to tables and figures appropriately, whether in the text of your report or its appendices, and to draw material from them into the discussion. It is a good idea to distribute evenly throughout the text illustrative material that may lie within it: making the reader encounter a 'brick wall' of tables or figures when trying to follow an argument may not be helpful. Those illustrations that form an essential part of your argument should go in the text; while those that merely support it should be placed in the appendices. Text cross-references, both to illustrations in the text and in the appendices, are essential.

The advice given in this section may be hard to apply when you are writing at length for the first time, or after a long break. The proposed length and complexity of your finished document may simply seem too daunting. Remember that a house is built one brick at a time, and it may be necessary for you simply to prepare your bricks (sentences, paragraphs, drafted sub-sections) and lay them out in front of you before you can see how they all fit together in the ways suggested above. Often it will become clear that a sub-section that was intended to fit in one place will fit better in another — with suitable minor re-wording — once other sub-sections have been written. It is also good practice to ask a colleague or friend to read drafts of what you have written, in order to comment on how well they can follow your argument, and what sections they find difficult to understand. In that way, you can see how easily your reader will follow the structure that you offer.

Language and 'voice'

The effectiveness of your research writing also depends upon your ability to select and and adopt a consistent and appropriate stance from which to write. In some areas of ethnographic research, and in case study research where a narrative approach is adopted (see Chapter 7) the use of the first person 'I' and 'we' is appropriate. In research where an objective viewpoint is paramount, a neutral third person stance, combined with use of the passive voice, will help to maintain objectivity. This does not mean that the language you use needs to be stilted: the statements, 'Five main-grade teachers were selected for interview . . .' or, 'The college has three main sites . . .' are no more difficult to follow than, 'I selected five main-grade teachers for interview . . .' or 'Our college has three main sites . . '. If you are not sure which 'person' to use, pay attention to the style of other writing in your discipline, and take advice from academic colleagues. In the end, as Blaxter *et al.* (1996: 221) comment 'Whether you use the first or third person will depend upon your discipline, your politics, your purpose and your audience.' You will find further advice on terminology in Chapter 1 of this book.

Researchers undertaking academic writing after a number of years away from study, or who may not have written formally at length for some considerable time, sometimes incorporate patterns of their own speech into their writing. Whilst this may enable the writer to 'break through' into the writing process, it is important that they move on to a more formal written style. As with gauging the level of presentation needed for your audience, it is advisable to read a range of academic writing in order to adopt a personal style with which you are comfortable, and which is appropriate for an academic reader.

Developing an appropriate viewpoint can merit as much attention as developing an appropriate style. Your viewpoint will be partly influenced by your reading of previous work on related subjects: you undertake a review of the literature in order to set your own work within its intellectual context. As your analysis both of the extant literature and of your own findings develops, you will find yourself developing a critical stance towards previous pieces of research, in order to incorporate them into your themes and arrive at your own conclusions. Taylor (1989: 67) offers a useful checklist of viewpoints which might be developed; these include:

- agreeing with, acceding to, defending or confirming a particular point of view;
- proposing a new point of view;
- reformulating an existing point of view, such that the new version makes a better statement;
- rejecting, rebutting or refuting another's arguments on various reasoned grounds; and
- reconciling two positions which may seem at variance by appeal to some 'higher' or 'deeper' principle. (1989: 67)

Note that these stances are developed on 'reasoned grounds' that is, by analysing the available evidence, either from other literature, or from your own findings; it is not enough simply to adopt a stance according to your own opinions.

Having carried through your piece of educational management research, the viewpoint you have reached may lead you to adopt a rather 'imperative' style in presenting the final stages of your analysis and your conclusions, saying that something 'must' be so or 'should' happen. Try very hard to avoid this stance. Think again about the scope of your research, the limitations of your methodology, and the wide range of un-investigated phenomena which may have had an impact upon the researched situation. A stance which balances confidence in making recommendations based upon the data whilst acknowledging the limitations and boundaries of the research is probably a wiser option.

Some students ask 'When can I express my own opinion? Surely that is important?' The simple answer is that your own opinion, unsupported by data, is not valid. The deeper answer is that your own opinion — in the form of your own interests, ethics and priorities — will shape the whole of your research: it will guide you in choosing what questions to ask, what literature to read, what methodology to adopt, what factors to analyse in your data and what importance to place upon your findings. It may lead you to set up a hypothesis which your research will explore in order to prove or disprove. The complexity for you the researcher lies in your ability to balance your opinion — what you feel is right or fitting — with an objective viewpoint that is prepared to accept a broad range of possible outcomes for the research.

Finally in this section there are some specific features of style to note. You should adopt a consistent model of referencing, both within the text and in your reference list, preferably a model such as the 'Harvard' system with which your readers will be familiar — and which examiners will expect to see. Abbreviations such as 'it's' and 'don't' should usually be avoided, but professionally used abbreviations such as 'SMT' for 'Senior Management Team' are acceptable, provided that they are written out in full and followed by their abbreviation, where they first appear in the text. Specialised terminology — which may include such simple phrases as 'subject leader' or 'homework club' — will need at least a brief explanation. Try to avoid using jargon that is very specific to your own institution — terms that may mean little to an outsider. Similarly, if you are writing for an international audience, remember that educational terminology varies from country to country, so it is good practice to offer a brief explanation of specific terms and abbreviations.

Whilst negotiating all these minefields and pitfalls of writing, do not lose sight of your own voice. Your own engagement with the topic investigated, and your own lively interest in it need not be lost in the process — indeed it is these features that will keep your readers engaged. You may choose to research and write from a particular ethical viewpoint or stance: a passionate interest in issues of equity or access to education may underlie your research, and lead you to 'theories and insights [which] can be used to improve [your] corner of the world' (Dadds, 1995: 137). But this does not mean that your investigation will be biased or lack rigour — as any other good research, it should be 'based on sound evidence, tested theory and workable philosophy'. (Locke, 1990: 202)

Authority

The previous section has explored some of the factors influencing your choice of language. There are aspects of language which are specifically important in presenting your analysed results. The scope of your investigation and the choice and design of your research tools dictate the limits of the authority with which you can report results. In reporting your research it is important, therefore, that your choice of language matches the scope of your investigation.

For example, a survey which involved all the teachers at one primary school could be reported as: 'Teachers at Sunnymead Primary School thought . . .', 'Three-quarters of the teachers at the school agreed that . . .' or 'Few of the teachers at the school considered X to be important.' Where the sample comprises the whole population, then, given reliable research tools, the results can be reported as representing the views of the whole population. It may still be wise to acknowledge that there may be personal variations in perception which the sampling design did not enable you to detect.

However, a survey which had sampled lecturers from two faculties of a further education college would be reported differently, for example: 'Half of the respondents agreed with the statement . . .', 'All of the staff sampled for the survey reported . . .' or 'The overall impression given by respondents from Faculty Y was . . .'. If robustly designed probability sampling has been used in your research, then inferences could be drawn for the whole of each faculty, or for a pair of faculties, but not for the college as a whole, unless the two faculties represented a reliable sample of the whole staff of the college.

Where the probability samples are small, or where non-probability sampling is chosen, assertions cannot be made about the whole population. Instead, the perceptions would be presented as a 'snapshot' of opinion, or as elements of a 'rich picture' of part of the school or college. Sampling design is fully discussed in Chapter 6 of this book, and the issues of reliability and validity of data in Chapter 4; both chapters will help you to understand the methodological issues underlying this advice. What is emphasised here is that the choice of words used to describe and present the data must match the parameters set by the research design. Your argument will be more convincing if you stay within the limits of the authority provided by your data.

Presenting your analysis

The specific examples discussed in the previous section lead us into a broader consideration of what will be at the heart of what you write: the analysis of the data you have collected. Other chapters in this book, particularly Chapters 14 and 15, will be valuable to you in conducting your analysis; this section focuses on the processes that enable you to present it appropriately to your audience. The rationale for presenting analysed data is rooted in the overall framework of research activity, and a brief recap of the processes that would normally precede analysis is therefore necessary at this point.

- *Research planning*. Here the key questions are developed and presented which the research is to clarify or answer, the context for the research is identified, and the broad methodology proposed for the investigation.
- *Literature review*. This sets the investigation within the context of existing research and published information about the phenomenon. It also enables the researcher to understand and discuss the key concepts which underpin the research, and to identify and develop themes and frameworks for analysis.
- *Developing the methodology*. Here the outcomes of the review are considered, together with the key research questions, in order to define the research approach and design the tools to be used. Research methodology texts (such as this one) are used to enable appropriate choices to be made and justified.
- *Collecting the data*. Data are collected which hopefully will provide insight into the research questions, and illustrate the key concepts. Guiding your analysis, therefore, will be both the research questions and the conceptual framework of your research.

The raw data — and you may be faced with a great deal of them, whether stored in boxes, on tapes or as computer files — will then be subject to two stages of analysis. The first stage enables you to see what the data indicate, and to identify patterns: likenesses, trends, differences and anomalies that are of relevance to the research. You will need to refer to Chapters 14 and 15 for more detailed advice on the analysis process, but your research outcomes may include graphs and charts, summaries of interviews, tables of concepts referred to by respondents, and the output of quantitative and qualitative analytical computer packages such as SPSS or NUD*IST. In a thesis or dissertation, much of these analysed data will need to be presented —

in the text and in the appendices of your report — in order to describe what you have found. In a journal article or conference presentation, it is likely that only selected data are presented: those that are germane to the argument proposed by the paper.

The second stage of analysis involves considering those discovered patterns — the likenesses, trends, differences and anomalies — in the light of the research questions and the frameworks of analysis derived from the literature. This is the most important part of your research, and it is where your own insight comes into play. At this stage, you are considering what your results 'mean' in terms of the desired outcomes of the research, guided by structures of thought which you have already explored in your literature review.

Whereas the outcomes of the first stage of analysis may seem static — they describe in different ways the research phenomenon that you have investigated — the second stage becomes increasingly dynamic. Arguments are built up which move you towards the 'answers' to your research questions, and to meaningful conclusions about your research area. Along the way you may develop models of the processes you have investigated, or ways of presenting the patterns that you have found, and evaluating their importance. The analysis — and your emergent conclusions and recommendations — is firmly rooted in the research context and aims, the literature and the primary data. It is the interaction of these elements, through the medium of the researcher, that leads the analysis towards new insights and understanding.

This second stage takes time, mental energy — and space on the page. An easy error is to spend most of the analysis section of your writing in simply presenting the results of your research. The real skill is in devising a concise but effective way of presenting those results, by making good use of tables, charts, explanatory comment and material cross-referenced in the appendices, for example, so that the reader has a secure grasp of what you have found, whilst reserving space for a substantial amount of secondary analysis. This part of your presentation, where your data are debated within the framework of your research questions and the key concepts from the literature, lies at the heart of your thesis, conference paper or journal article. It is where you and your reader engage with what is important in your research. Clarity of thought and presentation in this section will influence the confidence of your audience in the validity of your conclusions and recommendations. Presentation of analysis therefore merits time and care.

Dissemination

I hope that this chapter will have given some guidance in how to undertake the primary task with which you are faced: that of presenting your research. If you are engaged in completing a dissertation or thesis, probably the last thing that you wish to consider is undertaking further writing on the same subject. But consider a moment. Your thesis may be read by close family and colleagues. While a copy may be held in an academic library where other scholars may consult it; but on the whole its readership will not be wide; in addition it may well be too long to be read easily. To refer to Nisbet and Entwistle (1984: 256) quoted at the head of this chapter: 'Research in isolation serves no purpose'. For many practitioner researchers, the main object of their research is to achieve improvement in practice at their own school or college. To read about the experiences of other practitioner researchers, and to understand more about their potential impact, consult Middlewood *et al.* (1999) or Halsall (1998). For the purpose of your research to be fulfilled, the findings need to be disseminated. This could be through the medium of:

- an oral report or developmental workshop based on the research, presented to colleagues or staff from neighbouring educational institutions;
- a brief written summary of the research, its findings and recommendations, distributed internally — on paper or via an Intranet — to colleagues;
- a summary of the research and findings, with explanatory contextual detail, posted on an appropriate Internet discussion group or web page;
- a research paper published on the Internet;
- an article submitted to an educational newspaper or magazine;
- a paper submitted to an educational or academic conference; or
- a paper submitted to an academic journal.

You will probably be able to think of other dissemination routes, but one important principle is to match the route you choose to the message you are offering, and the other is not to under-rate yourself. If you choose to write a paper for an academic journal or a conference, your writing will be subjected to academic scrutiny before it can be disseminated. Do not let this put you off, even if you do not succeed first time. If the research was worth doing, it is worth disseminating, and if that means a 'lifetime first' of speaking at an academic conference, or of re-drafting your journal article for publication, so be it.

Whatever route you choose, you will probably be surprised at the amount of interest your research generates, and the stimulus you receive to undertake more research. Pushing forward the frontiers of understanding, even in a small way, can be addictive!

And finally . . .

If, even after reading all this good advice, you find it difficult to get started with your scholarly writing, don't panic — you are not alone! Even accomplished writers can find the process of writing difficult. There are many useful study guides which will help you to prioritise and plan your work — take from them what advice makes sense to you in your own circumstances. For me, the best advice is the simplest: 'Just write something!' Whatever you write will have to be re-drafted, probably three or more times, so the quality of the first draft is not really important. Once you have written something, and start to look at it critically, you will begin to see what is missing, what is in the wrong place, what needs to be better expressed. It is the engagement with the topic that even a clumsy attempt at writing can produce, that is the key to successful communication.

At some point in the writing process there often comes the moment when, in the words of Blaxter *et al.* (1996: 229): 'You have become so familiar with a group of ideas or theories that they now appear to you to be no more than common sense.' In other words, you appear to be going through the pointless process of presenting facts and perceptions and conclusions which you feel should be perfectly obvious to anyone. The advice wisely given is: 'Remind yourself of how far you have travelled on your intellectual journey.' (Blaxter *et al.*,1996: 229). Your task in writing is to trace that journey as you write, and engage your reader in it. No-one else has handled those concepts and those data in combination before. You therefore have a story worth telling.

References

Bassey, M. (1999) *Case Study Research in Educational Settings*, Buckingham: Open University Press.

Blaxter, L., Hughes, C. and Tight, M. (1996) *How to Research*, Buckingham: Open University Press.

Dadds, M. (1995) *Passionate Enquiry and School Development*, London: Falmer Press.

Halsall, R. (ed.) (1998) *Teacher Research and School Improvement*, Buckingham: Open University Press.

Locke, M. (1990) 'Methodological reflections', in Saran, R. and Trafford, V. (eds.), *Research in Education Management and Policy*, London: Falmer Press.

Middlewood, D., Coleman, M. and Lumby, J. (1999) *Practitioner Research in Education: Making a difference*, London: Paul Chapman.

Nisbet, J. D. and Entwistle, N. J. (1984) 'Writing the report', in Bell, J., Bush, T., Fox, A., Goodey, J. and Goulding, S. (eds.), *Conducting Small-scale Investigations in Educational Management*, London: Paul Chapman / Open University.

Taylor, G. (1989) *The Student's Writing Guide for the Arts and Social Sciences*, Cambridge: Cambridge University Press.

General index

Index of authors

293